Lecture Notes in Computer Scien

Edited by G. Goos and J. Hartmanis

Advisory Board: W. Brauer   D. Gries   J. Stoei

F. Meyer auf der Heide   B. Monien
A. L. Rosenberg (Eds.)

Parallel Architectures and Their Efficient Use

First Heinz Nixdorf Symposium
Paderborn, Germany, November 11-13, 1992
Proceedings

Springer-Verlag
Berlin Heidelberg New York
London Paris Tokyo
Hong Kong Barcelona
Budapest

Series Editors

Gerhard Goos
Universität Karlsruhe
Postfach 69 80
Vincenz-Priessnitz-Straße 1
W-7500 Karlsruhe, FRG

Juris Hartmanis
Cornell University
Department of Computer Science
4130 Upson Hall
Ithaca, NY 14853, USA

Volume Editors

Friedhelm Meyer auf der Heide
Burkhard Monien
Heinz Nixdorf Institut and FB Mathematik-Informatik
Universität-GH Paderborn, Postfach 16 21
W-4790 Paderborn, Germany

Arnold L. Rosenberg
University of Massachusetts, Computer Science Department
Lederle Graduate Research Center
Amherst, MA 01003, USA

CR Subject Classification (1991): F.1.2, B.2.1, B.6.1, C.1.2, F.2

ISBN 3-540-56731-3 Springer-Verlag Berlin Heidelberg New York
ISBN 0-387-56731-3 Springer-Verlag New York Berlin Heidelberg

© Springer-Verlag Berlin Heidelberg 1993
Printed in Germany

Typesetting: Camera ready by author/editor
45/3140-543210 - Printed on acid-free paper

Preface

The papers in this volume were presented at the

First Heinz Nixdorf Symposium:
Parallel Architectures and Their Efficient Use

in Paderborn, November 11–13, 1992, organized by the Heinz Nixdorf Institute of the University of Paderborn.

The symposium is the first in a series of Heinz Nixdorf Symposia, intended to cover varying subjects from the research spectrum of the Heinz Nixdorf Institute. As intended by the founder of this Institute – Heinz Nixdorf – its research spectrum is interdisciplinary and ranges from computer science to engineering and economics, including basics from natural sciences and related areas from humanistic and social sciences. Currently it focuses on research in the field of parallel computation and its applications in manufacturing technology.

Research in the field of parallel computer architectures and parallel algorithms has been very successful in recent years, and further progress is to be expected. On the other hand, the question of basic principles of the architecture of universal parallel computers and their realizations is still wide open. The answer to this question must be regarded as most important for the further development of parallel computing and especially for user acceptance. The First Heinz Nixdorf Symposium has brought together leading experts in this field to discuss the state of the art, promising directions of research, and future perspectives.

The symposium was organized as a "public day" followed by a "closed workshop" restricted to a smaller audience. The public day was attended by more than 200 participants; talks were given by Wolfgang Paul, Franco Preparata, Marc Snir, Charles Leiserson, and Tom Leighton.

The closed shop was split into four sections:

1. Parallel Computation Models and Simulations
2. Existing Parallel Machines
3. Communication and Programming Paradigms
4. Parallel Algorithms

In these proceedings, we have integrated the five talks from the public day in the appropriate sections. Surveys of the papers included in each section are given on the next pages (with the speakers' names capitalized).

We are in debt to all the people who helped us to make the symposium to something we are happy with and proud of:

– The invited participants:
   Fred Annexstein, Sandeep Bhatt, Michel Cosnard, Lennart Johnsson, Tom Leighton, Charles Leiserson, Fabrizio Luccio, David May, Ernst Mayr, Kurt Mehlhorn, Wolfgang Paul, Franco Preparata, Abhiram Ranade, Larry Rudolph, Marc Snir, Lawrence Snyder, Hal Sudborough, Eli Upfal, Leslie Valiant, Uzi Vishkin, Jean Vuillemin.

– The organizing group:
Bernhard Bauer, Astrid Burger, Michael Figge, Matthias Paul, Uta Schneider.

We are particularly indebted to the Westfalia Foundation for its generous support of the symposium.

Paderborn and Amherst, February 1993   Friedhelm Meyer auf der Heide
Burkhard Monien
Arnold Rosenberg

Survey of Papers

Section 1: Parallel Computation Models and Simulations

The major obstacle for achieving wide acceptance of parallel computers is the lack of a standard programming model for parallel computation, like the Von Neumann model for sequential computation. This section contributes to the discussion about the form such a parallel model could take.

LESLIE VALIANT has earlier proposed his bulk synchronous machine as a standard programming model, this model allows both (via simulations) the use of shared memory and direct interprocessor communication. In his paper he supports this model by presenting a combining mechanism that allows simulation of concurrent shared memory access in his model.

UZI VISHKIN argues in favor of the PRAM as one standard programming model. He discusses his thesis in the light of simplicity of programming and of (at least theoretically) efficient shared memory emulations on realistic parallel machines.

FRIEDHELM MEYER AUF DER HEIDE surveys the state of the art of shared memory simulations on distributed memory machines. The results show that simple, fast, simulations exist. This supports both the PRAM and the bulk synchronous machine as a standard model that can be used at the cost of only moderate loss in efficiency.

ARNOLD ROSENBERG advocates the thesis that parallel machines should consist of a very large number of very simple processors. More complex machines or programming paradigms should be added by sophisticated software. He illustrates this thesis by an examination of multigauging algorithms for SIMD bit-serial processor networks.

MICHEL COSNARD and Pascal Koiran contribute to the parallel complexity theory of computations over the real numbers. They introduce the Real PRAM, compare corresponding parallel complexity classes, and present P-completeness results in this framework.

FRANCO PREPARATA pinpoints the physical limits of the design of very large parallel machines, where the speed of light becomes a significant factor in the communication time. He argues that moderate size machines can use complicated networks, but very large machines should be built of meshes of such moderate size networks.

Section 2: Existing Parallel Machines

Massively parallel computers promise top performance for a wide range of applications at a price which is only a fraction of the price of conventional supercomputers. Such high performance is obtainable for an application only if the architecture of the machine and the communication primitives allow an efficient implementation of the underlying parallel algorithm.

WOLFGANG PAUL has developed a formal method to measure the cost-effectiveness of hardware architectures. Formella, Massone, and Paul use this method to compare the data flow machine Monsoon with the vector machines Cray I and Sparc 2.0.

CHARLES LEISERSON describes the communication networks of the Connection Machine CM-5. The machine contains three such networks: a data network, a control network, and a diagnostic network. The structure of the data network is based on the Fat Tree model.

LENNART JOHNSSON discusses techniques for preserving locality, especially the use of multidimensional address spaces and the partitioning of irregular grids. He also describes the communication primitives which are implemented on the Connection Machine.

BURKHARD MONIEN, Reinhard Lüling and Falk Langhammer describe the interconnection network of the transputer system SC 320 which is organized as a 2-level Clos network. The paper introduces also a new type of network, the "fat mesh of Clos", which combines aspects of efficiency and of realizability.

Many algorithms can be described in the "loosely synchronous" model of parallel programming, where processors alternate between phases of local computation and global communications. LARRY RUDOLPH introduces a parallel architecture supporting this model of parallel programming.

P. Bertin, D. Roncin, and JEAN VUILLEMIN present a number of "programmable active memories" for several applications including long multiplication, RSA cryptography, and data compression. A programmable active memory is a universal hardware co-processor closely coupled to a standard host computer. It is made of a configurable array of up to 14K programmable active bits.

Section 3: Communication and Programming Paradigms

The realization of communication among processors by routers and the discussion of paradigms for the design of parallel algorithms are the topics of this section.

TOM LEIGHTON and Bruce Maggs examine networks and protocols for packet routing and propose adding (pseudo-)randomness to the design of networks in order to achieve fast and fault-tolerant routing networks.

LARRY SNYDER describes an adaptive router, i.e. a router which allows that paths of messages are modified during execution. His Chaos Router is compared with many known routers.

Sergio Felperin, Prabhakar Raghavan and ELI UPFAL study wormhole routing, a routing mechanism that is not well studied but that is widely used in practice. They present analytical and experimental results on the performance of several variants of this routing mechanism.

The next two papers deal with programming paradigms.

FABRIZIO LUCCIO, Linda Pagli, and Geppino Pucci describe three algorithmic scenarios in which parallel solutions can be made especially efficient.

MARC SNIR focusses on the important, but often ignored, issue of scalability of algorithms. He discusses parallel algorithms that are scalable over a wide range of machine sizes. Further, he discusses paradigms of parallel programming languages for expressing scalable parallel algorithms.

Section 4: Parallel Algorithms

During the short history of computer science, algorithms have been designed mainly for sequential computers. The availability of parallel machines presents new challenges. In this section, a few methods are described for using parallel machines efficiently.

Most applications that run well on existing machines do so because they have locality, which can be exploited in algorithms. ABHIRAM RANADE introduces a framework for analyzing locality. His measure of locality allows him to show that several simple problems are inherently nonlocal. His paper also lists several problems for which fast network implementations can be designed.

The divide-and-conquer approach is one of the most successful programming paradigms. ERNST MAYR and Ralph Werchner show how to implement divide-and-conquer algorithms without undue overhead on a wide class of networks; in particular, they give an optimal implementation on hypercubes.

One promising way to take advantage of the communication pattern of an algorithm during the compilation process is to have software that can reconfigure the physical architecture according to the specified logical interconnection topology. FRED ANNEXSTEIN shows that many networks can be efficiently embedded into a hypercube using simple parallel algorithms.

Pancake networks have better diameter and vertex degree than the popular hypercube. Mohammad Heydari and HAL SUDBOROUGH study the diameters of pancake networks. They give new bounds for sorting some conjectured hard "stacks of pancakes."

Contents

Section 4: Parallel Algorithms

A Combining Mechanism for Parallel Computers*

Leslie G. Valiant

Aiken Computation Laboratory, Harvard University, Cambridge, MA 02138

Abstract. In a multiprocessor computer communication among the components may be based either on a simple router, which delivers messages point-to-point like a mail service, or on a more elaborate combining network that, in return for a greater investment in hardware, can combine messages to the same address prior to delivery. This paper describes a mechanism for recirculating messages in a simple router so that the added functionality of a combining network, for arbitrary access patterns, can be achieved by it with reasonable efficiency. The method brings together the messages with the same destination address in more than one stage, and at a set of components that is determined by a hash function and decreases in number at each stage.

1 Introduction

A general purpose parallel computer needs to have a mechanism for realizing concurrent memory accesses efficiently. Several or all of possibly thousands of processors may wish to read the same memory address at the same time. Alternatively, several or all may wish to write a value into the same address, in which case some convention needs to be adopted about the desired outcome. In either case, the requests will have to converge from the various parts of the physical system to the one location.

If each request is sent directly to the component containing the relevant address, then this component will require time to handle them proportional to the number arriving there. In general, this becomes unacceptable if the number of processors p is large. This overhead, potentially linear in p, can be overcome by implementing the requests in more than one stage. In the first stage, for example, the requests to any one ultimate destination will converge in groups at various intermediate components, where each group is *combined* into a single request to be forwarded in the next stage. In the last stage all extant requests to an address finally converge to the chosen location. Thus the requests can be viewed as flowing from the leaves of a tree to the root. In some instances, as when the concurrent requests implement a read statement, a flow of information in the reverse direction, from the root to the leaves, needs to follow. In these instances, whenever requests are combined at a component, the sources of the requests in that stage are stored at that component, so that a complete record of the structure of the tree is maintained. In a general pattern of requests, accesses to several memory addresses may be present. In that case a combining tree has to be maintained for each address.

What is the most efficacious way of providing a multiprocessor computer with a combining facility that is acceptably efficient for the widest range of concurrent

---

* This research was supported in part by a grant from the National Science Foundation, NSF-CCR-89-02500.

access patterns? In this paper we shall describe one proposed solution, and provide some analytic, experimental and, also, qualitative arguments in its favor.

In [12] we proposed the BSP model of parallel computation in which the basic medium of inter-processor communication is a *router*, that delivers messages among the components point-to-point, but performs no combining or ther computational operations itself. It was shown that shared memory with arbitrary concurrent accesses could be simulated on a p-processor BSP machine with only constant loss in efficiency asymptotically, if the simulated program had $p^{1+\epsilon}$ fold parallelism for some positive constant ϵ. One important advantage of having as the communication medium this simplest option is that it makes possible a competition for the highest throughput router among the widest possible range of technologies, including optical ones. In contrast, a medium that is required to perform more complex operations, imposes more constraints on the technology. The crucial question is whether the extra capabilities of more complex hardware can be simulated in practice on the simple router, with acceptable loss of efficiency.

In this paper we lend support to the position that simple routers can indeed implement concurrent accesses efficiently, by describing an algorithm for this that is more efficient and practical than previous solutions [8], [13]. Experiments suggest, for example, that for $p = 4096$ and with each processor making 32 requests, the cost of arbitrary concurrency patterns as compared with no concurrency is no more than a factor of about 3.5, even if nothing is known about the pattern. If the degree of concurrency is known then this factor is even smaller.

We conclude that it is indeed efficacious to invest the bulk of ones resources for communication in building a simple router with maximal throughput. Although every general purpose parallel machine needs to have mechanisms for implementing arbitrary patterns of concurrent accesses, if, as it appears, difficult access patterns occur rarely enough, then our proposed mechanism for dealing with them is efficient enough that substantial investments in combining networks are not warranted.

2 Multi-Phase Combining

We consider a system consisting of p *components*, each of which has some memory and processing capabilities. A *(q,r)-pattern* among the p component is a set of communication requests in which each component sends at most q requests, each request has a destination that is a memory *address* in a particular component, and at most r requests are addressed to any one component. Distinct components contain disjoint memory addresses. Several requests may share the same address (and therefore by implication also the same component.) We call the set of requests sharing the same address a *group*. The *degree* of a request is the number of elements in its group, and the degree of the pattern is the maximum degree of its elements. Thus if the pattern consists of n groups, of respective sizes $d_1, ..., d_n$ and destinations $t_1, ..., t_n$, then the *degree* of the pattern is $d = \max\{d_1, ..., d_n\}$. Although various alternatives may be considered, in this paper we shall charge $\max\{q, r\}$ units for executing directly a (q, r)-pattern on a router (as in the variant of the BSP model considered in [2].)

The proposed *multi-phase combining* algorithm implements patterns of high degree by decomposing them into a sequence of patterns of low degree. In each phase at each component, the requests having the same destination address that arrive there, are combined into a single request in the phase to follow. For example, if every processor wishes to read the same word in memory then the requests form a $(1, p)$-pattern consisting of a single group, and has degree p. If implemented directly our charging policy would charge it p units of time. It can be decomposed, however, into two $(1, \sqrt{p})$–patterns, each costing $\sqrt{p}$ units. The first allows each of $\sqrt{p}$ sets of $\sqrt{p}$ requests to converge to a separate component. The second sends the $\sqrt{p}$ requests, that are each formed from one of these sets, to their common destination. For simplicity we shall assume that any two requests to the same destination address are combinable. This is true if, for example, we are executing at any one time either read or write statements, but not both. Our algorithm and analysis can be easily extended to cases in which more than one species of request cohabit.

We shall now describe our multi-phase algorithm for implementing arbitrary patterns on a simple router efficiently. For concreteness we shall describe the instance that we analyzed and implemented. Many variants with comparable performance are possible and we shall discuss some of these in Section 5.

The algorithm has a *basis sequence* $(b_1, ..., b_m)$ of integers such that $\Pi_{i=1}^{m} b_i = p$ Suppose the space of possible addresses is denoted by M and that the components are numbered $\{0, ..., p-1\}$. Suppose also that $\{h_1, ..., h_m\}$ are hash functions where $h_i : M \rightarrow \{0, ..., b_1 \cdots b_i - 1\}$ and $\{k_1, ..., k_{m-1}\}$ are random functions where $k_i : \phi \rightarrow \{0, ..., b_{i+1} \cdots b_m - 1\}$. The important distinction is that for each pattern the hash functions h_i are chosen *once*, randomly from certain sets of hash functions, while the random functions k_i have values that are independently chosen randomly *at each invocation*, and do not depend on any argument. The ith phase of the algorithm will at each component combine into one all the requests it has to any one destination t_j and send it to component $h_i(t_j)b_{i+1} \cdots b_m + k_i$. Note again that the requests to the same t_j will have the same value of $h_i(t_j)$, but will have k_i chosen randomly and independently for each of them at each component. It can be easily verified that, after i phases, among the requests destined for any t_j, sets of up to $b_1 \cdots b_i$ may have been combined into one. Also, if $i < m$, the resulting requests have been scattered randomly over $b_{i+1} \cdots b_m$ components, whose identities are determined by the hash function h_i. In particular after the last phase the request destined for t_j has been delivered to the hashed address $h_m(t_j)$. It turns out that the most promising mechanisms known for simulating a shared memory, PRAM, or BSP model on multiprocessor machines use a hashed address space (e.g. [12], [13]). Hence the algorithm as described implements hashing exactly as required in that context. As noted in Section 5, however, the algorithm can be adapted easily to deliver to actual rather than hashed addresses.

An alternative algorithm with similar properties is obtained by replacing the random function k_i in the above by the deterministic function $k_i^* : \{0, \cdots, p-1\} \rightarrow \{0, \cdots, b_{i+1} \cdots b_m - 1\}$ defined as $k_i^*(s) = s \bmod b_{i+1} \cdots b_m$, and in the ith phase sending a request originating at component s and destined for address t_j to component $h_i(t_j)b_{i+1} \cdots b_m + k_j^*(s)$. This requires no randomization beyond the hash functions h_i, but evens out the load among the processors more slowly if the spread of the original requests is uneven.

3 Asymptotic Analysis

We shall establish the following property of the multi-phase algorithm, that holds asymptotically as the number of processors $p \to \infty$.

Theorem 1. *For any constant $\varepsilon > 0$, any integer $m \geq 1 + \lfloor \varepsilon^{-1} \rfloor$, and any constant $\delta > 0$, there is an m-phase algorithm that can realize any (q,r)-pattern with $q \leq p^\varepsilon$ in a number of steps that exceeds $(1+\delta)mp^\varepsilon$ with probability less than $e^{-\Omega(p^{\varepsilon-1/m})}$.*

The result assumes that the address space is hashed, as previously described, and for that reason does not depend on r. Also, the proof assumes that when choosing the hash functions, we are choosing from a set of functions that allow the chosen one to behave randomly and independently for the various arguments at which it is evaluated.

The result as stated improves on the constant multiplier in the runtime of the best previously known method based on integer sorting [8], [13]. In particular the experimental results show that small values of δ can be attained with overwhelming probability.

We shall use the following bound on the tail of the sum of independent random variables due to Littlestone [9], and also derivable from [10].

Lemma 2. *If $\xi_1, \cdots, \xi_n$ are independent random variables each taking values in the range $[0,1]$ such that the expectation of their sum is E, then for any $\delta > 0$,*

$$Prob\left(\sum_{i=1}^{n} \xi_i \geq (1+\delta)E\right) \leq \left(\frac{e^\delta}{(1+\delta)^{1+\delta}}\right)^E .$$

Proof of Theorem

In the analysis we shall assume, for simplicity, that $b = p^{1/m}$ is an integer. We choose as basis sequence $(b_1, \cdots, b_m)$ where $b_1 = b_2 = \cdots = b_m = b$. We consider how the algorithm behaves on an arbitrary (q,r)-pattern with $q \leq p^\varepsilon$, and with n destination addresses $t_1, \cdots, t_n$ and degrees $d_1, \cdots, d_n$, respectively. If we let $v = \sum_{i=1}^{n} d_i$ then clearly $v \leq qp \leq p^{1+\varepsilon}$.

At the start of phase i the jth group of requests, namely those destined for t_j, will have been combined into at most

$$\min\{d_j, p/b^{i-1}\}$$

requests. For $i > 1$ these will be distributed randomly among the p/b^{i-1} components numbered $h_{i-1}(t_j)b^{m-i+1} + x$ for $0 \leq x < b^{m-i+1}$.

Now consider some fixed component numbered $yb^{m-i} + z$ where $0 \leq y < b^i$ and $0 \leq z < b^{m-i}$. Let η_j be the number of requests with destination t_j arriving at this component at the end of phase i. Then

$$Prob(\eta_j \geq u) \leq Prob(h_i(t_j) = y) \cdot B(\min\{d_j, p/b^{i-1}\}, b^i/p, u) \qquad -(1)$$

where $B(w, P, u)$ denotes the probability that in w independent Bernoulli trials, each with probability P of success, there are at least u successes. The first term gives the probability that the randomly chosen hash function h_i maps t_j to y, and equals b^{-i} clearly. The second bounds the probability that at least u of the requests are mapped by the invocations of the random function k_i, to the chosen value of z, and, by the Lemma above, can be upper bounded by

$$\left(\frac{e^\delta}{(1+\delta)^{1+\delta}}\right)^b \leq e^{-\Omega(p^{1/m})} \qquad -(2)$$

if $u = (1+\delta)b$ and $\delta > 0$, since the mean is at most $(p/b^{i-1})(b^i/p) = b$.

We shall now define new random variables $\xi_1, \cdots, \xi_n$ where

$$\xi_j = \begin{cases} \eta_j/((1+\delta)b) & \text{if } \eta_j < (1+\delta)b, \\ 1 & \text{otherwise.} \end{cases}$$

These satisfy the condition of the Lemma that $0 \leq \xi_j \leq 1$, and model the behavior of $\eta_1, \cdots, \eta_n$ exactly, except for the range $\eta_j \geq (1+\delta)b$, which is a very rare event by virtue of (2). Since, by (1), the expected value of η_j is at most $b^{-i} \cdot \min\{d_j, p/b^{i-1}\} \cdot b^i/p$, it follows from the definition of ξ_j that the sum of the expectations of $\xi_1, \cdots, \xi_n$ is

$$E \leq \frac{1}{(1+\delta)b} \sum_{j=1}^n \frac{d_j}{p}$$

$$\leq \frac{p^{1+\epsilon}}{(1+\delta)bp} \leq \frac{p^{\epsilon-1/m}}{(1+\delta)}.$$

Applying the Lemma to $\xi_1, \cdots, \xi_n$ then gives that

$$Prob\left(\sum_{j=1}^n \xi_j \geq (1+\delta) \cdot \frac{p^{\epsilon-1/m}}{(1+\delta)}\right) \leq \left(\frac{e^\delta}{(1+\delta)^{1+\delta}}\right)^{p^{\epsilon-1/m}/(1+\delta)}$$

$$\leq e^{-\Omega(p^{\epsilon-1/m})} \qquad -(3)$$

if $\delta > 0$. But, by the definition of ξ_j, the lefthand side is

$$Prob\left(\sum_{j=1}^n \eta_j \geq (1+\delta)p^\epsilon\right) - \sum_{j=1}^n \mu_j \qquad -(4)$$

where μ_j is less than the probability that η_j exceeds $(1+\delta)b$, which by relations (1) and (2) is at most $e^{-\Omega(p^{1/m})}$. Hence we deduce from (3) and (4) that the probability that the number of requests $\sum_{j=1}^n \eta_j$ arriving at the chosen node at the end of phase i exceeds $(1+\delta)p^\epsilon$ is still $e^{-\Omega(p^{\epsilon-1/m})}$, since $n \leq p^{1+\epsilon}$.

As there are p components and m phases, the probability that this charge is exceeded anywhere in the run is therefore pm times this same quantity, which is also $e^{-\Omega(p^{\epsilon-1/m})}$. Hence the result claimed in the Theorem follows.

For completeness we now prove the same result for the alternative algorithm in which in phase i any request originating at component s and destined for address t_j is sent to $h_i(t_j)b^{m-i} + k_i^*(s)$ where $k_i^*(s) = s \bmod b^{m-i}$. Here at the start of phase i the group of requests destined for t_j will have been combined into at most $\min\{d_j, b^{m-i+1}\}$ requests, which are distributed among the b^{m-i+1} components numbered $h_{i-1}(t_j)b^{m-i+1} + x$ for $0 \le x \le b^{m-i+1}$. For any fixed component numbered $yb^{m-i} + z$ where $0 \le y < b^i$ and $0 \le z < b^{m-i}$ define η_j to be the number of requests with destination t_j arriving at this component at the end of phase i. Let X_j be the number of requests at the start of phase i destined for t_j from addresses with $k_i^*(s) = z$. Then clearly $X_j \le b$ and $\sum X_j \le p^\epsilon b^i$. Also $\eta_j = X_j$ with probability b^{-i} (i.e. if $h_i(t_j) = y$) and $\eta_j = 0$ otherwise. If we define $\xi_j = \eta_j/b$ then the sum of the expectations of ξ_j is

$$ E \le b^{-i-1} \sum_{j=1}^{n} X_j \le b^{-i-1} p^\epsilon b^i \le p^{\epsilon-1/m}. $$

The result then follows from the Lemma as before.

4 Experimental Results

The multi-phase combining algorithm with the k_i chosen to be random functions was implemented as follows. In the basis sequence we used only powers of 2 (i.e. $b_i = 2^{a_i}$ for integers $a_i, 1 \le i \le m$). We used a pseudo-random number generator to generate new values of the functions k_i at each invocation. We also used a pseudo-random number generator to generate for each pattern the set of values $\{h_i(t_j) \mid 1 \le i \le m, 1 \le j \le n\}$. In particular we had the binary representation of $h_i(t_j)$ to be the prefix of the binary representation of $h_{i+1}(t_j)$, so that only a_{i+1} random new bits were chosen when determining the latter.

We ran experiments for the case $p = 2^{12}$ and $v = \sum_{j=1}^n d_j = 2^{17}$. We implemented (q,r)-patterns with $q = 32$, but with degrees varying from 2^{12} down to 1. Thus typically we had $n = 2^{17}/d$ groups each of degree d, for $d = 2^{12}, 2^{11}, \cdots, 2^0$. The reported results are all averages over 500 runs.

At one extreme we had 2^{17} groups of degree one and therefore no combining was required. The patterns were $(32,r)$-patterns where r depended on the maximum number of requests that the hashed address space placed into one component. The average value of r was determined experimentally to be 54.4. This is just the expected number of objects in the bucket having the most objects, if 2^{17} objects are placed randomly into 2^{17} buckets. Since this is the baseline performance of a pure router with a hashed address space, we computed the runtime of all our experiments as multiples of this basic unit, and call this multiple the *performance factor*.

At the other extreme we had 32 groups of degree 2^{12}, which corresponds to each of the components sending requests to the same set of 32 addresses. This requires the highest amount of combining.

We note that the $m = 1$ version of our algorithm (i.e. basis sequence (4096)), is the solution proposed in [12] for patterns of low degree. From Table 1 we see that if the degree is no more than the slack (*i.e.* $v/p = 32$) then the performance is indeed quite good, the runtime factor being no worse than 3.7. This factor improves rapidly as d decreases. On the other hand, the degree is clearly a lower bound on the runtime of the one-phase algorithm, and for $d = 2^{12}$ gives a performance factor greater than $4096/54.4 > 75$, which is unacceptable.

If the case $d = 1$ is implemented in several phases, then each phase performs hashing with no combining and contributes a factor of about 1 to the overall runtime. (The contribution is actually slightly more since we are charging $\max(q, r)$ rather than r for a (q,r)-pattern.) This is also the case in early phases of the algorithm if d is small enough that little combining is done in that phase. In phases where much combining is done the performance factor can exceed one considerably. If the necessary combining is achieved in early phases, however, later phases may execute very fast since only few requests remain in the system. These phenomena can be discerned easily in Table 2, where for various values of d we give basis sequences that achieved factors below 3.

We note that the motivation for the charging policy in the BSP model is that some routers may achieve a satisfactory rate of throughput only when they have enough work to do (i.e. q is high enough when implementing a (q,r)-pattern) in one superstep. Hence the BSP model has a lower bound on the time for a superstep, determined by some parameters. Where this lower bound is relevant, we may give preference to basis-sequences that distribute the time cost evenly among the phases. On the other hand there are circumstances, for example, when the phases are implemented asynchronously as discussed below, when this issue does not arise.

Degree	4096	2048	1024	512	256	128	64	32	16	8	4	2	1
Performance	82	53	35	20	13	8.1	5.3	3.7	2.6	1.9	1.5	1.2	1.0

Table 1. Performance factors for basis sequence (4096), i.e. one-phase, for various degrees for $p = 2^{12}$ and $v = 2^{17}$.

Degree	Basis Sequence	Phase 1	Phase 2	Phase 3	Phase 4	Performance
4096	(8,8,8,8)	1.51	.64	.37	.17	2.7
2048	(16,8,8,4)	1.60	.67	.38	.10	2.8
1024	(32,8,4,4)	1.71	.71	.26	.14	2.8
512	(32,8,4,4)	1.46	.92	.32	.16	2.8
256	(128,8,4)	1.84	.73	.20		2.8
128	(256,4,4)	1.90	.52	.25		2.7
64	(512,8)	1.95	.66			2.6
32	(1024,4)	1.98	.46			2.4
16	(1024,4)	1.58	.64			2.2

Table 2. Performance factors for various basis sequences for various degrees for $p = 2^{12}$ and $v = 2^{17}$. The factors are given separately for each phase, as well as in total.

Degree	4096	2048	1024	512	256	128	64	32	16	8	4	2	1
(32,8,4,4)	3.4	3.0	2.8	2.8	3.0	3.2	3.4	3.6	3.8	4.0	4.1	4.1	4.1
(32,16,8)	3.4	3.1	3.0	3.1	3.3	3.3	3.3	3.4	3.4	3.4	3.3	3.2	3.0

Table 3. Performance factors for basis sequences (32,8,4,4) and (32,16,8) for various degrees for $p = 2^{17}$.

Tables 1 and 2 show that if we have information about the degrees of the patterns then we can find a good basis sequence that brings the performance factor of our algorithm below 3 in the whole range, and below 2 if $d \leq 8$. The only assumption here is that the requests all have the same degree, which is the case we tested. If we have no knowledge about the degree of concurrency, then, as Table 3 shows, the basis sequences $(32, 8, 4, 4)$ and $(32, 16, 8)$ are good compromises and achieve performance factors of at most about 4 and 3.5 respectively throughout the whole range.

5 Variants of the Algorithm

The algorithm as described is "bulk-synchronized" in the sense that each phase has to finish before the next one starts. The correctness of the algorithm, however, does not require this. As each request in a phase arrives at a component, a check can be made to determine whether any other to the same address has been previously received, and if none has then the request can be sent on immediately to the next phase, without waiting for the previous phase to complete. Where it is permissible, such an *asynchronous* implementation can only improve performance. The actual performance in that case depends, however, on the order in which the router delivers the requests. Asynchrony may be introduced also if the requests are transmitted bit-serially.

The algorithm can be adapted to models of parallel computation other than the simple router. One candidate is what is called the S*PRAM in [13] that has been suggested as a model of various proposals for optical interconnects [1],[6]. Here at each cycle any component can transmit a message to any other, but only those receive messages that have just one targeted at them in that cycle. The senders find out immediately whether their transmission succeeded. Known general simulations of the BSP on the S*PRAM with slack $\log p$ or slightly more are known [3], [13] and these imply constant factor optimal implementations of our combining algorithm on the S*PRAM. There are clearly several possibilities for more efficient direct implementations also.

So far we have discussed versions of the algorithm that implement (q,r)-patterns in a hashed address space. The performance has been independent of the value of r because of the hashing. Suppose now that, we wish to send requests directly to actual addresses as, for example, when implementing a "direct BSP algorithm" [2]. We can clearly do this by sending the requests to hashed addresses first by the algorithm described, and then in one extra phase sending them to the correct destinations. This last phase will be a pattern of degree 1, from randomly distributed sources. Also we can expect that the targets are distributed approximately uniformly among the components, since that is the purpose of using a direct algorithm. Hence this extra phase of the algorithm will run fast on the simple router. In particular, if the added last phase is a (q', r')-pattern, and the previous one is a (q'', r'')-pattern then clearly $q' \leq r''$. Also $r' \leq r^*$ where r^* is the maximum number of distinct destination addresses targeted in any component . Hence the cost $\max\{q', r'\}$ will be dominated by r'', which is controlled by randomization, and by r^* which is controlled by the programmer.

As an alternative to adding an extra phase to our multi-phase combining algorithm, we can also consider replacing its last phase by one that sends the requests directly to the actual rather than the hashed addresses. This will be efficient if the number of requests destined for each physical component, is small enough. When counting this number here, we have to allow for the multiplicity of each request group as defined by its degree in the last phase of the basic algorithm.

When implementing this multi-phase algorithm, provision has to be made by software or hardware or some combination, for storing at each phase the sources of the converging requests, so that this trace can be used for any necessary reverse flow of information. These provisions are also useful for implementing concurrent accesses when the decomposition of the pattern into phases is handcrafted by a programmer. This may be worthwhile for the sake of greater efficiency, for patterns that have a structure well-known to the programmer. Our algorithm, therefore, is also consistent with such direct implementations of concurrent accesses.

Finally, we note that our combining mechanism can be used for applications other than accesses. When requests are combined it is meaningful to perform almost any operation on their contents that is commutative and associative. The method can be used, for example, to find the sum, product, minimum, or Boolean disjunction over arbitrary sets of elements simultaneously.

References

1. R.J. Anderson and G.L. Miller. Optical communication for pointer based algorithms. TR CRI-88-14, Computer Science Department, University of Southern California, 1988.
2. A.V. Gerbessiotis and L.G. Valiant. Direct bulk-synchronous parallel algorithms. *Third Scandinavian Workshop on Algorithm Theory, Lecture Notes in Computer Science*, Vol 621, Springer-Verlag (1992) 1-18.
3. M. Geréb-Graus and T. Tsantilas. Efficient optical communication in parallel computers. *Proc. 4th ACM Symp. on Parallel Algorithms and Architectures*, June 29-July 1, (1992) 41-48.
4. A. Gottlieb et al. The NYU Ultracomputer - Designing an MIMD shared-memory parallel computer. *IEEE Trans. on Computers*, C-32:2, (1983) 175-189.
5. A. Hartmann and S. Redfield. Design sketches for optical crossbar switches intended for large scale parallel processing applications. Optical Engineering, 29:3 (1989) 315-327.
6. A. Karlin and E. Upfal. Parallel hashing – an efficient implementation of shared memory. *Proc. 18th ACM Symp. on Theory of Computing* (1986) 160-168.
7. R.M. Karp and V. Ramachandran. A survey of algorithms for shared-memory machines. In *Handbook of Theoretical Computer Science*, (J. van Leeuwen, ed.), North Holland, Amsterdam, (1990) 869-941.
8. C.P. Kruskal, L. Rudolph and M. Snir. A complexity theory of efficient parallel algorithms. *Theor. Comp. Sci.*, 71 (1990) 95-132.
9. N. Littlestone. Manuscript (1990).

10. P. Raghavan. Probabilistic construction of deterministic algorithms. *Proc. 27th IEEE Symp. on Foundations of Computer Science* (1986) 10-18.

11. A. Ranade. How to emulate shared memory. *In Proc. 28th IEEE Symp. on Foundation of Computer Science* (1987) 185-194.

12. L.G. Valiant. A bridging model for parallel computation. CACM *33* : 8 (1990) 103-111.

13. L.G. Valiant. General purpose parallel architectures. In *Handbook of Theoretical Computer Science* (J. van Leeuwen, ed.), North Holland, Amsterdam (1990) 944-971.

A Case for the PRAM As a Standard Programmer's Model

Uzi Vishkin[*]

University of Maryland &
Tel Aviv University

Abstract

The paper advocates that the PRAM model of parallel computation will be a standard (but not exclusive) programmer's model for computers whose hardware features various kinds of parallelism.

1 Introduction

The parallel random-access machine (PRAM) model of computation is an idealization that strips away levels of algorithmic complexity concerning synchronization, reliability, data locality, machine connectivity, and communication capacity, latency and contention and thereby allows the algorithm designer to focus on the combinatorial properties of the problem at hand. The result has been a substantial body of efficient algorithms designed in this model, and a growing number of design paradigms and utilities for designing such algorithms.

For this paper the PRAM represents a family of models of parallel computation with the following common denominators: a set of synchronous processors all having access to a shared memory (or bulletin board); differences among members of this family are suppressed as they are of secondary importance. We will use the following, somewhat informal, definition for efficiency of algorithms. Consider two PRAM algorithms. For inputs of length n, one runs in $T_1(n)$ time and $W_1(n)$ work (or total number of operations), and the other runs in $T_2(n)$ time and $W_2(n)$ work. As a rule-of-thumb we say that the first algorithm is the *more efficient* among the two if it performs less work than the second, or if the algorithms are equal on the work account, but the first needs less time. In other words, we define a lexicographic order on the asymptotic behavior of the pair $(W_1(n), T_1(n))$ versus the pair $(W_2(n), T_2(n))$ This definition should be taken with a "grain of salt", since, for instance, we do not want to categorically prefer an algorithm that runs in $O(n)$ work and $O(n)$ time to another algorithm with $O(n \log n)$ work and $O(1)$ time.

---

[*]Partially supported by NSF grants CCR-8906949 and 9111348.

Throughout the paper, we refer to parallelism expressed in the PRAM model as **algorithm-parallelism**. In contrast, **hardware-parallelism** is an attribute of the physical machine.

Our primary interest is in *how to make effective use of hardware-parallel machines*. The *main agenda item of this paper* is as follows:

- Have the PRAM as a standard programmer's model to be effectively supported by hardware-parallel machines.

We emphasize that we do not advocate the PRAM as an exclusive programmer's model. For instance, it will be reasonable to let sophisticated programmers, who are willing to invest the time, take advantage of some "closer-to-the-real-machine" (possibly ad-hoc) features, as long as they consider it cost-effective.

2 The need

For over two decades there has been an understanding that fundamental physical limitations on processor speed will eventually force high-performance computing to be targeted principally at the exploitation of parallelism. Today, just as the fastest cycle times are approaching these fundamental barriers, new generations of parallel machines are emerging. The main question is how to design such machines so that they will lend themselves to effective use.

A paramount component is software and algorithms. To facilitate an appropriate overall design, some accepted underlying model of such machines needs to be known in advance. We explain this by way of example. While the serial RAM is a programmer's model, several procedural high-level languages (such as C, FORTRAN, or PASCAL) enable implementation of it. New general-purpose (serial) machines are generally considered unacceptable unless they support the RAM model of computation.

There are several issues that need to be addressed in looking for a programmer's model.

- *Reusability.* Explanation by way of example is used again. The 1993 budget for the United States High Performance Computing and Communications (HPCC) Initiative is nearly $800,000,000. Out of this, nearly $350,000,000 is allocated for software technology and algorithms. This should lead to many algorithms and even more lines of code. The initiative states: "software library efforts will focus on development of common architectures and interfaces to increase the potential for reusability despite multiple underlying models of computation, the diversity of programming languages in use, ...". I have not yet heard any satisfactory suggestion on *how they are going to cope with the reusability issue.*

- *Simplicity.* The programmer's model should be as simple as possible to make it accessible to people who do not have the time to master advanced, complex computer science skills.

Does everybody agree on the nature of the problem? We revisit the HPCC example. A focal point has been to make progress towards a wide range of scientific and engineering "grand challenge" problems. There appear to be two conflicting opinions:

(i) Some argue that several existing huge software packages are not really "replaceable" and suggest that it will be cost-effective to focus the effort on developing software systems that will enable to emulate these software packages on current and future parallel machines (e.g., David Kuck, "The greatest of the grand challenges", keynote address, International Conference on Supercomputing, July 1992, Washington, D.C.).

(ii) The other extreme suggests that existing code and standard serial algorithms typically do not exhibit sufficient parallelism, and the problem is much more fundamental. That is, new code will have to be written based on new (parallel) algorithms. The issue of emulating the new code on available machines is of fundamental importance for this direction, as well. This paper supports the second opinion.

3 A possible general approach

It should be clear that agreeing on a standard programmer's model of computation to be supported by current and future parallel machines answers the reusability concern. Such "robust" model will have to be as simple as possible. An analogy to serial computation is useful again. There the RAM is used as one of the programmer's models, in addition to more architecture-related models, such as some features in the C programming language, or assembly languages.

Understanding the imperfection of the PRAM and other possible programmer's models A PRAM algorithm suppresses several important machine parameters. To better match a multi-processor computer, a parallel algorithms designer needs to take into account many parameters relating to issues such as synchronization, reliability, data locality, machine connectivity, and communication capacity, latency, and contention. We see two main problems in coping with all parameters at once: (1) The programmer's job becomes prohibitively difficult. (2) Since multi-processor computers can be very different (in terms of the parameters that need to be considered), a better match for one may be worse for another.

Therefore, in comparing parallel computing solutions with serial solutions, an evaluator must remember that: (1) the analogous problems are much more involved in the parallel case, (2) not reaching agreement on even a tentative solution to the above need may cause stalemate and therefore have a grave impact on the advancement of the field.

This also explains why it is not unreasonable to ask critics to suggest a true alternative (i.e., substantiate claims for improvement), as part of their criticism.

4 Pillars of the case for the PRAM as a Programmer's Model

- *Relevance for hardware-parallelism.* Algorithm-parallelism is formally emulatable on some multi-processor architectures. Such efficient emulation results suggest that the PRAM is not overly simplistic. See also the section on processor-parallelism.
  A later section, which is entitled machine-parallelism, happens to be the longest in the present paper, since it overviews some more recent perspectives. The main point there is as follows. Potentially, the resource of algorithm-parallelism can be traded for effective use of "machine-parallelism" which is more general than "processor-parallelism". The possibility of a more evolutionary (and less revolutionary) shift towards effective use of hardware-parallelism is also presented.

- *Successful theory.* A knowledge-base of algorithm-parallelism of considerable extent has been developed. Several books, [Akl-89], [GR-88], [J-92] and [R-92], and a few review papers, [EG-88], [KR-90], [KRS-90] and [Vi-91a], attest to a unique and comprehensive knowledge-base of PRAM algorithms, methods, techniques and paradigms. Note that some of these publications consider as efficient only algorithms whose running time is poly-logarithmic (i.e., asymptotically bounded by a polynomial in the logarithm of the problem size). Our notion of algorithm efficiency, which is exactly the same as in an 1983 position paper [Vi-83], categorically prefers poly-logarithmic time parallel algorithms to slower parallel algorithms only if their work complexity (i.e., total number of operations) is not larger. We view the fact that many of the known techniques provide poly-logarithmic running time as circumstantial (though, remarkable).

- *By default.* Knowledge-bases in non-PRAM parallel algorithms fall short on one or both of the above accounts, in spite of many attempts by able researchers over more than two decades. The acute need for a robust programmer's model and this *lack of competition* make the PRAM the only reasonable choice at the present time.

5 Hardware-parallelism

Hardware-parallelism can come in several flavors. We start by a short review of **processor-parallelism**, where parallelism is due to a large number of processing elements.

Later, we provide a more general definition of **machine-parallelism**. It is argued that: (1) only few (if any) new and future computers are likely to escape this definition, and (2) algorithm-parallelism relates to effective use of this wider concept of machine-parallelism as well. Therefore, the recent paper [Vi-91b] argues that there are more reasons for considering algorithm-parallelism than merely its relationship with massive processor-parallelism. Furthermore, gradual adoption of the algorithm-parallelism paradigm in education and practice will enable a less abrupt transition to the long term goal of massive processor-parallelism.

5.1 Processor-parallelism

It appears that most of the research activity on parallelism in the theory and algorithms community, among others, has focused on processor-parallelism. We summarize in one paragraph a relationship between algorithm-parallelism and this well-studied kind of hardware-parallelism.

The following observation, which is due to the companion papers [MV-84] and [Vi-84], discusses this relationship. *The PRAM model can be formally emulated, in an efficient manner, by a synchronous distributed computer, where each processor is connected to a small number of others in a fixed pattern.* This observation was useful for enhancing the interest of the academic computer science community (theoretical and other) in PRAM algorithmics. Elegant and insightful refinements and enhancements of this observation were given in [KU-86], [R-87], [U-89] and [ALM-90]. For more on this topic and machine designs that relate to it see [L-92a] and [L-92b], and references therein.

5.2 Machine-parallelism

For background we note the following,

- The new generation of "serial machines" is far from being literally serial. Each possible state of a machine can be described by listing the contents of all its *data cells*, where data cells include memory cells and registers. For instance, pipelining with, say, s single cycle stages may be described by associating a data cell with each stage; all s cells may change in a single cycle of the machine. More generally, a transition function may describe all possible changes of data cells that can occur in a single cycle; the set of data cells that change in a cycle define the *machine-parallelism* of the cycle; a machine is *literally serial* if the size of this set cannot be more than one. We claim that literally serial machines hardly exist and that considerable increase in machine-parallelism is to be expected. Machine-parallelism comes in such forms as pipelining, or in connection with the Very-Long Instruction Word (VLIW) technology, to mention just a few.

- In contrast to this, textbooks on algorithms and data-structures still educate students, who are about to join the job market for at least forty years, to conceive of computers as literally serial; such textbooks are not to blame, of course, since software for currently widely available machines does not enable the typical user to express parallelism.

- Parallel algorithms can be exploited to make more effective use of machine-parallelism; the paper [Vi-91b] demonstrates how to use parallel algorithms for prefetching from slow memories (using pipelining); other means include using the parallelism offered by VLIW; there, a CPU can process simultaneously several operands and potentially provide the same effect as having separate processors working in parallel on these operands.

This wider understanding of parallelism suggests a multi-stage implementation strategy.

- The agenda for the first stage (or stages) consists of the following.

  - *Agenda for the education system:* Teach students in undergraduate courses, as well as computer science graduates that work as professional programmers, parallel algorithms and data-structures and educate them to do their programming in parallel. Explain to them that algorithm-parallelism is a resource that can be traded in several ways to take advantage of machine-parallelism.

  - *Agenda for computer manufacturers:* Update the design of (serial) machines, including software, so that parallel algorithms can be implemented on them; a particular emphasis should be given to allowing parallel algorithms to take advantage of machine-parallelism. The intention is that the first few generations of such computers will still provide competitive support for serial algorithms (including existing code). We note that Fortran 90, the new international standard described in [MR-90], requires that manufacturers continue to provide support for serial algorithms, and at the same time to provide support for new array instructions that essentially enable implementing PRAM algorithms. Needless to say that this support should be effective.

- Later stages will advance from aiming at moderate machine-parallelism to massive parallelism. These stages coincide with the massive processor-parallelism approach.

The main advantages of the multi-stage machine-parallelism approach are:

- A gradual, rather than abrupt, transition of general purpose computing from serial to parallel algorithms. Using the terminology of [HP-90], this gives the advantage of being **more evolutionary** in its demands from the user (and **less revolutionary**).

- The first generations of machines that will be built this way will cost much less than massively parallel machines. (These first generations can be nicknamed a "poor-person's" parallel computer, as opposed to a massively parallel approach that can be called a "rich-person's" one.)

- A much wider access to implementation of parallel algorithms. This will enable students and professional programmers to be trained, over a period of several years, towards the emerging age of parallel computing.

As was explained above, the multi-stage approach does not mean to replace the effort for building massively parallel machines, but rather augment it, since both approaches share the same ultimate goal. We refer the reader to [Vi-91b] for more details and references.

6   Conclusion

A "divide-and-conquer" strategy to the advancement of parallel computing has been suggested in several theoretical and practical publications. The Parallel-Design Distributed-Implementation (PDDI) machine scheme of [Vi-84], and the position paper [Vi-83] advocate that software and algorithms people work on the PRAM as a programmer's model, while machine builders focus *separately* on implementing the PRAM. Valiant [Va90a] and [Va90b] used the term "bridging model" for describing a whole spectrum of possibilities for such a programmer's model. (The general idea of trading algorithm-parallelism for more effective implementation has also been discussed in these four papers.) Such a "divide-and-conquer" strategy also led to Fortran 90, the new computer language international standard [MR-90], which guides machine designers to support Fortran 90 in the future. As mentioned above, Fortran 90 enables coding PRAM algorithms, much in the same way that Fortran 77 enables coding of RAM algorithms.

Is it possible to come up with an alternative to the PRAM for algorithm-parallelism? We certainly do not have a proof that this is impossible. Many have tried to develop algorithms for quite a few models of parallel computation. Still, we are not aware of a theory of a similar (or even slightly lesser) magnitude for any other alternative model. Following the lesson of the last two decades, I would like to point out that there is little merit in simply stating a "new more realistic model" and quitting there. Formulating a new model will do little good unless it comes with a knowledge-base of algorithms, similar in magnitude and extent to the PRAM one. The current lack of competition to the PRAM model adds circumstantial evidence to it importance.

Acknowledgement. Helpful comments by Clyde Kruskal, Yossi Matias, Bill Pugh, and Neal Young are gratefully acknowledged.

References

[Akl-89]   S.G. Akl. *The Design and Analysis of Parallel Algorithms.* Prentice Hall, Engelwood Cliffs, New Jersey, 1989.

[ALM-90]   S. Arora, T. Leighton and B. Maggs. On-line algorithms for path selection in a nonblocking network. In *Proc. of the 22nd Ann. ACM Symp. on Theory of Computing*, pages 149-158, 1990.

[EG-88]   D. Eppstein and Z. Galil. Parallel algorithmic techniques for combinatorial computation. *Ann. Rev. Comput. Sci.*, 3:233–283, 1988.

[GR-88]   A. Gibbons and W. Rytter. *Efficient Parallel Algorithms.* Cambridge University Press, Cambridge, 1988.

[HP-90]   J.L. Hennessy and D.A. Patterson. *Computer Architecture a Quantitative Approach.* Morgan Kaufmann, San Mateo, California, 1990.

[KR-90]   R.M. Karp and V. Ramachandran. A survey of parallel algorithms for shared-memory machines. In Handbook of Theoretical Computer Science: Volume A, Algorithms and Complexity (Editor J. van Leeuwen), MIT Press/Elsevier, 1990, pages 869–942.

[KRS-90] C.P. Kruskal, L. Rudolph, and M. Snir. A complexity theory of efficient parallel algorithms. In *Theoretical Computer Science*, 71:95-132, 1990.

[J-92]   J. JáJá. *Introduction to Parallel Algorithms.* Addison-Wesley, Reading, MA, 1992.

[KU-86]   A. Karlin and E. Upfal. Parallel hashing – an efficient implementation of shared memory. In *Proc. of the 18th Ann. ACM Symp. on Theory of Computing*, pages 160–168, 1986.

[L-92a]   F.T. Leighton. *Introduction to Parallel Algorithms and Architectures: Arrays, Trees, Hypercubes.* Morgan Kaufmann, San Mateo, California, 1992.

[L-92b]   F.T. Leighton. Methods for message routing in parallel machines. In *Proc. of the 24th Ann. ACM Symp. on Theory of Computing*, pages 77–96, 1992.

[MR-90]   M. Metcalf and J. Reid. *Fortran 90 Explained.* Oxford University Press, New York, 1990.

[MV-84]   K. Mehlhorn and U. Vishkin. Randomized and deterministic simulations of PRAMs by parallel machines with restricted granularity of parallel memories. *Acta Informatica*, 21:339–374, 1984.

[R-87]   A.G. Ranade. How to emulate shared memory. In *Proc. of the 28th IEEE Annual Symp. on Foundation of Computer Science*, pages 185–194, 1987.

[R-92]   J.H. Reif, editor. *Synthesis of Parallel Algorithms.* Morgan Kaufmann, San Mateo, California, 1992.

[U-89]   E. Upfal. An $O(\log N)$ deterministic packet routing scheme. In *Proc. of the 21st Ann. ACM Symp. on Theory of Computing*, pages 241–250, 1989.

[Va90a]   L.G. Valiant. A bridging model for parallel computation. *Comm. ACM*, 33,8:103–111, 1990.

[Va90b]   L.G. Valiant. General purpose parallel architectures. In Handbook of Theoretical Computer Science: Volume A, Algorithms and Complexity (Editor J. van Leeuwen), MIT Press/Elsevier, 1990, pages 942–971.

[Vi-83]   U. Vishkin. Synchronous parallel computation - a survey. Technical Report TR 71, Dept. of Computer Science, Courant Institute, New York University, 1983.

[Vi-84]   U. Vishkin. A parallel-design distributed-implementation (PDDI) general purpose computer. *Theoretical Computer Science*, 32:157–172, 1984.

[Vi-91a] U. Vishkin. Structural parallel algorithmics. In *Proc. of the 18th Int. Colloquium on Automata, Languages and Programming*, pages 363–380, 1991, Lecture Notes in Computer Science 510, Springer-Verlag.

[Vi-91b]   U. Vishkin. Can parallel algorithms enhance serial implementation? TR-91-145, University of Maryland Institute for Advanced Computer Studies (UMIACS), College Park, Maryland 20742-3251, 1991.

Hashing strategies for simulating shared memory on distributed memory machines

Friedhelm Meyer auf der Heide*

Heinz Nixdorf Institute and
Computer Science Department
University of Paderborn
4790 Paderborn, Germany

Abstract. We survey shared memory simulations on distributed memory machines (DMMs), that use universal hashing to distribute the shared memory cells over the memory modules of the DMM. We measure their quality in terms of delay, time-processor efficiency, memory contention (how many requests have to be satisfied by one memory module per simulated step) and simplicity. Further we take into consideration different access conflict rules to the modules of the DMM, in particular the c-Collision rule motivated by the idea of communicating between processors and modules using an optical crossbar.

It turns out that simulations with very small delay require more than one hash function. Further, simple simulations on DMMs with the c-Collision rule are only known if more than one hash function is allowed.

1 Introduction

Parallel machines that communicate via a shared memory, so called *parallel random access machines* (PRAMs) represent the most powerful parallel computation model considered in the theory of parallel computation. Further, it is relatively comfortable to program, because the programmer does not have to specify interprocessor communication, or to allocate storage in a distributed memory; rather she can even use common data structures, stored in the shared memory.

On the other hand, PRAMs are very unrealistic from the technological point of view; large machines with shared memory can only be built at the cost of very slow shared memory access. A more realistic model is the *distributed memory machine* (DMM), where the memory is partitioned in modules, one per processor. In this case a parallel memory access is restricted in so far that only one access to each module can be performed per parallel step. Thus *memory contention* occurs if a PRAM algorithm is run on a DMM; parallel accesses to cells stored in one module are sequentialized.

Therefore many authors have investigated methods to simulate PRAMs on DMMs. Often it is assumed that processors and modules are connected by a bounded degree

---
* Supported in part by DFG-Forschergruppe "Effiziente Nutzung massiv paralleler Systeme, Teilprojekt 4", and by the Esprit Basic Research Action Nr. 7141 (ALCOM II).

network, and packet routing is used to access the modules. (See e. g. ([11], [14], [14], [9], for a survey on packet routing see [15], [16]).

In this survey we focus on DMMs with a complete interconnection between processors and modules.

The most promising approaches are based on hashing: One or more hash functions, randomly drawn from a suitable universal class, are used to distribute the shared memory cells (we shall say "keys" for short) among the modules.

If one hash function h is used, the *delay* of the simulation, i. e. the time needed to simulate one PRAM step is governed by

- The *evaluation time* of h.
- The *memory contention*, i. e. the maximum number of memory accesses of a PRAM step that are mapped to the same module under h.
- The *quality of the access schedule.* If we want to benefit from the effect of parallel slackness, i. e. if we simulate a large PRAM on a smaller DMM, or if we have restricted access conflict resolution rules at the modules (e. g. as motivated by a realization of the communication among processors and modules via an "optimal crossbar", see below), we need a protocol that specifies how (e. g. when, by whom, in which order) the requests are sent to the modules. The time needed for the access is clearly bounded from below by the memory contention; the aim is to come close to this bound. Further, it is desirable that such schedules are *simple*, i. e. do not make complicated computations to decide which request to try to satisfy next, and do not distribute the requests among the processors before sending them to the modules.

In Chapter 5 we shall get to know several simulations that use two or three hash functions, i. e. that store each shared memory cell in two or three modules. It turns out that it is not necessary to access all copies of a requested cell in order to obtain a simulation. In this case, memory contention is constant with high probability, if an "ideal" access schedule can be found which specifies, for each keys to be accessed, which copies to access. Thus, in this case the *access schedule* is of particular importance.

The rest of the paper is organized as follows: In Chapter 2 we define the computational models and discuss several criteria for measuring the quality of simulations. In Chapter 3 we briefly sketch results on universal hashing.

In Chapter 4 we survey the simulations using one hash function, in Chapter 5 those using two or three hash functions.

In this paper we restrict ourselves to describing simulations, we do not give any hint towards the (in most case complicated) proof techniques used for proving the delay bounds.

2 Computation models and criteria for the quality of simulations

A parallel random access machine (PRAM) consists of processors $P_1, \ldots, P_m$ and a shared memory with cells $U = \{1, \ldots, p\}$, each capable of storing one integer. The processors work synchronously and have random access to the shared memory cells.

We distinguish PRAM models according to their capabilities of handling concurrent accesses to the same shared memory cell. We distinguish between the following rules:

- *exclusive read (ER)*: concurrent reading to the same shared memory cell forbidden
- *concurrent read (CR)*: concurrent reading allowed
- *exclusive write (EW)*: concurrent writing forbidden
- *concurrent write (CW)*: concurrent writing allowed.

In case of concurrent write we have to specify the semantics of a concurrent write access to a shared memory cell. There are many rules of resolving such write conflicts considered in literature.

Write conflict resolution rules: The result of the attempt of processors $P_{i_1}, \ldots, P_{i_s}, i_1 < \ldots < i_s, s > 1$, to write concurrently $x_1, \ldots, x_s$ to cell j is, for example, as follows.

Tolerant: cell j remains unchanged

Arbitrary: cell j contains any of $x_1, \ldots, x_s$, all of these choices have to lead to a correct result of the algorithm

Priority: cell j contains x_1

Minimum: cell j contains $\min\{x_1, \ldots, x_s\}$.

In [13], it is shown that all the above rules are almost identical, if concurrent read is allowed: an $n \log^*(n)$-processor CRCW-PRAM with the strongest rules, Minimum, can be simulated in a randomized fashion on a n-processor CRCW-PRAM with the weakest rule, Tolerant, such that the delay is $O(\log^*(n))$ with probability $1 - 2^{-n^\varepsilon}$, for some $\varepsilon > 0$.

In this paper we therefore only distinguish between exclusive-read exclusive-write PRAMs (EREW-PRAMs) and concurrent-read concurrent-write PRAMs (CRCW-PRAMs). It is convenient to assume the arbitrary rule in our considerations.

A *distributed memory machine* (DMM) consists of n processors $Q_1, \ldots, Q_n$ and n memory modules $M_1, \ldots, M_n$. Each module has a communication window where it can read from or write into. For the processors, these windows act like shared memory cells.

Again we distinguish DMM model with respect to how concurrent accesses at the communication windows are handled. It is easily checked that the result from [13] also implies that the computation powers of these CRCW-models are almost identical. In this paper we assume the arbitrary rule if we refer to CRCW-DMMs.

In case of DMMs we take into consideration a further rule for handling read/write collisions, which is motivated by the idea of using an optical crossbar to communicate between processors and (communication windows of) modules, compare [12], [17], [23]. Here a processor that wants to access module M directs a beam of light to it. If M only gets one message (i.e. only one beam is directed to its window), it acknowledges it, or, in case of read, sends back the requested data. If more than one processor sends a message to M, all of them get back a collision message.

We generalize this concept by assuming that a module can handle not only just one, but a constant number c of concurrent accesses. If at most c requests arrive, all of them are satisfied, otherwise, all issuing processors get a collision message. We refer to this model as a *c-Collision-DMM*.

In this paper we consider step by step simulations of PRAMs by DMMs. In all these simulations we use 1, 2, or 3 hash functions $h : U \rightarrow \{1, \ldots, n\}$ that specify in which module(s) each shared memory cell is maintained. We consider the following criteria for the quality of our simulations.

- **delay:** We want to simulate a PRAM fast on a DMM, i.e. we want that the delay, the (perhaps amortized) time needed to simulate one PRAM step, is small.
- **time-processor-efficiency:** If an m-processor PRAM is simulated on an n-processor DMM the smallest possible delay is $\frac{m}{n}$. We want to come close to this delay. If we achieve delay $O(\frac{m}{n})$ we talk about a *time-processor-optimal* simulation.
- **memory contention:** Assume that the PRAM processors access large blocks of data in a read or write request. In this case it is important to find access schedules that guarantee that each memory module only has to process few request, i.e. to keep memory contention as small as possible. This may even be of advantage if a (fast) precomputation for finding the schedule is necessary.
- **access conflict rules:** We aim to simulate a strong PRAM, i.e. a CRCW-PRAM on a weak DMM, i.e. a EREW-DMM or 1-Collision-DMM, or find simulations which come close to this ideal.
- **simplicity:** We want to have very simple simulations, in particular very simple access schedules. In particular, we prefer schedule in which processors that issue an access request, do not send it to another processor, but pass it to the module(s) itself.

3 Universal Hashing

Let $U = \{1, \ldots, p\}$ be the shared memory cells of the PRAM. In all simulations they are distributed among the modules of the DMM using one or more hash functions $h : \{1, \ldots, p\} \rightarrow \{1, \ldots n\}$, randomly drawn from a *universal class of hash functions*.

The analyses of the simulations require high performance universal classes, a randomly chosen function of which has properties very much like a random function. On the other hand they have to be generated fast using little space, and have to be evaluated in constant time, at least if time-processor optimality is desired. Suitable classes are introduced in [10] and in [3], [4]. In [19] a combination of the above classes is introduced. This is necessary for all simulations presented in this paper which use more then one hash function.

We do not go into details about hashing in this survey, and refer the reader to the above papers and to [2], [8] and [18] for information about polynomials as hash functions. To simplify understanding of the simulations below one should assume that the hash functions used are random functions.

4 Simulations using one hash function

Let $U = \{1, \ldots, p\}$ be the set of registers (or cells) of the shared memory of a PRAM, and let $M_1, \ldots, M_n$ be the memory modules of a DMM. Let $H_{n,p} \subseteq \{h : U \rightarrow \{1, \ldots, n\}\}$ be a high performance universal class of hash functions. In this chapter we assume that, for a randomly chosen $h \in H_{n,p}$, cell x is stored in $M_{h(x)}$.

4.1 Simulations of n-processor PRAM on n-processor DMMs using one hash function

Consider a PRAM with processors $P_1, \ldots, P_n$, to be simulated by a DMM with processors $Q_1, \ldots, Q_n$. Let $X = \{x_1, \ldots, x_n\} \subseteq U$. In a given PRAM step, P_i wants to access cell x_i. Q_i simulates P_i, i.e. has to simulate P_i's access to cell x_i, for $i = 1, \ldots, n$. It can be shown that the maximum bucket size of X under a randomly chosen $h \in H_{n,p}$ is $\Theta(\frac{\log(n)}{\log\log(n)})$ with high probability, i.e. that $\text{Prob}(\max_{1 \le i \le n}\{|h^{-1}(i) \cap X|\} = \Theta(\frac{\log(n)}{\log\log(n)}))$ is very large. In other words: with high probability each module is only accessed by at most $D\frac{\log(n)}{\log\log(n)}$ different requests. As $\frac{\log(n)}{\log\log(n)}$ is also a lower bound, $\Theta(\log(n)/\log\log(n))$ delay and memory contention is the best we can hope for.

n-processor CRCW-PRAM $\rightarrow$ n-processor CRCW-DMM. In this case the access schedule is very simple. (Recall that we assume an Arbitrary-rule at the modules.) In each round, each Q_i that was not yet successful tries to access $M_{h(x_i)}$. Each M_j answers one request. Q_i is successful if it gets an answer from $M_{h(x_i)}$, or if a Q_j with $x_i = x_j$ gets the answer.

Thus delay and contention equal the maximum bucket size $O(\frac{\log(n)}{\log\log(n)})$, and the schedule is very simple.

n-processor CRCW-PRAM $\rightarrow$ n-processor EREW-DMM. In this case we use the $O(\log(n))$-time sorting algorithm from [20] for sorting n numbers with an n-processor EREW-PRAM. As this algorithm uses space $O(n)$, it can be implemented on a n-processor EREW-DMM with constant delay.

The *access schedule* first sorts $(h(x_1), x_1), \ldots, (h(x_n), x_n)$ according to the lexicographic order. Now it is obvious how to schedule the requests such that no collisions happen.

This needs time $O(\log(n))$ with high probability, i.e. the delay is by a factor $O(\log\log(n))$ away from the maximum bucket size. The contention is still $O(\frac{\log(n)}{\log\log(n)})$, with high probability. The schedule is very complicated, requests are not passed to the modules by the issuing processors because of the sorting; answers have to be redistributed.

4.2 Optimal simulations allowing parallel slackness, using one hash function

Consider a PRAM with $m = n \cdot t$ processors $P_{i,j}, i = 1, \ldots, n, j = 1, \ldots t$, and a DMM with n processors $Q_i, \ldots, Q_n$. Let $X = \{x_{i,j}, i = 1, \ldots, n, j = 1, \ldots, t\}$. $P_{i,j}$ wants to access cell $x_{i,j}$, $P_{i,1}, \ldots, P_{i,t}$ are simulated in Q_i. It can be shown that the maximum bucket size $\max_{1 \le i \le n}\{|h^{-1}(i) \cap X|\}$ is best possible, i.e. $\Theta(t)$, with high probability, only for $t = \Omega(\log(n))$. Thus, with one hash function, time-processor optimal simulations must have delay $\Omega(\log(n))$.

$n^{1+\epsilon}$-processor CRCW-PRAM $\rightarrow$ n-processor EREW-DMM. The following algorithm is presented in [6]. It assumes that p is polynomial in n. In this case it is possible to base the simulation on fast integer sorting, using a similar idea as in Section 4.1.2.

Based on the randomized EREW-PRAM algorithm for integer sorting from [21], in [22] a randomized algorithm is presented for sorting $n^{1+\epsilon}$ keys from $[1, \ldots, n^k]$ on a n-processor EREW-DMM in time $O(n^\epsilon k) = O(n^\epsilon)$ if k is constant. Using this algorithm a similar schedule as in 2.1.2 leads to an access schedule, which implies a randomized simulation of a $n^{1+\epsilon}$-processor-CRCW-PRAM on an n-processor EREW-DMM.

The simulation is time-processor optimal, but the delay is very high. Further the access schedule is very complicated, again requests are not passed to the modules by the issuing processors, a redistribution of answers becomes necessary.

$n \log n$-processor CRCW-PRAM $\rightarrow$ n-processor CRCW-DMM. The following algorithm is presented in [3]. We assume that we (virtually) have n further processors $W_1, \ldots, W_n$, the working processors, available in the DMM. The W_i do the following in each round: they randomly choose a Q_i to ask it for a new request x. Each Q_i delivers a constant number of keys to asking working processors. A working processor tries to deliver its key x to $M_{h(x)}$. Each $M_{h(x)}$ returns a constant number of answers, which are transmitted from the working processor to the Q_i that issued the request.

This schedule can be shown to run in expected time $O(\log(n))$, i.e. achieves optimal expected delay, if an EREW-PRAM is simulated.

The same optimal expected delay can also be achieved for simulations of CRCW-PRAMs on CRCW-DMMs using a complicated algorithm that searches for concurrent accesses during the competition of duplicates of a key x to access $M_{h(x)}$.

This simulation reaches expected optimal delay $O(\log(n))$, i.e. is best possible in this respect, if only one hash function is used. On the other hand the schedule is still complicated; even if EREW-PRAMs are simulated, keys have to be distributed among the processors.

$n \log n$-processor EREW-PRAM $\rightarrow$ n-processor CRCW-DMM. The analysis of the following simple simulation is shown in [25].

The access schedule is very simple: The processors satisfy their requests in the given order. In each round, each processor tries to pass its currently processed request to the module. Each module answers one (arbitrary) of the incoming requests per round.

This schedule needs optimal delay $O(\log(n))$ with high probability, if an $n \log n$-processor EREW-PRAM is simulated on a CRCW-DMM. The importance of this schedule lies in its simplicity.

$n \log n$-processor EREW-PRAM $\rightarrow$ n-processor 1-Collision-DMM. This simulation is shown in [17] based on an access schedule from [23]. This schedule works not only if the destinations of keys x, $M_{h(x)}$, are random, but already if no module gets more than $c \log(n)$ messages, for arbitrary constant $c > 0$.

In a first phase, in each round, each Q_i randomly chooses one of its not yet satisfied requests. With a certain probability, it passes it to the corresponding module. The attempt is successful if the module gets no other request at the same time.

A schedule based on the above idea is designed in [23]. The expected number of not yet satisfied request after $O(\log(n))$ rounds is shown to be $O(n)$.

It is easy to finish up the remaining accesses in time $O(\log(n))$ using a parallel prefix algorithm to distribute the remaining keys evenly among the processors and to define the schedule.

This simulation is optimal, has asymtotically best possible expected delay $O(\log(n))$, and works already on 1-optimal DMMs. The access schedule is still very complicated, in particular, in the second phase accesses are not processed by the issuing processors, and a redistribution of answers to read requests become necessary.

5 Simulations using two or three hash functions

In this section we consider simulations using two or three hash functions h_1, h_2 or h_0, h_1, h_2, randomly, independently drawn from some high performance universal class $H_{n,p} \subseteq \{h : h : \{1, \ldots, p\} \rightarrow \{1, \ldots, n\}\}$. Each key $x \in U$ will be stored in $M_{h_1(x)}, M_{h_2(x)}$, and, in case of three hash functions, in $M_{h_0(x)}$. We refer to the representants of x in the $M_{h_i(x)}$'s as its copies.

In some simulations we further assume that few, i.e. $O(n)$ keys may be intermediately stored at further positions. This will be done by using a perfect hash table of size $O(n)$. In [1] and [7] it is shown how to implement such a table on a CRCW-PRAM using space $O(n)$ in time not exceeding $O(\log^*(n))$ with high probability. Because of the space bound it also can be implemented on a CRCW-DMM within the same time bound, as long as only $O(n)$ keys have to be stored in it.

5.1 Fast simulations of n-processor PRAMs on n-processor DMMs

Consider a PRAM, DMM and a set X as described in the beginning of Section 4.1. Already if two hash functions are used, there is an access schedule that needs constant time, if only one arbitrary copy of each $x \in X$ has to be accessed. To see this consider the bipartite graph with node set $X \cup \{1, \ldots, n\}$, where each $x \in X$ is connected to $h_1(x)$ and $h_2(x)$. If h_1, h_2 are random and independent, then this graph is random. It is well known that the nodes in X can be covered by a constant number of matchings, with high probability. Thus a schedule that processes one matching after the other needs constant time, even on an EREW-DMM. In particular, the memory contention of such a schedule is constant. The problem is to find such a schedule efficiently.

n processor CRCW-PRAM $\rightarrow$ n-processor CRCW-DMM. This simulation is presented in [19]. It uses two hash functions and has delay $O(\log \log(n))$ with high probability. We present a variant which only has constant memory contention.

We distinguish between write- and read steps. For writing, we maintain two perfect hash tables SM_1, SM_2 of size $O(n)$, each. In order to update the copies of $x_1, \ldots, x_n$ w. r. t. $h_1, \{x_1, \ldots, x_n\}$ is added to SM_1 using the perfect hashing strategy mentioned above. Then, for each key x in SM_1 an attempt is made to update its copy in $M_{h_1(x)}$. Only constantly many of the updates directed to M_j are performed, and the corresponding keys are removed from SM_1. The time for such a step is governed by $O(\log^*(n))$, the time to set up a perfect hash table, as long as this table has size at most $c \cdot n$ for a suitable constant $c > 0$. It can be shown that this size bound is satisfied with high probability. The same procedure is executed w. r. t. h_2, using the hash table SM_2.

This write algorithm has delay $O(\log^*(n))$ with high probability.

The read algorithm is very simple. Note that the up-to-date value of x is stored in SM_1 and SM_2, if x is in one of these hash tables. Otherwise the copies of x in $M_{h_1(x)}$ and $M_{h_2(x)}$ are up-to-date. Thus, in the read algorithm, each Q_i inspects SM_1 and SM_2 to find the contents of cell x_i. This takes constant time by definition of perfect hashing. Each unsuccessful processor tries to access alternately the two copies of its key, until it gets an answer (no matter from which copy, both are up-to-date.) In each round, each module answers all requests, as long it only gets some constant c many. If it gets more it answers none of them.

Each of the above rounds takes constant time. It can be shown that $O(\log\log(n))$ rounds suffice to answer all requests, with high probability.

Thus we have got a simulation with delay not exceeding $O(\log\log(n))$ with high probability. The memory contention is only constant, and reading is very simple. On the other hand, writing is complicated because it uses perfect hash tables; again processors that process a request, i.e. pass the corresponding key to a module, are not those that issue the request, and redistribution of answers becomes necessary.

n-processor EREW-PRAM $\to$ n-processor c-Collision-DMM. This simulation is presented in [25].

The basic idea is borrowed from the deterministic simulation from [24]. We use three hash functions. In the write algorithm, arbitrary two of the three copies of each cell x_i are updated.

Thus, both for reading and writing, we need a schedule that accesses two arbitrary of the three copies of each x_i. This schedule is very simple.

Each round consists of three phases 0, 1, 2. In phase j, each Q_i tries to access the j'th copy of x_i. It skips an access to copy j, if it was earlier successful in accessing this copy. Q_i quits as soon as it gets two answers. Each module answers all request it gets in one phase, if it gets at most c requests. Otherwise it answers no request (this is the c-Collision rule).

It can be shown that this schedule finishes within $O(\log\log(n))$ rounds with high probability. Further it guarantees constant memory contention, is very simple, and runs on the weak c-Collision-DMM. The time bound $O(\log\log(n))$ already holds with reasonable probability for $c = 2$.

5.2 Optimal simulations allowing parallel slackness, using three hash functions

We use the notations introduced in the beginning of Section 4.2. Whereas, if only one hash function is used, the contention can be reduced to $O(\frac{m}{n})$ only if $m =$

$\Omega(n \log(n))$, this reduction is possible for all $m \geq n$ in case of two or more hash functions, as described in the beginning of Section 4.1. Again the problem is to find such schedule.

$n \log \log(n) \log^*(n)$-processor EREW-PRAM $\to$ n-processor CRCW-DMM. This simulation is shown in [19]. We do not go into details here. The simulation is based on the idea shown in Section 5.1.1. A simpler variant, also shown in [19] has delay not exceeding $O(\log \log(n) \log^*(n))$ with high probability, simulates even CRCW-PRAMs, but is by a factor $\log^*(n)$ away from time-processor optimality.

These simulations are very complicated, e. g. they still use perfect hashing.

$n \log(n)$-processor EREW-PRAM $\to$ n-processor c-Collision-DMM. This simulation is presented in [25].

It represents the simplest time-processor optimal simulation on a c-Collision-DMM.

The schedule is as in Section 5.1.2 with the extension that each processor starts processing its next key in the situation where it quits in Section 5.1.2. It now quits when all its accesses are satisfied.

This schedule has optimal delay $O(\log(n))$, with high probability. Further, it is very simple, and runs on the weak c-Collision-DMM. $c = 2$ is sufficient to make the delay bound reasonably reliable.

6   Conclusion

Simulations of PRAMs on DMMs that use more than one hash function have the disadvantage that they vaste storage (a factor 2 or 3) within the modules. (It is not required that the number of modules is enlarged!).

Nevertheless the simulations described in this paper show that the use of two or three hash functions has advantages that make them worth being considered more carefully, both theoretically and experimentally.

- The memory contention can be made constant.
- Simulations on c-Collision-DMMs (motivated by a communication technology using optical crossbars) become very simple, i. e. feasible for efficient implementation.
- Simulation with very small delay can be designed.

References

1. H. Bast and T. Hagerup. Fast and reliable parallel hashing. In *Proc. of the 3rd Ann. ACM Symp. on Parallel Algorithms and Architectures*, pages 50–61, 1991.
2. J. L. Carter and M. N. Wegman. Universal classes of hash functions. *J. Comput. Syst. Sci.*, 18:143–154, 1979.
3. M. Dietzfelbinger and F. Meyer auf der Heide. How to distribute a dictionary in a complete network. In *Proc. of the 22nd Ann. ACM Symp. on Theory of Computing*, pages 117–127, 1990.

4. M. Dietzfelbinger and F. Meyer auf der Heide. A new universal class of hash functions and dynamic hashing in real time. In M. S. Paterson, editor, *Proceedings of 17th ICALP*, pages 6–19. Springer, 1990. Lecture Notes in Computer Science 443.

5. A. Karlin and E. Upfal. Parallel hashing — an efficient implementation of shared memory. In *Proc. of the 18th Ann. ACM Symp. on Theory of Computing*, pages 160–168, 1986.

6. C. P. Kruskal, L. Rudolph, and M. Snir. A complexity theory of efficient parallel algorithms. *Theoret. Comput. Sci.*, 71:95–132, 1990.

7. Y. Matias and U. Vishkin. Converting high probability into nearly-constant time – with applications to parallel hashing. In *Proc. of the 23rd Ann. ACM Symp. on Theory of Computing*, pages 307–316, 1991.

8. K. Mehlhorn and U. Vishkin. Randomized and deterministic simulations of PRAMs by parallel machines with restricted granularity of parallel memories. *Acta Informatica*, 21:339–374, 1984.

9. A. G. Ranade. How to emulate shared memory. In *Proc. of the 28th IEEE Ann. Symp. on Foundations of Computer Science*, pages 185–194, 1987.

10. A. Siegel. On universal classes of fast high performance hash functions, their time-space tradeoff, and their applications. In *Proc. of the 30th IEEE Ann. Symp. on Foundations of Computer Science*, pages 20–25, 1989. *Revised Version*.

11. E. Upfal. Efficient schemes for parallel communication. *J. Assoc. Comput. Mach.*, 31(3):507–517, 1984.

12. L. G. Valiant. General purpose parallel architectures. In J. van Leeuwen, editor, *Handbook of Theoretical Computer Science, Vol. A: Algorithms and Complexity*, chapter 18, pages 943–971. Elsevier, Amsterdam, 1990.

13. T. Hagerup. The log-star revolution, proceedings. *STACS 92, LNCS 577*, pages 259–280, 1992.

14. A. Karlin, E. Upfal. Parallel Hashing, an efficient implementation of shared memory. *Proc. 18th ACM STOC*, pages 160–168, 1986.

15. F. T. Leighton. Introduction to parallel algorithms and architectures: arrays, trees, hypercubes. *Morgan Kaufmann Publishers*, San Mateo, 1992.

16. F. T. Leighton. Methods for packet routing in parallel machines. *Proc. 24th ACM STOC*, pages 77–96, 1992.

17. L. Valiant. A bridging model for parallel computation. *Communications of the ACM*, 33(8), pages 103–111, 1990.

18. M. Dietzfelbinger, A. Karlin, K. Mehlhorn, F. Meyer auf der Heide, H. Rohnert, R. E. Tarjan. Dynamic perfect hashing, upper and lower bounds. *Proc. 29th IEEE FOCS*, pages 524–531, 1988, extended version appears in SIAM J. Comp.

19. R. Karp, M. Luby, F. Meyer auf der Heide. Efficient PRAM simulation on distributed memory machine. *Proc. 24th ACM STOC*, pages 318–326, 1992.

20. R. Cole. Parallel merge sort. *SIAM J. Comp.* 17(4), pages 770–785, 1988.

21. J. Reif. An optimal parallel algorithm for integer sorting. *Proc. 26th IEEE-FOCS*, pages 496–504, 1985.

22. R. A. Wagner, Y. Han. Parallel algorithms for bucket sorting and the data dependent prefix problem. *Proc. Int. Conf. on Parallel Processing*, Illinois, pages 924–930, 1986.

23. R. J. Anderson, G. L. Miller. Optical communication for pointer based algorithms. *Tech. Rep.* CRI 88–14, Comp. Sci. Dpt, Univ. of Southern California, Los Angeles, 1988.

24. E. Upfal, A. Wigderson. How to share memory in a distributed system. *J. ACM 34*, pages 116–127, 1987.

25. M. Dietzfelbinger, F. Meyer auf der Heide. Simple, efficient shared memory simulations, preprint 1992.

Better Parallel Architectures via Emulations

Arnold L. Rosenberg
Department of Computer Science
University of Massachusetts
Amherst, Massachusetts

Abstract. As the processors and communication subsystems of parallel architectures become progressively faster, it is becoming increasingly cost-effective to build simple architectures that achieve complex behavior by emulating more complicated ones. We support this thesis by describing work by the author and collaborators [10] on algorithmically implementing, for pure SIMD bit-serial processor arrays, a multigauging capability that would be prohibitively expensive to implement in hardware.

1 Introduction

1.1 The Thesis

Present-day technology has seen great progress in making the processors and communication subsystems of parallel architectures ever faster. One corollary of this technological progress is that one can now relegate to software complex processes that, using earlier technologies, had to be realized in hardware for the sake of efficiency. Indeed, one already sees examples of architectures whose sophisticated capabilities result from a synergy of fast, simple hardware and efficient, complex software.

The thesis of the present note extrapolates directly from the synergistic architectures just alluded to. Specifically, the thesis asserts that the tools for efficiently emulating one processor array by another, as exemplified by the work in [1, 3, 5, 7], enable us to *algorithmically* build efficient architectures that cannot be built cost-effectively in hardware. The remainder of the note describes a case study that we believe supports this thesis.

1.2 A Validating Case Study

When searching for a testbed for the thesis of the preceding subsection, I recalled a series of papers discussing the desirability and difficulty of endowing a parallel architecture with a *multigauging capability*, i.e., the ability to change dynamically the (apparent) width of its datapath, ALU, and memory bus. Using examples drawn largely from the area of computer vision, it was argued in [6, 11, 14] that such a capability would enhance the efficient usefulness of an architecture. By carefully analyzing the costs of realizing such a capability, it was argued in [14, 15] that one could practically envisage implementing at most a couple of gauge sizes in hardware.

This, then seemed like the perfect testbed for the thesis. To wit, if one could algorithmically achieve an efficient multigauging capability for an architecture, it was (intuitively) rather unlikely that the efficiency would hold for only a few values of the gauge size. One would, therefore, have achieved algorithmically a useful architectural enhancement that one could not achieve in hardware.

The remainder of this note surveys the work of a research team (who were then all) at the University of Massachusetts, that studied the problem of devising algorithms that would endow a parallel architecture with an algorithmic multigauging capability. The work is described in detail in [10].

2 The Problem Formalized

The Computing Model. In order to comply with the architectures of many machines that were designed with computer vision in mind, we decided to restrict attention to the following genre of processor arrays: pure SIMD arrays of n identical bit-serial processing elements (PEs) that are interconnected via a one-bit-wide network. We assumed that each PE is capable of one-bit algebraic addition and one-bit logical operations. Each has a local memory comprising m one-bit words and one $(\log n)$-bit read-only processor-index register (for instruction masking); we decided to support memory access via direct addressing (access via address field), indirect addressing (access via address register), and implicit addressing (access via "end" of shift-register). We assumed that computations by the array alternate *computation* and *communication* steps.

Multigauge Behavior. Identifying the *gauge size* of an array as the common width of its datapath, ALU, and memory bus, we established as our goal the implementation — using emulations, with no hardware enhancements — of the meta-instruction

gauge k

(where k is any integer from 1 to n). The functionality of the meta-instruction is defined schematically as follows.

$$\left. \begin{array}{l} SIMD \\ bit\text{-}serial \\ n\text{-}PE\ array \\ \text{on a} \\ 1\text{-}bit\text{-}wide\ network, \\ m\ 1\text{-}bit\ words/PE \end{array} \right\} \implies \textbf{gauge } k \implies \left\{ \begin{array}{l} SIMD \\ k\text{-}bit\text{-}parallel \\ n/k\text{-}macro\text{-}PE\ array \\ \text{on a} \\ k\text{-}bit\text{-}wide\ network, \\ m\ k\text{-}bit\ words/macro\text{-}PE \end{array} \right.$$

The *macro-PEs* of the transformed array are to be capable of the following operations using k-bit words: (algebraic) addition, bitwise logical operations, and shifting operations; note that the former operations extend the bit-serial repertoire, while the last has no analogue in the bit-serial world. We decided to make the entire implementation a "black box" operation, so that the machine would not change its appearance in any way to the user; in particular we decided to retain the original, bit-serial I/O. A consequence of this decision is that datapath conversion would require "corner-turning". We did not cop out by insisting that the user corner-turn for us.

3 The Algorithmic Solution

3.1 The Overall Strategy

Our strategy for achieving multigauge behavior built on the common idea of representing the given n-PE array $\mathcal{A}$ as a graph G: nodes of G represent PEs of $\mathcal{A}$, while edges of G represent communication links of $\mathcal{A}$. As suggested earlier, our strategy prescribed partitioning $\mathcal{A}$ into *macro-PEs*, with k PEs each. We would then have the partitioned $\mathcal{A}$ act as an *n/k-PE macro-array of macro-PEs*, and we would have the PEs in each macro-PE "cooperate" to emulate a single k-bit-parallel PE.

The major challenges resided in finding a way to partition $\mathcal{A}$ so that the SIMD controller could "address" macro-PEs efficiently (including the issue of PE masking) and so that PEs within macro-PEs could "cooperate" efficiently.

3.2 The Ingredients of Success

Three ideas enabled our implementation of the meta-instruction. Note that these ideas are common ones to the computer theorist, yet less so to the computer architect. We view the success of the project as having resulted from a melding of the toolkits of the architect and the theorist.

A. Direct-Product Arrays

The Idea. The *direct product* of arrays $\mathcal{A}$ and $\mathcal{B}$, denoted $\mathcal{A} \times \mathcal{B}$, is the array whose nodes are all ordered pairs $\langle x, y \rangle$ where x is a node of $\mathcal{A}$ and y is a node of $\mathcal{B}$. The edges of $\mathcal{A} \times \mathcal{B}$ connect nodes $\langle x, y \rangle$ and $\langle x', y' \rangle$ just when (a) $x = x'$ and y is connected to y' by an edge in $\mathcal{B}$, or (b) x is connected to x' by an edge in $\mathcal{A}$ and $y = y'$. An important feature of the direct-product construction is that the copies of $\mathcal{A}$ and $\mathcal{B}$ retain their identities in the product.

The Application. We employ the notion of direct-product array in our implementation of the **gauge** macro-instruction by having *array $\mathcal{A}$ emulate a direct-product array both of whose factors are smaller versions of $\mathcal{A}$.* Specifically, if we let $\mathcal{A}_N$ denote the N-PE version of array $\mathcal{A}$, then we implement the macro-instruction **gauge** k by having array $\mathcal{A}_N$ emulate the direct product $\mathcal{A}_k \times \mathcal{A}_{N/k}$. For instance, if $\mathcal{A}_N$ were an N-node hypercube (so $N = 2^n$ for some n, which is the dimensionality of $\mathcal{A}_N$), and if $k = 2^r$ for some r, then $\mathcal{A}_k$ would be the r-dimensional hypercube, and $\mathcal{A}_{N/k}$ would be the $(n-r)$-dimensional hypercube. Our intention is: each instance of the array $\mathcal{A}_k$ will play the role of a k-bit macro-PE; the instance of array $\mathcal{A}_{N/k}$ that interconnects these macro-PEs will play the role of the N/k-macro-PE macro-array.

We have assumed in our general prescription, for simplicity, that k divides N and that array $\mathcal{A}$ has versions with N nodes, k nodes, and N/k nodes. Our specific example (the hypercube) shows that these assumptions may not hold; in such cases, we would have to restrict the values of k which we allow as target gauge sizes (i.e., as arguments to **gauge**). We consider such possible restrictions a small cost for the big gains we perceive from our prescription, which we describe now.

Having array $\mathcal{A}_N$ emulate the direct-product array $\mathcal{A}_k \times \mathcal{A}_{N/k}$ yields an elegant solution to many of the problems encountered in a quest for an *efficient, pure SIMD* implementation of the **gauge** macro-instruction. Specifically:

- The fact that the k-bit-parallel macro-array $\mathcal{A}_{N/k}$ has the same topology as the bit-serial array $\mathcal{A}_N$ should simplify the task of *programming the macro-array;* in fact, the same algorithms (especially those involving communication) should work for all gauge sizes.

- The fact that all of the k-bit macro-PEs are identical in structure, being copies of $\mathcal{A}_k$, renders *the "addressing" problem for the SIMD controller* simple: all macro-PEs have same node-set and topology.
- The fact that, in the direct-product construction, "logically" adjacent copies of node v of $\mathcal{A}_k$ are (up to the problem of emulation) "physically" adjacent to one another, renders the operation of *direct data-transfer* trivial and efficient.

B. Permutation-Routing

The Idea. In a *(partial) permutation route*, every node of $\mathcal{A}$ sends data to, and receives data from (at most) one other node. The source-destination pairs thus form a (partial) permutation of the nodes of $\mathcal{A}$. The importance of permutation routing to our task is twofold: many of the data transfers we shall have to do can be accomplished by (sequences of) *off-line* permutation routes; there are efficient *deterministic* off-line permutation routing algorithms for most popular interconnection networks (cf. [2, 9]).

The Application. We employ permutation routing to implement all internal data transfers within our macro-PEs, such as cyclic shifting on k-bit words. The most important use of permutation routing, however, is in the implementation of the datapath conversion (corner-turning) that begins each change of gauge size. Specifically, the corner-turning needed to implement **gauge** k reduces to k consecutive permutation routes, as illustrated in Figure 1.

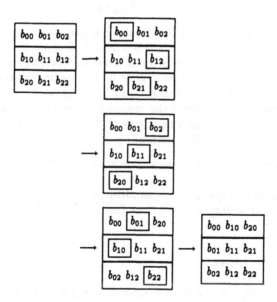

Fig. 1. Corner-turning via permutation routing.

The fact that we have a fixed repertoire of permutation routes that need to be implemented allows us to use *off-line deterministic* routing algorithms. We had to modify known routing algorithms (for the specific networks we considered) in a nontrivial way in order to cleave to the pure SIMD regimen of our study. However, we did *not* have to worry about implementing adaptive, randomized routing algorithms, because of the fixed repertoire.

C. Leveled Emulations of Complete Binary Trees

The Idea. The complete binary tree has long been known to be a useful structure for a variety of computations. Two genres of computations are of prime interest to us here.

Evaluation Trees. Say that one is given a binary associative "multiplication" * and any vector $\mathbf{x} = \langle x_0, x_1, \ldots, x_{m-1} \rangle$ of elements in the domain of *. If one loads the elements of $\mathbf{x}$ in the leaves of a complete binary tree, left to right, then one can evaluate the *-product $x_0 * x_1 * \cdots * x_{m-1}$ in $\lceil \log_2 m \rceil$ steps, by a single sweep up the tree: beginning at the parents of the leaves, one places in node v the *-product of the elements in its children.

Parallel-Prefix Trees. A simple extension of the evaluation-tree sweep algorithm allows one to compute the *parallel-prefix* of the "multiplication" * on the vector $\mathbf{x}$ [8], that is, the vector

$$\text{parallel-prefix}(\mathbf{x}; *) = \begin{pmatrix} x_0 \\ x_0 * x_1 \\ x_0 * x_1 * x_2 \\ \vdots \\ x_0 * x_1 * \cdots * x_{m-1} \end{pmatrix}$$

of all partial prefix-*-products of $\mathbf{x}$. Specifically, a single, $\lceil \log_2 m \rceil$-step upward sweep supplies each node of the tree with the *-product of all elements in the leaves of its subtree. The parallel prefix can now be computed in another $\lceil \log_2 m \rceil$ steps by having (in a pipelined fashion) each left sibling node in the tree broadcast its *-product to all of the leaves in the subtree rooted at its right sibling (cf. [9, 13]).

The Application. We implement the majority of evaluatory instructions in the repertoire of k-bit-parallel macro-PEs by having the macro-PEs emulate k-leaf complete binary trees, level by level. Specifically:

- We use the trees as evaluation trees in order to implement bit-wise logical operations.
- We use the trees to implement the parallel-prefix operator in order to implement comparisons and arithmetic operations (using carry-lookahead techniques) (cf. [4, 9]).

4 Testing the Ideas

In [10], we set out to test the ideas described herein in two ways, both involving implementing the ideas down to the level of pure SIMD pseudocode with single-bit masking (i.e., when we excluded certain PEs from a certain operation, we made sure that the exclusion was based on the value of a single bit in the PEs' processor-index registers). First, we implemented the prescribed algorithms in an architecture-independent way, thereby establishing the broad applicability of the techniques we were prescribing. The disadvantage of such broad implementation is that the timing analyses of our algorithms inevitably depended on a variety of unknown parameters relating to the time needed to accomplish certain crucial tasks (notably, emulating a direct-product array, emulating a complete binary tree level by level, and performing one of our special partial permutation routes). In order to obtain meaningful timing analyses, we therefore implemented the prescribed algorithms on (idealized) bit-serial, SIMD architectures based on three disparate networks: the hypercube [9], the de Bruijn network [12], and a specific mesh with reconfigurable buses that is being implemented at the University of Massachusetts as part of our Image Understanding Architecture [16].

What emerged from the architecture-independent phase of our study was the conclusion that we had achieved, algorithmically, a level of flexibility in changing gauge size that would be prohibitively expensive to achieve by hardware enhancement.

What emerged from the architecture-specific phase of our study was the conclusion that our solution may well be within the realm of practicality in many situations. We came to this conclusion by comparing the overhead of implementing the meta-instruction **gauge** k via our emulation-based strategy, as compared with trying to achieve the functionality of the meta-instruction via straightforward bit-serial implementation (when we could conceive of how to accomplish this). The results of our analysis are summarized, for the hypercube and de Bruijn networks, in the following table; presenting meaningful results for the reconfigurable mesh would require extra description of the architecture that is precluded by page limitations.

In reading the following table, the reader is reminded that the constants hidden in the big-O entries never exceed 5, and are often smaller.

| | Hypercube | | de Bruijn | |
	Emulated	*Bit-serial*	*Emulated*	*Bit-serial*?
I/O*	$O(k)$	$O(k)$	$O(k)$	$O(k)$?
Logical Operations*	1	$O(k)$	$O(1)$	$O(k)$?
Communication*	1	$O(k)$	$O(\log k)$	$O(k)$?
Arithmetic Operations*	$O(\log k)$	$O(k)$	$O(\log^2 k)$	$O(k)$?
Datapath Conversion†	$O(m \log k)$	0	$O(m \log^2 k)$	0?

* *recurring cost*
† *one-time cost*
? *not clear how to achieve at all!*

Acknowledgment of Support: This work was supported in part by NSF Grant CCR-90-13184.

References

1. F.S. Annexstein, M. Baumslag, A.L. Rosenberg (1990): Group action graphs and parallel architectures. *SIAM J. Comput. 19*, 544-569.
2. M. Baumslag and F.S. Annexstein (1991): A unified approach to global permutation routing on parallel networks. *Math. Syst. Th. 24*, 233-251.

3. S.N. Bhatt, F.R.K. Chung, J.-W. Hong, F.T. Leighton, B. Obrenić, A.L. Rosenberg, E.J. Schwabe (1991): Optimal emulations by butterfly-like networks. *J. ACM*, to appear.

4. G.E. Blelloch (1989): Scans as primitive parallel operations. *IEEE Trans. Comp. 38*, 1526-1538.

5. D.S. Greenberg, L.S. Heath and A.L. Rosenberg (1990): Optimal embeddings of butterfly-like graphs in the hypercube. *Math. Syst. Th. 23*, 61-77.

6. S.I. Kartashev and S.P. Kartashev (1979): A multicomputer system with dynamic architecture. *IEEE Trans. Comp., C-28*, 704-721.

7. R. Koch, F.T. Leighton, B. Maggs, S. Rao, A.L. Rosenberg, E.J Schwabe (1990): Work-preserving emulations of fixed-connection networks. Submitted for publication; see also, *21st ACM Symp. on Theory of Computing*, 227-240.

8. R.E. Ladner and M.J. Fischer (1980): Parallel prefix computation. *J. ACM 27*, 831-838.

9. F.T. Leighton (1992): *Introduction to Parallel Algorithms and Architectures: Arrays, Trees, Hypercubes.* Morgan Kaufmann, San Mateo, Calif.

10. B. Obrenić, M.C. Herbordt, A.L. Rosenberg, C.C. Weems, F.S. Annexstein, M. Baumslag (1991): Using emulations to construct high-performance virtual parallel architectures. Tech. Rpt. 91-40, Univ. Massachusetts. See also, Achieving multigauge behavior in bit-serial SIMD architectures via emulation. *3rd IEEE Symp. on Frontiers of Massively Parallel Computation* (1990) 186-195.

11. T.D. de Rose, L. Snyder, C. Yang (1987): Near-optimal speedup of graphics algorithms using multigauge parallel computers. *Intl. Conf. on Parallel Processing*, 289-294.

12. M.R. Samatham and D.K. Pradhan (1989): The deBruijn multiprocessor network: a versatile parallel processing and sorting network for VLSI. *IEEE Trans. Comp. 38*, 567-581.

13. J.T. Schwartz (1980): Ultracomputers. *ACM Trans. Prog. Lang. 2*, 484-521.

14. L. Snyder (1985): An inquiry into the benefits of multigauge parallel computation. *Intl. Conf. on Parallel Processing*, 488-492.

15. L. Snyder and C. Yang (1988): The principles of multigauging architectures. Typescript, Univ. Washington.

16. C.C. Weems, S.P. Levitan, A.R. Hanson, E.M. Riseman, D.B. Shu, J.G. Nash (1987): The Image Understand Architecture. *Intl. J. Computer Vision 2*, 251-282.

Relations between models of parallel abstract machines

Michel COSNARD and Pascal KOIRAN
Ecole Normale Supérieure de Lyon
46 Allée d'Italie 69364 LYON - FRANCE
e-mail: cosnard@lip.ens-lyon.fr

Abstract

We formally introduced a new model of computations the *RealRAM* and its parallel counterpart the *RealPRAM*. We study the relationship between these models, classical computational models and two recently proposed parallel machine models, the real machine from Blum, Shub and Smale and the analog neural networks from Siegelman and Sontag. We propose a classification using simulations by dynamical systems. We also generalise the *NC* class and *P-complete* problems to real computations.

1 Introduction

1.1 Historical viewpoint

Several parallel machines models have been introduced and their relations in term of complexity have been analysed [12] [1]. These machines are known to follow the Parallel Computation Thesis: whatever can be solved in polynomial space on a reasonable sequential machine model can be solved in polynomial time on a reasonable parallel machine model, and vice versa. The term reasonable can lead to various interpretations. It has been proposed to consider as reasonable, machines that can simulate each other within a polynomial overhead of time and a constant-factor overhead in space (Invariance Thesis). Classical models of reasonable sequential machines are the Turing machine and the random access machine. Hence we can define as sequential, machines which satisfy the Invariance Thesis with respect to the Turing machine model and parallel, machines which satisfy the Parallel Computation Thesis with respect to the Turing machine model. Various models including the vector machines, the array machines, the SIMDAG, the tree machine, the well known parallel random access machine, the uniform circuit model, finite cellular automata, the systolic computation model, finite-state devices in an arbitrary interconnection pattern satisfy this last requirement and hence can be reasonably called parallel. One can ask whether there are models of parallel computations that do not belong to this class.

Surprisingly numerical algorithms have been studied and analysed using the previous models either in sequential or in parallel. Until recently no formal theory of the computability and the complexity of problems using real numbers was available. In [2] such a theory has been proposed. One can now consider the relationship between models based on the real numbers and models based on the integers. Neural networks can be seen as an alternative computational model. Neural networks with real weights have been studied in this framework in [11] and shown to have super-Turing capabilities. These networks have been proposed as models for parallel analog machines. Using real numbers in computations can be discussed. However, one can argue that there exist physical or biological systems in which real quantities which may not be measurable can have a non negligible effect on the behavior of the system. A tentative model of such systems would consist of abstract machines using real numbers for internal computations but discrete, although unbounded, inputs and outputs. Neural networks appear to be ideal candidates

In this paper, we review the relationship between several parallel machine models and show that they can be ultimately studied using the dynamical system theory of real functions. We also introduced a new model for computations with real numbers and show that it is equivalent to the model introduced by Blum, Shub and Smale. We also extend this model to parallel computations.

1.2 Definitions

We shall not recall the definition of a Turing machine. However we give in the following the definitions of various parallel abstract machines.

Definition 1 *A Parallel Random Access Machine consists of several independent sequential processors, each with its own private memory, communicating with one another through a global memory. In one unit of time, each processor can read one global or local memory location, executes a single RAM operation, and writes into one global or local memory location [6].*

PRAMs can be classified according to their capabilities on global memory accesses. In the remaining, we shall only consider the most common model, namely the Concurrent Read Exclusive Write (*CREW*) model. A *PRAM* is a straigtforward generalization of the *RAM* to the shared memory parallel computers. It is possible to extend this model to distributed memory parallel machines [3].

One of the oldest models of parallel machines are the cellular automata model and the model of *boolean circuits* (or networks) based on the theory of boolean functions.

Definition 2 *A boolean circuit is a labeled directed acyclic graph (DAG). Nodes are labeled as input, output, constant, AND, OR or NOT nodes. Each node has bounded fan-in and fan-out.*

A boolean network with n input nodes and m output nodes computes a boolean function $f : \{0,1\}^n \rightarrow \{0,1\}^m$. The *size* of the network is the number of gates; the *depth* is the length of the longest path in the *DAG*.

Definition 3 *A one dimensional cellular space is a collection of cells associated to every point of Z. In a cellular automata each cell is a finite automaton with a finite set of states Q and a local transition function δ depending upon the cell itself and some neighboring cells. The transition function and the neighborhoods are the same for all the cells (uniform neighborhoods). In one unit of time, each cell computes its new state using the transition function.*

Cellular automata have an infinite memory with an infinite number of identical finite control units working in parallel and synchronously. In the remaining we shall restrict ourselves to the case where the neighbors of a cell are the two adjacent cells. Hence $\delta : Q^3 \rightarrow Q$. The configuration space is $C = Q^Z$, and the global transition function $T : C \rightarrow C$ is defined by: $(T(x))_i = \delta(x_{i-1}, x_i, x_{i+1})$.

An immediate generalization of the cellular automata consists in considering that the underlying net is no longer homogeneous but an arbitrary digraph and that the local transistion function can vary from cell to cell. *Discrete neural nets* are an attempt in this direction. However, mainly for biological analogy reasons, in the classical discrete neural nets the local transition functions first compute weighted sums of inputs from neighboring cells, which makes the cells unable to detect where specific inputs come from.

Definition 4 *A (discrete) neural net is a quadruple $(Q, X, U, \{f_i\})$ consisting of an activation set $Q \subseteq R$, a countable (finite or infinite), locally finite, arc weighted digraph X, a set of inputs nodes, and a family of activation functions $f_i : R \rightarrow Q$, one for each vertex i in D. The local dynamics is defined by*

$$x_i(t+1) = f_i\left(\sum_j a_{ij} x_j(t) + \sum_j b_{ij} u_j(t) + \theta_i\right)$$

where the first summation is taken over all neigbor cells j of cell i and the second is taken over all inputs.

Following [11], we shall consider $Q = [0, 1]$ and for f_i the saturated-linear function:

$$f_i(x) = \sigma(x) = x \quad if \quad 0 \leq x \leq 1, 0 \quad if \quad x < 0, 1 \quad if \quad x > 1$$

A subset O of X will consist of the output cells which communicate the outputs of the network to the environment. These networks are often called *recurrent first-order neural nets*. The networks are discrete if the inputs and output are boolean values and real if they are real.

These networks have been generalized in [2] in order to introduce a powerful model of computation over the real numbers. In the *BSS model*, real-valued inputs are allowed and values can be compared for exact equality. The model has originally been defined on an ordered ring commutative with unit. We shall simplify the definition by considering only R.

Definition 5 *A BSS machine is a 5-uple $\{I, O, S, X, f_i\}$ where I is the input space identified with R^l, O is the output space identified with R^m, S is the state space identified with R^n, X is a directed graph and $f_i : S \rightarrow S$ are rational functions. The nodes of X are divided into one input node with no incoming edge and one outgoing, ouput nodes with no outgoing edge, computation nodes with one incoming and one outgoing edges and branch nodes with one incoming and two out going edges. The input node puts the input into the machine and the output nodes transfer the results to the environment. To each computation node is associated a rational function. The computation nodes apply their rational function to their state and transmit the new state to the next node. To a branch node is associated a polynomial. If the value of the polynomial in the current state is positive the state is transmitted to the left son else to the right.*

The *BSS* machine has been extended to deal with data in R^∞ with the restriction that a point $x = (x_1, ..., x_n, ...)$ in R^∞ satisfies $x_k = 0$ for all k sufficiently large. In an infinite machine the definition is modified to allow input and output in R^∞, and the rational functions associated to computation nodes and to branch nodes are supposed to depend of at most k variables and coordinates :

$$f_i(x) = x_i \quad if \quad i > k \quad and \quad \delta f_i(x)/\delta x_j = 0 \quad if \quad i \leq k \quad and \quad j > k$$

In order to allow to use x_i for large i in the computation, the authors introduce a *fifth node* which possesses one outgoing edge and operates on an element $(x_1, ..., x_i, ..., x_j, ...,)$ by replacing it by $(x_1, ..., x_j, ..., x_j, ..,)$.

2 A new model

In this section we introduce a model called *RealRAM*, show that the *BSS* model is equivalent to the *RealRAM* and generalize it in order to model parallel real computations by defining a *RealPRAM*. A *RealRAM* is simply a RAM in which we allow computations on real numbers. Is has been used already in [5] for studying the complexity of some problems in the *BSS* models, and in application fields like computational geometry (see [9] and [13]). It was also largely used for studying numerical problems. However as noted in (*BSS*) there is no formal development of a theory of such a model. Our aim is to give some contributions to this subject.

Definition 6 *A RealRAM model consists of a finite control where a program is stored, accumulator registers and an infinite collection of memory registers. In* *each register a real number can be stored. The instruction repertoire of the Real-RAM is composed of input and ouput instructions, instructions for performing integer and real arithmetic, conditional and unconditional jump statement, and instructions for transport of data between accumulator and memory. The time for performing any arithmetic operation is assumed to be constant and is taken equal to 1.*

We can consider the *BSS* model as a generalization of the Turing machine model and the *RealRAM* as a generalization of the *RAM*. Both models are equivalent in their corresponding class. More precisely we can state:

Lemma 1 *A BSS machine can be simulated in constant time and size by a RealRAM. Reciprocally, to any program on a RealRAM executed in time T with M registers, we can associate a BSS machine with $O(M)$ nodes taking a time $O(T)$.*

Proof. For the first part of the proof, we show that any node of the *BSS* machine can be executed on a *RealRAM* in constant time and with a constant number of registers. This is trivial for input, output and fifth nodes. For computation nodes, we compute the rational function by using a standard RAM algorithm. Since the degree of the function is bounded independently of the size of the input and the size of the machine, the algorithm takes a constant time and uses a constant number of registers. A similar argument applies for branch nodes. For the reciprocal, we construct a *BSS* machine by replacing any instruction of the program by a node which executes the same operation. For this it suffices to show that this is true for any instruction of the repertoire of the *RealRAM*. □

The *BSS* machine is sequential by nature. In order to get a model of parallel machines which operate on real numbers, we have only to generalize the *RealRAM* to the *RealPRAM*. For this, take the definition of the *PRAM* of the previous section and replace the sentence "executes a single *RAM* operation" by executes a single *RealRAM* operation". In the same way one can generalize the *XRAM* model to the *RealXRAM*.

3 Relations between models

In this section we are interested in comparing the computational power of the machine models we have introduced in the two previous sections. We shall concentrate on new or non classical results for the parallel machine models.

3.1 *PRAMs* and cellular automata

The usual definition of the power of the *PRAM* is defined by means of the Uniform Boolean Circuits. More precisely the following type of result can be obtained (see [6] for a detailed presentation). Let $UCKT(C(n), D(n))$ be the set of problems solved by an unbounded fan-in circuit of size $C(n)$ and depth $D(n)$ and $CRCW(P(n), T(n))$ be the set of problems solved by a CRCW *PRAM* in time $T(n)$ with $P(n)$ processors. Then we have :

$$UCKT(C(n), D(n)) \subseteq CRCW(C(n), D(n)) \subseteq UCKT(polyC(n), D(n))$$

The notion of uniformity of the family of circuits is central since it is necessary to correlate the size and depth of a family that solves a problem P with the parallel time and hardware complexity of P. The notion of uniformity that is commonly accepted is *logspace uniformity* which insures that the description of the nth circuit of the family can be described by a Turing machine using $O(logn)$ workspace.

The universality of the *PRAMs* as a programming system is proved in general with reference to the Uniform Boolean Circuits or with Alternating Turing Machine. However both have their drawbacks, namely a somewhat complicated uniformity condition for the former and sequentiality for the latter. In [8], the author proposes to prove the universality with reference to an intrinsically uniform and parallel model of computation. The cellular automata constitute such a model. More precisely the author proves that:

Lemma 2 *There exists a CREW PRAM which can simulate in constant time any given two-ways and totalistic cellular automaton A with any finite initial configuration and finite evolution time.*

From this point of view the cellular automata are a better reference model for the *PRAM*. Moreover if we allow the *PRAM* to possess an infinite number of processors, the two models are completely equivalent.

3.2 Computability properties of neural networks

In [10], the authors show that if one restricts to nets whose weights are rational numbers (called rational nets *rNN* for short), then one obtains a model that can simulate a multi-tape Turing machine in linear time. Linear time simulation means that the transition function of the Turing machine can be computed in constant time by the network. Clearly the inverse simulation can be done in polynomial time.

In a subsequent paper [11], the authors analyse the computational properties of neural networks with real weights (real neural network). They prove that real neural networks can solve in polynomial time the same class of discrete problems that can be solved by Turing machines that consult sparse oracles in polynomial time (namely the class $P/poly$). Moreover they can solve all discrete problems, including non-computable ones, in exponential time. It is then shown that almost every problem requires exponential time. The proofs of these results are based on the equivalence between neural networks and non-uniform circuits.

Let $RNN(T(n))$ be the class of all functions computed by real neural networks in time $T(n)$ and $NUC(S(n))$ be the class of all functions computed by non-uniform circuits of size $S(n)$. If $T(n) \geq n$ then

$$RNN(T(n)) \subseteq NUC(Poly(T(n))) \subseteq RNN(Poly(T(n)))$$

It can be deduce that $P_{RNN} = P_{NUC}$ and that $EXP_{RNN} = EXP_{NUC}$. The class P_{NUC} is often called *P/poly* which coincides with the class of problems solved by Turing machines with advice sequences in polynomial time and with the class of problems solved by Turing machines that consult oracles where the oracles are sparse sets (the number of oracles of size n is bounded by a polynomial in n). These results can be generalized to nondeterministic circuits and neural networks to prove that $NP_{RNN} = NP_{NUC}$.

We deduce that any function from $\mathbf{N} \to \{0, 1\}$ can be computed in at least exponential time, ... even non computable ones!

3.3   Models as dynamical systems

The global transition function of a *rNN* or a *RNN* with d analog units is a piecewise-linear function $F : [0, 1]^d \to [0, 1]^d$. In [10], it is shown that $d = 1058$ is sufficient for a *rNN* to simulate a universal Turing machine. Hence the evolution of the *RNN* can be seen as a real dynamical system in a d-dimensionnal space, acting on rational inputs. Along the same line, the *BSS* machine can also be considered as a dynamical system in a possibly infinite dimensional real space. The dynamical system is governed by piecewise rational functions called *the register equations* in the original paper.

The relations between computability theory and dynamical system theory were never studied in many details. These results raise the problem of finding the minimum dimension d for which Turing machine simulation by iteration of piecewise-linear functions is possible. In [4], we show that $d = 2$ is sufficient. Our construction can be used to give another proof of the existence of universal neural networks. We also compare simulation of cellular automata to simulation of Turing machines.

Definition 7 *Let F be the transition function of a machine $\mathcal{M}$ (which may be a Turing machine or a cellular automaton). A function $f : I^d \to I^d$ simulates $\mathcal{M}$ if there is an f-stable subset $D \subset I^d$ and a bijective function $\phi : C \to D$ such that*

$$F = \phi^{-1} \circ f \circ \phi.$$

Intuitively, this means that in order to apply F, one can encode the configuration with ϕ, apply f, and then decode the result with ϕ^{-1}. For cellular automata, we shall make the additional assumption that ϕ is a homeomorphism. We refer the reader to [4] for a complete definition in this case. A machine $\mathcal{M}_1$ is usually said to simulate another machine $\mathcal{M}_2$ in real time (resp. linear time, quadratic time,...) if a computation of $\mathcal{M}_2$ for t time units can be performed by $\mathcal{M}_1$ in time

t (resp. $O(t)$, $O(t^2)$,...). Since the class of piecewise-linear (resp. piecewise-analytic, piecewise-monotone) functions is closed under composition, linear time simulation is equivalent to real time simulation. With this definition, we show that:

Theorem 1 *1. An arbitrary Turing machine can be simulated in linear time by a 2-dimensionnal piecewise-linear continuous function with rational coefficients (rPL_2).*

2. There exist a Turing machine that cannot be simulated by a 1-dimensionnal piecewise-linear continuous function (PL_1).

3. An arbitrary Turing machine can be simulated in linear time by a 1-dimensionnal countably piecewise-linear function with rational coefficients.

4. An arbitrary Turing machine can be simulated in linear time by a 1-dimensionnal continuous piecewise-monotone function with rational coefficients.

5. There exist a cellular automaton that cannot be simulated with a continuous encoding by a 2-dimensionnal piecewise-linear continuous function.

6. There exist a cellular automaton that cannot be simulated with a continuous encoding by a 1-dimensionnal countably piecewise-monotone function.

7. An arbitrary cellular automaton can be simulated by a 1-dimensionnal continuous function.

4 On the power of the *RealRAM* and *RealPRAM*

The *BSS* machine model was introduced to construct a theory of the computability and the complexity over the real numbers. Another motivation was to bring the theory of computation into the domain of analysis, geometry and topology. The mathematics of these subjects can then be put to use in the systematic analysis of algorithms.

Since *BSS* and *RealRAM* are equivalent, we shall use the latter in this section in order to give a new insight in this theory. We first go along different lines by examining the power of the *RealRAM* for computing discrete functions (over **N**). We have already seen in the previous section that *RNN* can compute any discrete function in exponential time. Is the *RealRAM* more powerful than a *RNN* for these problems? The problem is still open but we can show the following:

Theorem 2 *Any discrete function $f : \mathbf{N} \rightarrow \{0,1\}$ can be computed in exponential time using a RealRAM. Any function in P/poly can be computed in polynomial time using a RealRAM.*

The proof will not be presented here but can be found in [7]. In fact, contrarily to *RNN*, the *RealRAM* model allows for real-valued inputs rather than only binary, performs exact comparisons and allows for an infinite range of values in registers. It is still an open problem to know the time to compute on a *RealRAM* any discrete function of P. In [2], the *4-Feasibility problem* which consists in finding if a given n-variable *4*-degree polynomial equation has a real solution, is shown to be NP_R-complete. The class of NP_R-complete problems has been extented in [5].

Clearly the *NC*-class of problems that can be solved on a *PRAM* in polylogarithmic time using a polynomial number of processors can be extented to *RealPRAM*. Any discrete problem in NC_D belongs to NC_R. In the same way, we can extend the notion of *P-reduction* to *P_R-reduction*. As in the discrete case there exist P_R-complete problems.

Theorem 3 *The Real Arithmetic Circuit Value Problem is P_R-complete.*

RACVP is a direct extension of *CVP*. Consider a circuit with real inputs, one boolean output and where each of the n nodes is labeled by either an input, a comparison or an arithmetic operation. The answer is *Yes* if the output of the circuit is 0. The proof follows the classical proof for *CVP* and will be omitted.

To conclude this section let us come back to simulations by dynamical systems. We can extend the results of the previous section by the following theorem whose proof can be found in [7].

Theorem 4   *1. An arbitrary function $F : \{0,1\}^+ \rightarrow \{0,1\}$ can be computed by an iterated $f \in PL_1$ in exponential time.*

   2. A family $C = (C_n)_{n \in N}$ of circuit of non-decreasing sizes $S(n)$ can be simulated in time $n.poly(S(n))$ by an iterated function of PL_2.

   3. An arbitrary function $F : \{0,1\}^+ \rightarrow \{0,1\}$ in P/poly can be computed by an iterated $f \in PL_2$ in polynomial time.

5   Conclusion

We have introduced new models for real computations and studied their relationships with already existing ones. Analysing the computational power of these models is a very interesting area in particular in wiew of the super-Turing capabilities that they demonstrate. Most of the problems are still open. As an example let us mention that we do not know if P_D in included into NC_R.

References

[1] J.L. Balcázar, J. Diáz, and J. Gabarró. *Structural Complexity I.* EATCS monographs on theoretical computer science. Springer-Verlag, 1988.

[2] L. Blum, M. Shub, and S. Smale. On a theory of computation and complexity over the real numbers : NP-completeness, recursive functions and universal machines. *Bulletin of the American Mathematical Society*, 21(1):1–46, July 1989.

[3] M. Cosnard and A. Ferreira. On the real power of loosely coupled parallel architectures. *Parallel Processing Letters*, 1(2):103–112, 1991.

[4] M. Cosnard, M. Garzon, and P. Koiran. Computability properties of low-dimensional systems. In *Proceedings of STACS'93*, Lecture notes in computer science to appear. Springer Verlag, 1993.

[5] F. Cucker and F. Rossello. On the complexity of some problems for the Blum, Shub and Smale model. In *Proceedings of Latin'92*, Lecture notes in computer science, pages 530–545. Springer Verlag, 1992.

[6] R.M. Karp and V. Ramachandran. Parallel algorithms for shared-memory machines. *Handbook of Theoretical Computer Science, Vol. A Algorithms and complexity*, pages 870–941, 1990.

[7] P. Koiran. On the relations between dynamical systems and boolean circuits. Research Report in preparation, LIP, Ecole Normale Supérieure de Lyon, 1992.

[8] B. Martin. A universal parallel random-access machine based on cellular automata. Research Report , LIP, Ecole Normale Supérieure de Lyon, 1992.

[9] F.P. Preparata and Shamos M.I. *Computational Geometry*. Springer, 1985.

[10] H. T. Siegelman and E. D. Sontag. Neural networks with real weights: analog computational complexity. COLT92 and SYCON Report 92-05, Rutgers University, September 1992.

[11] H. T. Siegelman and E. D. Sontag. On the computational power of neural nets. In *Proc. Fifth ACM Workshop on Computational Learning Theory*, July 1992.

[12] P. van Emde Boas. Machine models and simulations. *Handbook of Theoretical Computer Science, Vol. A Algorithms and complexity*, pages 3–66, 1990.

[13] F.F. Yao. Computational geometry. *Handbook of Theoretical Computer Science, Vol. A Algorithms and complexity*, pages 345–389, 1990.

Frontiers of parallel computing

Franco P. Preparata

Computer Science Department
Brown University
Providence, RI 02912

Attention is given to the ultimate impact of physical limitations - such as speed of light and device size - on parallel computing. Although an innovative and gradual evolution to the limiting situation is to be expected, it is provocative to explore the consequences of the accomplished attainment of the physical bounds. The main result is that scalability holds only for neighborly interconnections, such as the mesh, of bounded-size synchronous modules, presumably of the area-universal type. To be discussed are also the ultimate infeasibility of latency hiding, the violation of intuitive maximal speed-ups, and the emerging novel processor-time trade-offs.

Cost Effectiveness of Data Flow Machines and Vector Processors

Formella A., Massonne W. and Paul W.J.

Computer Science Department
Universität des Saarlandes
e–mail : {formella,massonne,wjp}@cs.uni–sb.de

At the 1st Nixdorf symposium a survey talk was given by the third author. The model from [PM90] was reviewed. This model permits to treat computer architecture as a formal optimization problem. The construction of cost effective PRAMs (scalable shared memory machines) from [AKP91], their physical realization [BGP92, DS92] and possible applications were discussed. New results concerning the cost effectiveness of vector machines and data flow machines were announced. This paper only covers the new material.

Abstract. Proponents of data flow machines always emphasize the high potential for parallelization and the high performance on numerical applications reachable by that kind of architecture. On the other hand opponents critisize the additional overhead during run time and the difficulties of the memory management. In order to evaluate the cost effectiveness of dynamical data flow machines we compare a well known representative, the MONSOON designed at the MIT, with two vector processors, the CRAY I and the SPARK 2.0. This comparison is based on a theoretical model, which provides measures for the run time and the cost of the machines. As numerical workload we have chosen some kernels from the *Livermore Loops* benchmark. In this paper we briefly review the evaluation model, we describe the machines under consideration and finally we present our results of the comparison.

1 Introduction

Vector processors are able to execute identical operations on large sets of data using pipelined functional units with a high throughput. Usually, only one machine instruction is sufficient to deal with three vectors out of a fast intermediate memory (vector registers). Chaining, functional units working in parallel and multiple load/store pipes increase the performance significantly. In this paper we will compare the CRAY I, a classical vector processor, and the SPARK 2.0, a special purpose vector processor with flexible addressing of the vector memory, to the data flow machine MONSOON.

Data flow machines are designed to exploit the inherent parallelism of programs. A global program counter responsible for a more or less sequential program flow has been omitted. Execution of all operations is controlled by the availability of the data. If all input data of an operation have been computed this operation can take place. It generates new data which then is used for the next pending operation.

MONSOON [Pa88, PACU90] is a dynamical data flow machine. The design is based on the theoretical model MIT–TTDA (tagged token dataflow architecture) [AN87]. However, MONSOON does not use an associative memory which is included or simulated both in the model or in other implementations [GKW85, HSS87]. Instead of such a memory an explicit token store (ETS) is used [CP90]. Points to synchronize tokens are determined during compile time relatively to a frame, whose location in memory is calculated dynamically during run time.

Section 2 briefly reviews the formal model for computer architectures from [PM90] which allows for a quantitative comparison of different machines. The model includes both the hardware and the compiler. Comparisons can only be done on a workload, section 3 introduces the selected kernels of the *Livermore Loops* we used for our analysis. In section 4 we describe the three machines under consideration. Section 5 summerizes some of the results.

2 Model

According to [PM90] an architecture $\mathcal{A}$ is defined as:

$$\mathcal{A} = (\mathcal{H}, \mathcal{M}, \mathcal{C}, \mathcal{P})$$

where $\mathcal{H}$ is the hardware, $\mathcal{M}$ is the machine language, $\mathcal{C}$ is a set of compilers and $\mathcal{P}$ the corresponding high level languages.

As a means to compare two architectures the quality is defined as the quotient of the performance on a benchmark and cost of the hardware. The cost is the sum of all the costs of the components of the hardware measured in *gates*. The performance is the quotient of all floating point operations (weighted according to [Mc84]) and the execution time of the program. The time is measured in gates delays within a fixed technology. As unit of the quality we use the *nodg* (nano operations per delay and gate).

In what follows we will describe in more detail the different parts of an architecture for two vector processors and one data flow machine.

2.1 Hardware

Figure 1 shows a simplified block diagram of the hardware of a vector processor. The address bus A and the two data busses DI and DO are connecting main memory (MM) to the data paths (DP). Main memory is not part of the hardware. It is modelled in the way how the data can be accessed, i.e. how much time is needed to read or write sequences of data according to their corresponding sequences of addresses. The model simplifies the access time for a address sequence A of length n to:

$$t = S[A] + n * B[A]$$

$S[A]$ is an averaged start up time and $B[A]$ an averaged inverse bandwidth depending on the address sequence. Within the kernels there occur only two types of address sequences: standard addressing and indirect addressing. Usually, high bandwidth for standard addressing implies low bandwidth for indirect addressing because main memory has to be interleaved. Furthermore, the start up time increases if interleaving is implemented. This is modelled in the following way. Let $I = B[A_i]/B[A_s]$ be the quotient of the averaged bandwidths for indirect (A_i) and standard (A_s) addressing of main memory. In an interleaved memory with n banks we have $I = n/2$. We model the start up time generally with

$$S[A] = S + \begin{cases} 0 & \text{if } I = 1 \\ \lceil I * B[A_s]/\tau \rceil & \text{if } I > 1 \end{cases}$$

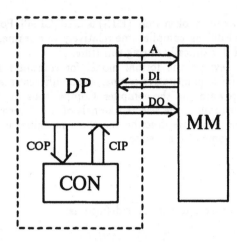

Fig. 1. Hardware of a processor

The time S stands for a start up time which depends only on the hardware of the vector processor and the implementation of the data exchange operation. τ is the cycle time of the machine in *delays*.

The data paths of the hardware consist of circuits including registers and memories. The interconnections are built according to rules which are an obvious extension of circuit theory, with the restriction that no clock or enable signals can be generated in the data paths. Those signals are derived exclusively by the control logic CON and are passed through the bus CIP to the data paths. All components are constructed using basic gates listed in table 1. For each type of gate the cost c measured in *gates* and the propagation delay d measured in *delays* is given for the technology M [Mo91] we used throughout this investigation.

Because the cost of the hardware should reflect the space occupied by a circuit being implemented on a chip (size of the die) we use certain packing factors (see table 2). We distinguish four types of structures. Every gate of a hardware belongs to a structure which has one of the types. Its costs are weighted with the appropriate factor. The corresponding factors were derived by analyzing data of given macro components of the manufacturer [Mo91].

The propagation delay of a combinatorial path is calculated by adding up all delays of basic components on that path. The longest path between two registers determines the time interval needed to clock the register at the end of the path safely. The control logic which generates all clock and enable signals will not be considered. We assume that the cost of the control logic can be neglected and that the length of the critical path lies in the data paths. Some examples of components are given in the section 4.

The hardware of a data flow machine is modelled in the same manner. One essential difference occurs in the connection to main memory. This will be explained in the description of MONSOON (see section 4.3).

2.2 Machine language

The machine languages of vector processors are quite different from those of data flow machines. Therefore, we describe them separately.

basic gate	c	d	remark
AND	2	2	
OR	2	2	
NAND	1	1	
NOR	1	1	
EXOR	4	3	
EQUI	4	3	
INV	1	1	
HA	6	3	half adder cell
FA	10	4	full adder cell
GP	5	4	generate/propagate cell
CC	8	6	conditional carry cell
MUX	3	2	2:1 multiplexer
TR	4	2	tranceiver
REG	8	4	flipflop
M1	5	3	see below
M2	8	10	see below

The costs c_m and the delay d_m of a memory block (RAM or ROM) are modelled using the two parameters M_1 and M_2 of the table:

$$c_m = (M_1^c * 2^a + M_2^c * \sqrt{2^a}) * d$$
$$d_m = M_1^d * a + M_2^d$$

whereas a is the width of the address bus and d is the width of the data bus.

Table 1. Costs and delays of the basic gates

structure	factor	value
logical	ρ_l	1.00
arithmetical	ρ_a	0.80
RAM	ρ_m	0.40
ROM	ρ_r	0.07

Table 2. Packing factors

Vector processors Each instruction of the machine language of a vector processor is an encoding of a register transfer graph which allows for a stepwise clocking of all registers by the control logic. In most of the cases such an encoding consists purely of an operation part (opcode) and an addressing part. We will not give any detailed description of the machine languages of the two processors CRAY I and SPARK 2.0, instead we refer to [Cr82] and [Sch89]. This is modivated by the fact that the control logic is omitted anyway. The size of an instruction word and, thus, the size of intermediate instruction memories are counted within the data paths.

MONSOON A program for a data flow machine is represented by a directed graph. The nodes hold the operations and the arcs specify the data dependencies. On program execution the graph is traversed by operands i.e. tokens. A node in a data flow graph is executed only if the required operands are available. In a data flow machine the nodes are coded as instructions and the arcs are coded as address lists. An instruction consists of the opcode and the address list of the destination instructions. A token generated by the execution of an instruction receives the result of the operation and the address of of its destination instruction.

Static and dynamic data flow machines differ by the number of tokens that traverse an arc at a time. Static data flow machines permit at most one token per arc at a time. Dynamic data flow machines allow for several tokens on one arc simultaneously. Unique tags identify matching tokens. The matching of tokens with the same tag and the same target instruction is realized by a special functional unit of the machine: the wait–matching unit. With tagging it is possible to parallelize loops and to implement subroutines, recursive functions etc.

MONSOON is a dynamic data flow machine.

2.3 Compiler

Given a program written in a high level language the compiler generates a program in machine language. For the vector processors we use VectorPASCAL as high level language [FRS91]. Thus vectorization is done by the programmer and must not be performed by the compiler. MONSOON is programmed in ID–90 [Ni90, Tr86].

Vector processors In order to determine the run times of the kernels on the vector processors we have not used existing compilers. The compiler was modelled in a way described in [Fo92]. The compiler generates only certain assembler sequences. The run time of such a sequence has to analyzed for each of them.

The front end of the compiler generates a data flow graph as first intermediate representation. The nodes of the graph contain information about the operations that have to be executed. The edges of the graph are labeled with address sequences of the operands which participate in the operation. Those addresses are calculated according to the location of the operands in main memory. In the data flow graph the ordering of the operations is still not fixed yet. Now, chaining possibilities can be detected. All of the kernels of the *Livermore Loops* can be compiled using a static management of main memory, i.e. the location of every operand is known at compile time.

The data flow graph is transformed into an operational graph. On the way strip mining is performed, i.e. long vector operations are cut into parts that fit into the vector memory of the data paths. Furthermore, spilling is performed, which means that intermediate results which can't be kept in the vector memory are written back to main memory. They are reloaded again if the appropriate operation comes to execution. The address sequences which refer to locations in main memory are mapped on the addressing modes of the hardware. In the operational graph the partial ordering of the operations is changed into a total ordering. This ordering is characterized by a sequence of basic code blocks, which are executed one after the other.

Such a basic code block is a sequence of assembler instructions. The execution time of every sequence is fixed and known to the compiler during the code generation phase [Fo92]. The overall run time can be calculated by summing all times needed to execute the blocks in the operational graph. During the transformation of the data flow graph into an operational graph the register allocation is performed, too.

MONSOON The ID–90 compiler translates a program in ETS code blocks. An ETS *code block* is a directed graph $G = (E, V, I, O)$, where $v_j \in V$ is an instruction with a maximum indegree and outdegree of two, and $(v_j, v_k) \in E$ implies $v_j \to v_k$, i.e. a data dependency between v_j and v_k. $e_i \in I$ is an input arc that is directed towards v_i (e_i has no source vertex), and $e_o \in O$ is an output arc that is directed away from v_o (e_o has no destination vertex).

It is required that,

1. G is either acyclic or it can be shown that any order of execution of G that obeys the dependency constraints E will never have more than one token on a given arc.
2. G is self-cleaning. When tokens are present on all output arcs in O it must be the case that no tokens are present on the arcs in E or I.

The compiler does not produce code blocks according to the above definition but target code for TTDA. The outdegree of nodes is not bound by two and there are instructions with indegree three. It is easy to reorganize the TTDA graph by insertion of additional nodes (fanout trees) or by splitting nodes. In all other cases the transformation of TTDA instructions into MONSOON code is trivial (see [Pa88]).

3 Benchmark

As benchmark we chose some of the kernels of the *Livermore Loops* (see [Mc84, Mc86, Mc88, Fe87]). The *Livermore Loops* are a collection of inner loops and they are widely accepted as a good representative of a real workload for a processor dealing with numerical data. Originally, they are written in FORTRAN77, but we have ported them to VectorPASCAL and ID–90 respectively.

In order to compare vector processors with a data flow machine we have only taken 3 of the 24 kernels. It seems to be obvious, that on totally vectorizable programs data flow machines are inferior to that of vector machines. We use one vectorizable kernel, namely the matrix multiplication in kernel 21). The data flow graphs of the other two selected kernels are quite large and indirect addressing is used (kernel 13 and 14), too. The analysis in section 5 considers only kernel 13 and 21, but all results of kernel 14 are similar to those derived for kernel 13.

Kernel 21 of the *Livermore Loops* in ID–90 is given by:

```
Def kernel21 A B C D n =
 { For i <- 1 to n do
  {For j <- 1 to n do
   s = C[i,j];
    D[i,j] =
    { for k <- 1 to n do
      next s = s+A[i,k]*B[k,j];
      Finally s }}};
```

4 Architectures

We will present three architectures: two vector processors, SPARK 2.0 and CRAY I, and the dataflow machine MONSOON. To allow for a fair comparison some of the parameters of the machines have been set to equal values. For instances, the width of the fixed point units is 64 bit, and the width of the address bus to main memory is 24 bit. The floating point units have been designed identical. Moreover, the instruction sets of the processors concerning floating point operations have been unified. The bandwidth to main memory is measured in bits per delay. Thus, the widths of the data busses are taken into consideration.

4.1 SPARK 2.0

Figure 2 illustrates the main data paths of SPARK 2.0 (see [AP86, Fo89, Ob89, Sch89, FRS91]). One can distinguish three main parts: the floating point unit FU, the fixed point unit XU and the branch unit BU. The functional units of the floating point part are pipelined processors (adder/subtractor and multiplier/divider) which are connected in such a way to the floating point memory FM that every machine cycle two operands can be read and one result can be written. The fixed point part is designed in a similar manner, but the processors (ALU and multiplier) are not pipelined. The address generators of both parts are able to produce standard addressing sequences which makes vector operations easy. A special feature of the architecture which was designed for applications in molecular dynamics is the possibility of the fixed point unit to generate address sequences for the floating point unit while a floating point operation takes place. This allows to implement indirect vector operations of the following form (VectorPASCAL):

```
A[1:N] := B[I[1:N]] + C[1:N];
```

Such operations can be executed without bubbles in the pipelines. The branch unit always works in parallel with all other units and takes care of the program flow by clocking each machine cycle a new instruction into the instruction register (BI). Vector operations are implemented as single instruction loops.

Loading of the memories XM, FM and BM with data out of main memory is performed by move operations. While such a blockwise data transfer is performed no other operation can take place. One exception is the generation of address sequences for main memory, which makes it possible to scatter or gather data during a move operation. Chained loading of a floating point operand is possible, too.

With some of the parameters of the SPARK 2.0 being adjusted to the *Livermore Loops*, e. g. the size of BM is set to 256 and the length of FM is set to 64 data words, one gets the costs of the processor as given in table 3.

type	unit	costs	
		unpacked	packed
M	FM	49152	19661
	XM	40448	16179
	BM	90112	36045
A	XALU	5810	4648
	XMUL	4837	3870
	FALU	13615	10892
	FMUL	52594	41835
	BU	15558	12446
R		8220	8220
$\sum$		280346	154036

Table 3. Costs of the SPARK 2.0

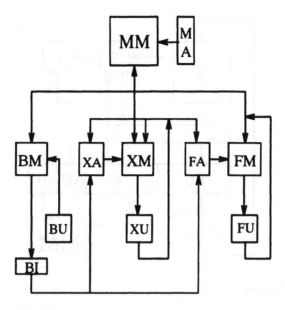

Fig. 2. Datapaths of the SPARK 2.0

The cycle time of the modelled SPARK 2.0 is $\tau = 111$ *delays*. The critical path within the first phase of the machine cycle is determined by the fixed point unit and within the second phase of the machine cycle by the instruction unit. The bandwidth $B[A_s]$ to main memory for standard addressing is equal to 111 *delays*, i.e. every machine cycle a word can be read or written. Indirect addressing of main memory requires $B(A_i) = 2 * B(A_s)$ *delays* and therefore we have $I = 2$. The run time of move operations measured in machine cycles equals

$$\lceil B[A_s] * I/\tau \rceil + 3 = 5$$

for a scalar value and

$$\lceil B[A_s] * I/\tau \rceil + 2 + B[A_s]N/\tau = 4 + N$$

for a standard addressed vector and finally

$$\lceil B[A_s] * I/\tau \rceil + 3 + 2B[A_s]N/\tau = 5 + 2N$$

if indirect addressing of a vector is used.

4.2 CRAY I

Figure 3 shows the main data paths of a reverse engineered CRAY I. The core of the hardware consists of the vector registers V, which can be addressed only starting at their first location, and the pipelined functional units. All units which are not required for the *Livermore Loops* have been dropped. The connection to main memory is implemented using a blockwise data exchange method, too. Load chaining is possible. Moreover, different functional units can either work in parallel on different sets of registers or they can operate in a chain with one operand of a unit as a result of another one.

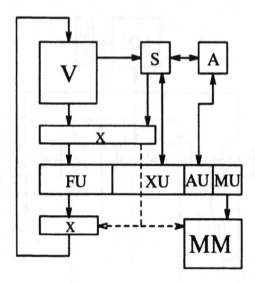

Fig. 3. Datapaths of the CRAY I

Indirect addressing is not possible. The components have to be loaded one after the other out of main memory and are manipulated in the scalar functional units.

Some of the parameters of the CRAY I were adjusted to the *Livermore Loops*: only four vector registers each with 32 entries are used. The T- and B–register blocks have been omitted. One gets the costs of the processor as given in table 4.

type	costs	
	unpacked	packed
M(V)	134400	107520
A	184308	147446
R	91099	91099
Σ	409807	346065

Table 4. Costs of the CRAY I

Whenever a register is clocked, this is done at the some point of the machine cycle. The length of such a cycle is $\tau = 21$. The critical path is dominated by addressing the instruction memory. The bandwidth $B[A_s]$ for standard addressing equals 21 *delays*, i. e. every cycle an item can be read or written. This is achieved by an eightfold interleaved main memory. Thus we have $I = 4$. The run times for move operations measured in machine cycles equals

$$\lceil B[A_s] * I/\tau \rceil + 7 = 11$$

for a scalar value and

$$\lceil B[A_s] * I/\tau \rceil + 5 + B[A_s]N/\tau = 9 + N$$

for a vector. Indirect accesses are not possible.

4.3 MONSOON

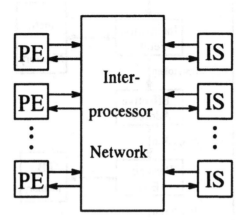

Fig. 4. MONSOON overview

MONSOON is a general purpose parallel machine with ETS. (Figure 4). The pipelined processing elements (PE's) and the I–structure modules (IS's), managing data structures are connected by a multistage network.

The basic idea of ETS is as follows: each code block gets its own memory frame by the compiler to do the synchronization. If a code block is activated during run time, a context manager computes the start address of the corresponding memory frame.

A token has the following structure: $t = $ <PE:FP.IP,v>, v is the value, PE:FP.IP is the tag of the token. IP is a pointer to the actual instruction. FP is the start address of the activation frame of a certain code block. PE is the destination processor.

The actual instruction contains the opcode, the offset in the activation frame and the offset of the destination instructions. One obtains the matching address by adding FP to the activation frame offset (e. g. FP+5). In the same way addresses of destination instructions are obtained (e. g. IP+1 und IP+150).

Each slot of an activation frame owns associated presence bits. The token synchronization is managed by status transitions of these presence bits. For a dyadic operation (e. g. add) the status of the corresponding presence bits is initially *empty*. Upon arrival of the first token the status is switched to *present*. The value of the token is stored in the slot. The second token of the operation recognizes the status *present*, extracts the value of the first token and switches the status back to *empty*. Now the operation is executed. The transition function and the compiler strategy guarantee that all slots are *empty* after the execution of a code block. The memory frame may be reused.

One frame is allocated for each iteration of a loop. This allows the parallel execution of loop iterations. Efficient algorithms for frame allocation applied to loop iterations are described by Culler [Cu90]. A context manager schedules the dynamic allocation and disallocation of frames.

token = [tag,value]

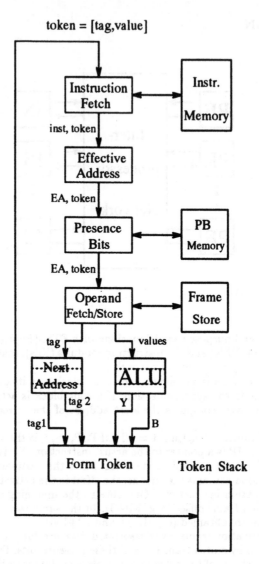

Fig. 5. Data paths of the MONSOON PE

Each code block allocation is completely executed by one PE. This reduces the network load and simplifies the implementation of context managers. The parallelism within code blocks and the simultaneous activation of many code blocks keep the PE pipeline full, if there is enough inherent parallelism in the dataflow graph.

The execution of tokens within the PE pipeline is as follows (cf. fig. 5):

The instruction memory is addressed using the IP of the token. The effective address of the slot in the frame store is computed by adding the offset fetched from the instruction memory to FP. In the third stage the presence bits are manipulated according to the transition function. Subsequently the access to the slot is performed.

The ALU executes the actual operation on values. The tags for the generated tokens are computed in the next address generation unit parallely to the ALU execution. The destination addresses are built from IP and the offsets fetched from the instruction memory. The ALU and the next address generation are multistaged for balancing the whole PE pipeline. The new tokens are finally constructed by the result values and the computed tags. One token can directly be recirculated in the pipeline. Tokens for other PE's are sent into the network. The token stack buffers the remaining tokens.

The LIFO order restricts a flooding of the token store caused by breadth first unfolding. Additionally the LIFO order strategy simplifies the use of possible caches for the frame store and the token store. In each machine cycle 0, 1, or 2 new tokens are generated and one token is able to enter the PE pipeline. No new tokens are generated in the last pipeline stage, if no token entered the pipeline previously (idle cycle) or if the first token of a dyadic operation was computed. In the latter case a bubble was created below the operand fetch/store unit. The overhead caused by bubbles is about 30% of the execution time of a program [PACU90].

On MONSOON the handling of data structures like arrays is radically different from the implementation on machines using a program counter. It is not possible to guarantee that a read access to global data gets the right value, if the attached data structure is changed repeatedly. ID–90 offers I–structures. I–structures are data structures allowing for reading values many times. Any position in an I–structure may not be written more than once. I–structures are used for producer/consumer synchronization. Like the PE, each word of an I–structure memory is equipped with presence bits. It is both possible to handle I–structures in the IS or in the frame stores of the PEs [Pa88]. An additional status *sticky* has to be coded in presence bits beside *empty* and *present*. The *sticky* status remains unchanged as soon as a value is written. It is possible to distribute I–structures to several PEs.

Read accesses to I–structures are split into two transactions. One sends the read request, a token with the address of the element and the tag of the destination instruction. The other replies with the value as the read request is satisfied. In the interim, the pipeline is not blocked — other instructions are free to execute.

The run time of a program is the number of cycles multiplied by the cycle time of the MONSOON pipeline.

The number of cycles was estimated by the simulator GITA in the ID–world [Ni87] development and simulation system. GITA simulates the MIT-TTDA. The simulation results must be transformed in order to count the number of MONSOON cycles. Especially the TTDA allows the activation of any number of tokens in one cycle. The maximum number of MONSOON tokens per cycle is two. Therefore identity trees were introduced in order to duplicate tokens. This results in additional tokens i. e. additional machine cycles. Other additional tokens result from the simulation of some TTDA instructions which have no directly corresponding instructions in MONSOON. If the pipeline is always full (i. e. one token enters the pipeline in each cycle), the number of cycles equals the number of tokens generated. Otherwise the run time of a program is increased by the number of idle cycles.

A MONSOON PE has been reverse engineered except for some function units like the exception unit, the statistic unit and the hardware type checking unit.

The MONSOON pipeline works with a system of four main memories. These are the instruction memory, the frame store, the presence bits memory, and the token stack. The token stack is decoupled from the main memory system by a memory internal to the PE. A direct access to main memory for each token stacked would decrease the memory bandwidth. An overflow or an underflow of the intermediate memory results in block moves to or from the main memory. The overhead by block moves

was not taken into account. Instead a mechanism for contolling the number of tokens in the stack and for smoothing the unprocessed token profile has been designed:
Each token carries a flag. This flag marks the number of tokens, that are possibly activated by the execution of the token. Two token stacks of a constant length 32 are introduced. The first stack holds the tokens possibly activating 0 or 1 token. The second stack holds the tokens, which will possibly activate 2 new tokens. If the stacks risk to overflow, tokens from the first stack are pushed into the pipeline. If the stacks risk to be empty, tokens from the second stack are entered into the pipeline. Because bubbles occur in 30% of all cycles and because the bubbles are fairly evenly distributed, there are frequent occasions to apply this mechanism. We presently do not have a formal analysis or simulations for this mechanism. If it does not succeed in reducing drastically traffic to the part of the token stacks which is kept in main memory, then our present estimates for the quality of MONSOON are too good.

The cycle time of a PE depends directly on the memory bandwidth. High memory bandwidth results in more ALU (and next address generation) stages. The other functional units are not pipelined. The cost of a MONSOON PE with two ALU stages is shown in table 5.

For a multi PE MONSOON a butterfly network was designed. Now the PEs have additional costs caused by the network connection and by enlarged tokens. The address of the destination PE is included in the tokens. It is assumed that I–structures are held in the PEs.

type	unit	costs	
		unpacked	packed
M	Stacks	45567	18226.8
	ROMs	23088	1539.2
A	ALU	60542	48433.6
	other	1095	876
R		20744	20744
$\sum$		151036	89891.6

Table 5. Cost of the MONSOON PE

5 Analysis

Figure 6 shows the quality of the three architectures as a function of the bandwidth $B[A_s]$ to main memory for kernel 13. The vector length is set to 104 and the ratio $I = B[A_i]/B[A_s]$ is set to 2, which corresponds to a fourfold interleaving of main memory. With decreasing bandwidth the quality of the data flow machine drops down significantly. This effect does not occur for the vector machines. For an unbounded bandwidth (i.e. $B[A_s] = 0$) the run time is determined only by the cycle time of the machines. At this point MONSOON has the best quality. The main reason for this is the fact that the cycle time of MONSOON has been adapted to the available bandwidth, which was not done for the vector machines. Thus, it is possible to construct a dataflow machine MONSOON which reaches a higher quality than the unchanged vector machines using the same bandwidth (21 *delays* for 64–bit words).

The quality achieved is higher than the quality reachable by a CRAY I even with a very high bandwidth. The bandwidth of the SPARK 2.0 has been modelled with 111 *delays* for standard addressing and with 222 *delays* for indirect addressing. The corresponding point in the curve shows a larger quality which is not reached by the CRAY I within the whole interval under consideration. The capability of addressing the vector memory within the data paths seems to increase the quality in any case for kernel 13.

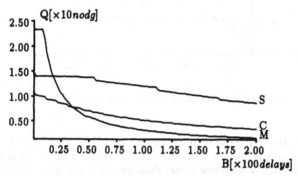

Fig. 6. Quality for kernel 13 depending on the bandwidth to main memory

Figure 7 illustrates for the same parameter range the quality for kernel 21. Here, the vector length is set to 40. Advantages for MONSOON can only be noticed for a very high bandwidth to main memory ($B[A_s] \geq 14$). Once again it is demonstrated that the SPARK 2.0 with its flexible addressing facilities is not effected much by a decreasing bandwidth. The declining of the curve for the CRAY I is explained by the load chaining strategie, which slows down the operation time as bandwidth decreases.

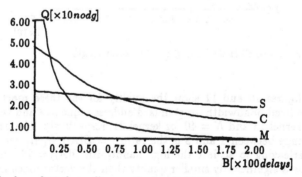

Fig. 7. Quality for kernel 21 depending on the bandwidth to main memory

In figure 8 the quality is drawn depending on the vector length for kernel 13. The bandwidth is fixed to $B[A_s] = 28$ *delays*, which is almost the real bandwidth of a CRAY I. In that case the cycle of our reverse engineered MONSOON is 92 *delays*. As one can see SPARK 2.0 has always the highest quality. The MONSOON is better than the CRAY I if the vector length is greater than 30.

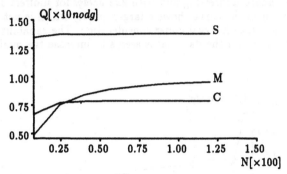

Fig. 8. Quality for kernel 13 depending on the vector length

Looking at the matrix multiplication (figure 9) the CRAY I has the best quality if the vector length is greater than 16. The bandwidth has been fixed to $B[A_s] = 28$ *delays*, too. MONSOON becomes better than SPARK 2.0 if the vector length is greater than 40.

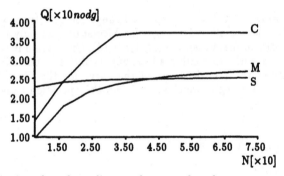

Fig. 9. Quality for kernel 21 depending on the vector length

The two figures 10 and 11 show the quality for the three machines and both kernels with a fixed bandwidth for standard address sequences and vector lengths of $N = 104$ for kernel 13 and $N = 40$ for kernel 21, respectively. The parameter being varied in a range between 1 and 9 is the ratio $I = B[A_i]/B[A_s]$, which models the degree of interleaving to achieve the high bandwidth $B[A_s] = 28$ *delays*. For $I \geq 2$ MONSOON has a significantly smaller quality than the vector machines.

The last diagram (figure 12) shows the ratio of a multiple processor MONSOON to a MONSOON with a single PE on kernel 21 with a fixed vector length of $N = 40$. The loss of quality upgrading from one to two PEs is determined by the additional costs within the PEs. Afterwards the interconnection network and the increasing idle times of the PEs are responsible for the decreasing quality. Nevertheless, for a wide range there is a sufficient amount of inherent parallelism to keep the loss of quality for a moderate number of PEs quite small.

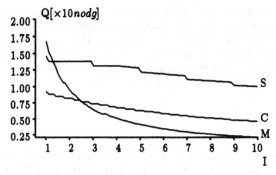

Fig. 10. Quality for kernel 13 depending on the ratio of the bandwidths

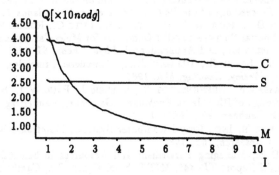

Fig. 11. Quality for kernel 21 depending on the ratio of the bandwidths

6 Conclusion

We used the method from [PM90] to compare the vector computer SPARK 2.0 and CRAY I with the dataflow machine MONSOON. We chose some kernels of the *Livermore Loops* as benchmarks to compare the numerical power. The comparison showed that the cost effectiveness of MONSOON strongly depends on the memory bandwidth. MONSOON is only as good as SPARK 2.0 and CRAY I, if the memory bandwidth in case of random addressing is quite large. Because MONSOON uses only random ad-

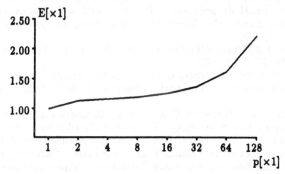

Fig. 12. Efficiency for a n PE MONSOON on kernel 21

dressing the advantage of interleaving is greater for the vector computers. By using caches for MONSOON one can increase the real bandwidth for random addressing, but that increases the cost. We plan to investigate this in the future. The transition to a multiprocessor MONSOON shows that it is possible to use the inherent parallelism very efficiently over a wide area. The slowly growing loss of quality indicates run time in half by duplicating the number of PEs.

References

[AKP91] ABOLHASSAN F., KELLER J., PAUL W.J.; On the Cost–Effectiveness of PRAMs; Proc. of the 3rd IEEE Symposium on Parallel and Distributed Processing, IEEE Computer Society Press, 2-9, 1991

[AN87] ARVIND, NIKHIL R.S.; Executing a Programm on the MIT Tagged–Token Dataflow Architecture; Proceedings of the PARLE Conference, Netherlands 1987

[AP86] AUERBACH D.J., PAUL W.J., BAKKER A.F., LUTZ C., RUDGE W.E. AND ABRAHAM F.F.; A Special Purpose Parallel Computer for Molecular Dynamics: Motivation, Design, Implementation, and Application; J. Phys. Chem., 91, 4881–4890, 1987

[ASU85] AHO A.V., SETHI R., ULLMAN J.D.; Compilers: Principles, Techniques, and Tools; Addison–Wesley, Reading, MA, 1985

[BGP92] ABOLHASSAN F., DREFENSTEDT R., KELLER J., PAUL W.J., SCHEERER D.; On the Physical Design of PRAMs; in Buchmann, Ganzinger, Paul (Hrsg.): Teubner–Texte zur Informatik, Teubner 1992, Bd. 1, 1-19

[Cr82] CRAY RESEARCH, INC.; Cray I Computer Systems, Mainframe Reference Manual HR–0029; Cray Research, Inc., 1982

[Cu90] CULLER D.E.; Managing Parallelism and Resources in Scientific Dataflow Programs; Technical Report TR–446, MIT Lab. for Comp. Sci., Cambridge MA, 1990

[CP90] CULLER D.E., PAPADOPULOS G.M.; The Explicit Token Store; CSG Memo 312, MIT Lab. for Comp. Sci., Cambridge MA, 1990

[DS92] DREFENSTEDT R., SCHMIDT D.; On the Physical Design of Butterfly Networks for PRAMs; Proceedings of the 4th Symposium on the Frontiers of Massively Parallel Computation, McLean, Virginia, IEEE Computer Society Press, Los Alamitos, CA, 202–209, 1992

[Fe87] FEO J.T.; An Analysis of the Computational and Parallel Complexity of the Livermore Loops; Parallel Computing, Vol. 7, 163–185, 1988

[Fo89] FORMELLA A.; Entwurf, Bau und Test eines Vektor–Prozessors mit parallel arbeitenden Operationseinheiten, SPARK 2.0 Teil I; Diplomarbeit, Universität des Saarlandes, FB14 Informatik, 1989

[Fo92] FORMELLA A.; Leistung und Güte numerischer Vektorrechnerarchitekturen; Dissertation, Universität des Saarlandes, FB14 Informatik, 1992

[FRS91] FORMELLA A., OBÉ A., PAUL W.J., RAUBER T., SCHMIDT D.; The SPARK 2.0 System — A Special Purpose Vector Processor with a VectorPASCAL Compiler; Proceedings of the Hawaii 25th International Symposium on System Science HICSS–25, Vol. 1, 547–558, 1992

[GKW85] GURD, KIRKHAM, WATSON; The Manchester Prototype Dataflow Computer; Comm. of the ACM, 28, 1985

[HSS87] HIRAKI, SEKIGUCHI, SHIMADA; The SIGMA–1 Dataflow Supercomputer : A Challange for New Generation Computing Systems; Journal of Information Processing, 10(4), 1987

[HJ90] HOCKNEY R.W., JESSHOPE C.R.; Parallel Computers 2: Architecture, Programming and Algorithms; Adam Hilger, Bristol and Philadelphia, 1990

[HP90] HENNESSY J.L., PATTERSON D.A.; Computer Architecture: A Quantitative Approach; Morgan Kaufmann Publishers, Inc., San Mateo, California, 1990

[Ma88] MARTIN J.L., Editor; Performance Evaluation of Supercomputers; Elsevier Science Publishers B.V., Amsterdam, 1988

[Mc84] McMAHON F.H.; Fortran Kernels, MFlops, file modicikation date Feb 29; *Lawrence Livermore National Laboratory, 1984*

[Mc86] McMAHON F.H.; L.L.N.L. FORTRAN Kernels: MFLOPS; *Lawrence Livermore National Laboratory, 1986*

[Mc88] McMAHON F.H.; The Livermore Fortran Kernels Test of the Numerical Performance Range; *Lawrence Livermore National Laboratory, 1988*

[Mo91] MOTOROLA; H4C Series Design Reference Guide; *Motorola Inc., 1991*

[Ni87] NIKHIL R.S.; ID WORLD Reference Manual; *CSG Memo 317, MIT Lab. for Comp. Sci., Cambridge MA, 1987*

[Ni90] NIKHIL R.S.; ID VERSION 90.0 Reference Manual; *CSG Memo 284-1, MIT Lab. for Comp. Sci., Cambridge MA, 1990*

[Ob89] OBÉ A.; Entwurf, Bau und Test eines Vektor–Prozessors mit parallel arbeitenden Operationseinheiten, SPARK 2.0 Teil III; *Diplomarbeit, Universität des Saarlandes, FB14 Informatik, 1989*

[Pa88] PAPADOPOULUS G.M.; Implementation of a Gerneral Purpose Dataflow Multiprocessor; *Technical Report TR–432, MIT Lab. for Comp. Sci., Cambridge MA, 1988*

[PACU90] PAPADOPULOS G.M., CULLER D.E.; Monsoon : An Explicit Token Store Architecture; *CSG Memo 306, MIT Lab. for Comp. Sci., Cambridge MA, 1990*

[PM90] PAUL W.J., MÜLLER S.M.; Towards a Formal Theory of Computer Architecture; *Parcella 90, Research in Informatics, Akademie Verlag, S. 157–169, Berlin 1990*

[Ru78] RUSSELL M.R.; The CRAY I Computer System; *Comm. ACM, Vol. 21, no. 1, 63–72, 1978*

[Sch89] SCHMIDT D.; Entwurf, Bau und Test eines Vektor–Prozessors mit parallel arbeitenden Operationseinheiten, SPARK 2.0 Teil II; *Diplomarbeit, Universität des Saarlandes, FB14 Informatik, 1989*

[TPB91] TRAUB K.R., PAPADOPOULOS G.M., BECKERLE M.J., HICKS J.E., YOUNG J.; Overview of the Monsoon Project; *Motorola Technical Report MCRC–TR–15, Cambridge MA, 1991*

[Tr86] TRAUB K.R.; A Compiler for the MIT TTDA; *Technical Report TR–370, MIT Lab. for Comp. Sci., Cambridge MA, 1986*

The Networks of the Connection Machine CM-5

Charles E. Leiserson*
Laboratory for Computer Science
Massachusetts Institute of Technology
Cambridge, Massachusetts 02142

The Connection Machine Model CM-5 Supercomputer is a massively parallel computer system designed to offer performance in the range of 1 teraflops (10^{12} floating-point operations per second). The CM-5 obtains its high performance while offering ease of programming, flexibility, and reliability. The machine contains three communication networks: a data network, a control network, and a diagnostic network. The organization of the CM-5 and its networks is shown in Figure 1.

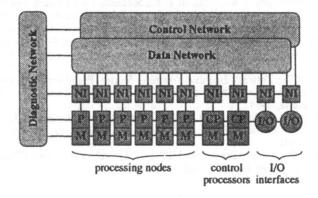

processing nodes   control   I/O
processors interfaces

Figure 1: The organization of the Connection Machine CM-5. The machine has three networks: a data network, a control network, and a diagnostic network. The data and control networks are connected to processing nodes, control processors, and I/O channels via a network interface.

The CM-5 contains between 32 and 16,384 *processing nodes*, each of which contains a 32-megahertz SPARC processor, 32 megabytes of memory, and a 128-megaflops vector-processing unit capable of processing 64-bit floating-point and integer numbers. System administration tasks and serial user tasks are executed by a collection of *control processors*, which are Sun Microsystems workstation computers. There are from one to several tens of control processors in a CM-5, each configured with memory and disk according

---

*Charles E. Leiserson is also a Corporate Fellow of Thinking Machines Corporation.

to the customer's preference. Input and output is provided via high-bandwidth *I/O interfaces* to graphics devices, mass secondary storage, and high-performance networks. Additional low-speed I/O is provided by Ethernet connections to the control processors. The largest machine, configured with up to 16,384 processing nodes, occupies a space of approximately 30 meters by 30 meters, and is capable of over a teraflops (10^{12} floating-point operations per second).

The processing nodes, control processors, and I/O interfaces are interconnected by the data network, the control network, and the diagnostic network. The data network provides high-performance point-to-point data communications between system components. The control network provides cooperative operations, including broadcast, synchronization, and *scans* (parallel prefix and suffix). It also provides system management operations, such as error reporting. The diagnostic network allows "back-door" access to all system hardware to test system integrity and to detect and isolate errors.

Further details about the CM-5 networks can be found in [1] and [2].

References

[1] C. E. Leiserson, Z. S. Abuhamdeh, D. C. Douglas, C. R. Feynman, M. N. Ganmukhi, J. V. Hill, W. D. Hillis, B. C. Kuszmaul, M. A. St. Pierre, D. S. Wells, M. C. Wong, S.-W. Yang, and R. Zak. The network architecture of the Connection Machine CM-5. In *Symposium on Parallel and Distributed Algorithms '92*, June 1992.

[2] Thinking Machines Corporation, 245 First Street, Cambridge, MA 02154-1264. *The Connection Machine CM-5 Technical Summary*, October 1991.

Massively Parallel Computing: Data distribution and communication

S. Lennart Johnsson
Division of Applied Sciences
Harvard University
Cambridge, MA 02138
and
Thinking Machines Corp.
johnsson@harvard.edu

Abstract

We discuss some techniques for preserving locality of reference in index spaces when mapped to memory units in a distributed memory architecture. In particular, we discuss the use of multidimensional address spaces instead of linearized address spaces, partitioning of irregular grids, and placement of partitions among nodes. We also discuss a set of communication primitives we have found very useful on the Connection Machine systems in implementing scientific and engineering applications. We briefly review some of the techniques used to fully utilize the bandwidth of the binary cube network of the CM–2 and CM–200, and give some performance data from implementations of communication primitives.

1   Introduction

Massively parallel computing systems today all have the memory distributed among the processors. The processors with their memory modules and communication circuitry, collectively referred to as nodes, are interconnected by a network of some type. Networks currently in use include two- and three-dimensional meshes, binary cubes, two levels of rings, and fat–trees. Some systems are programmed as a shared memory machine, others have a shared address space but are programmed in a single program multiple data mode, while others still are programmed as a collection of local address spaces with message passing libraries for data interchange and synchronization. Much of the motivation for massively parallel architectures is their promise to deliver extreme performance. Locality of reference and routing are key issues in accomplishing this goal. The mapping of the index space to the memory units, the data allocation, determines the communication need. Below we briefly discuss some of the techniques we have employed for effective data placement and routing on the Connection Machine systems [61, 62].

Many problems in science and engineering are solved using regular discretizations in two, three, or more dimensions. Discretizing differential operators leads to difference *stencils* forming a weighted sum of values at grid points in a local neighborhood. The size and shape of the neighborhood is a function of the differential operator being approximated by a discrete representation and the order of the approximation. Stencils in the solution of (partial) differential equations serve the same role as convolution kernels in signal and image processing. Solving the resulting set of algebraic equations by an iterative method, such as Jacobi and SOR with various coloring schemes [8, 20], or carrying out the convolution through direct evaluation (as opposed to using Fourier transforms), requires communication in a local neighborhood of each grid point as defined by the stencil or convolution kernel (which may vary from grid point to grid point). The source of the communication requirement in these methods is a matrix–vector multiplication. Other methods, such as the conjugate gradient method, in addition, requires global communication in each step (through inner products). Hierarchical or divide–and–conquer methods, such as the multigrid method and the fast multipole and related methods [2, 6, 21], require communication over successively increasing (decreasing) distances in the index space. The communication is also often represented as quad–trees (two spatial dimensions) or oct–trees (three spatial dimensions). The Fast Fourier Transform also requires communication over successively increasing (decreasing) distances, as represented by a butterfly network. Well-known algorithms such as Gaussian elimination and QR factorization require global communication among (decreasing) subsets of nodes. Techniques for maximizing the size of the subsets (for load balance) for as large a part of the computation as possible are presented in [41, 42, 43].

Many problems in scientific and engineering computations yield solutions that cover a wide range of scales in the spatial domain, the time domain, or in both. Multiscale problems in the spatial domain are usually handled by nonuniform, and often unstructured, grids. Multiple scales in the time domain are handled by dynamic grids. Thus, the efficient handling of arbitrary discretizations, for instance, of complex three–dimensional geometries that may change over time is very important in many real scientific applications, such as the computation of the airflow around complete aircraft.

Matrix multiplication, using the standard algorithm requiring $2N^3$ arithmetic operations, is often used for evaluating compilers for conventional computers. It is a simple computation that also is a good example for understanding some of the critical operations on distributed memory architectures. Unlike the FFT, or relaxation methods, matrix multiplication involves three operands that typically are of different shapes. The relative allocation of the indices from the different operands has a profound impact on the performance. We will discuss this issue in some detail; in particular, we will consider how generic communication primitives may be employed.

The outline of this paper is as follows. We will first justify a simplified model of the memory hierarchy in massively parallel computer systems, then present some of the techniques used on the Connection Machine systems to choose a suitable data allocation with respect to the memory hierarchy and locality of reference. Then, we discuss some of the communication primitives we have found useful in programming the Connection Machine systems for performance and some of the techniques used to achieve high performance for these primitives.

2 Locality of reference – packaging technology

It is well–known that exploiting locality of reference may enhance performance significantly in many architectures. For vector architectures, such as the Cray YMP series, the use of techniques such as loop unrolling may yield a performance enhancement by a factor of two to five [11]. The experience on many cache–based architectures is that loop unrolling, loop partitioning and loop skewing may yield similar performance enhancements [40]. The reason for these performance enhancements is the underlying memory hierarchy, and the ability of the mentioned techniques to exploit this hierarchy.

The memory hierarchy in computer systems is largely determined by the storage and packaging technologies used. The latter introduces bottlenecks in the system. Today, a processor with a moderate size register set, floating–point arithmetic, and a small cache, all fit on a single chip. The ability to move data on a chip is considerably higher than the ability to communicate off chip. Chip packages typically have a few hundred pins, while there may be several thousand wire channels on each of a few layers on the chip. Each channel across the chip may be shared by several wires on different parts of the chip. Thus, the data motion capacity on a chip may be two orders of magnitude higher than the ability to move data between a chip and its environment. The situation is similar with respect to printed circuit boards. The dimensions of wires, pins, and boards are larger, but the ratio of on–board data motion capacity to off–board capacity is similar.

Thus, one set of issues a designer faces in choosing an interconnection network is the tradeoff between few but wide channels per node, or many narrow channels [9, 50]. The communications bandwidth of nodes with few, wide channels is often relatively easy to exploit, except that the associated network may exhibit severe contention for important computations, as, for instance, in computing the FFT on a mesh of low dimension, in particular a one–dimensional array. A higher dimensional array may support such computations with significantly less contention, but the capacity of each channel is less. The mapping of high dimensional arrays to lower dimensional arrays was studied, for instance, in [53]. Whichever design is preferable is a tradeoff between latency and bandwidth.

For fine grain architectures, hardware techniques have been devised to create low latency communication systems, such as in the Caltech Mosaic system [44, 15] and the MIT J-machine [10]. In systems of coarser granularity, there is often sufficient excess parallelism, or slack, to use pipelining and lookahead techniques to diminish the significance of the latency issue. We focus on data allocation for preservation of locality of reference, and thus, reduced need for communications bandwidth, and the efficient exploitation of the communications bandwidth in high degree networks, such as large binary cubes, through the use of multiple embeddings.

3 Data allocation

The data motion requirements, and the performance, depend strongly upon the data allocation. The Connection Machine systems are programmed with a global address space. Below, we first discuss the techniques used for allocating arrays used in matrix–like computations, then we report on some early experiences with using a technique for allocation of irregular grids.

3.1 Regular arrays

On the Connection Machine systems, each array is by default distributed as evenly as possible over all nodes. In the default array allocation mode, the collection of nodes is configured for each data array as a nodal array with the same number of axes as the data array. The ordering of the axes is also the same. When there are more matrix elements than nodes, consecutive elements along each data array axis (a block) are assigned to a node. The ratios of the lengths of the axes of the nodal array are approximately equal to the ratios between the lengths of the axes of the data array [63]. The lengths of the local segments of all axes are approximately the same, and the number of off–node references minimized when references along the different axes are equally frequent, i.e., the surface area for a given volume is minimized. The default array layout is known as a *canonical layout*.

The canonical layout minimizes the data to be sent or received by each node in LU and QR factorization [43]. The canonical layout is also optimal with respect to communication for the standard matrix multiplication algorithm parallelized with respect to two of the three index axes [45]. The "standard" matrix multiplication algorithm in this context is the familiar textbook algorithm requiring $2N^3$ arithmetic operations for the multiplication of two $N \times N$ matrices. The multiplication can be performed by keeping either one of the three operands stationary. The communication requirements are minimized when the matrix with the largest number of elements is stationary. The nodal array shape for two–dimensional nodal arrays shall be congruent to the stationary matrix in order to minimize the off–node references [45]. In parallelizing the computations along all three axes, the optimal nodal array shape is congruent to the shape of the index space [29], i.e., the index space allocated to each node is as close to a cube as possible. For relaxation methods with an equal number of references along the different axes, the number of off–node references is minimized for a consecutive mapping [28] in which the lengths of the segments of the different axes mapped to a node are as equal in length as possible.

Remark 1: Note that the shape of the nodal array is important not only for communication operations but also for entirely local operations, since it effects strides and the lengths of axes, which are important with respect to loop overhead, vector lengths, cache hit ratios, and DRAM page faults. The arithmetic efficiency may vary by a factor of two or more.

Remark 2: Allocating contiguous segments of axes to a node, i.e., *consecutive allocation*, is a preferred way of aggregating data with respect to communication for computations in which nearest neighbor references dominate, such as in relaxation. In others, the consecutive allocation may yield poor load balance due to computations being nonuniform across the index space, or it may result in excessive communication. Thus, in the proposed High Performance Fortran standard [16], *cyclic* and *block-cyclic* allocation are also supported. In computations such as factorization and triangular system solution, the traversal of the index space can be matched with the chosen method of aggregation, thus creating an equal load balance for consecutive and cyclic allocation [27, 43]. But, for computations where the order of traversal of the index space is fixed, such as the FFT, a cyclic allocation may reduce the communication needs by a factor of two [37, 38, 58, 64].

For a number of important computations on regular arrays, the canonical layout indeed minimizes the number of off–node references for a given number of data elements per node. However, when references along the different axes are not uniform, other nodal array shapes may result in a reduced number of off–node references. On the Connection Machine systems, the canonical layout can be altered through compiler directives. An axis can be forced to be local to a node by the directive SERIAL, if there is sufficient local memory. The length of the local segment of an axis can also be changed by assigning *weights* to the axes. High weights are used for axes with frequent communication and low weights for axes with infrequent communication. A relatively high weight for an axis increases the length of the local segment of that axis at the expense of the lengths of the segments of the other axes. The total size of the subarray is independent of the assignment of weights for sufficiently large arrays. Only the shape of the subarray assigned to a node changes.

In many computations, more than one array is involved and the relative allocations of the arrays are often important. For instance, in solving a linear system of equations, there are at least two arrays involved: the matrix to be factored and the set of right–hand sides. The ALIGN compiler directive may be used to assure that different data arrays are assigned to nodes using the same nodal array shape for the allocation. Alignment corresponds to a reshaping of the nodal array (compared to the canonical layout). The associated data motion corresponds to a generalized shuffle operation.

Number of partitions	Number of shared edges	%of total	Number of shared nodes	% of total
8	188	0.8	195	2.4
16	381	1.6	396	4.8
32	752	3.1	773	9.3
64	1483	6.0	1479	17.8
128	2154	8.8	2101	25.3

Table 1: Partitioning of a planar mesh with inner boundary in the form of a double ellipse.

Number of partitions	Number of shared edges	%of total %of total	Number of shared nodes	% of total
8	5186	2.4	2735	13.4
16	8005	3.7	4095	20.1
32	11553	5.3	5747	28.2
64	16055	7.3	7721	37.9
128	21502	9.8	9827	48.2

Table 2: Partitioning of a tetrahedral mesh between concentric spheres.

3.2 Irregular grids

The consecutive, cyclic, and block–cyclic allocation schemes are easily evaluated and implemented for computations with regular data reference patterns on one or multidimensional arrays. For data structures corresponding to irregular grids, partitioning the grid for preservation of locality of reference is a much more difficult task. Partitioning unstructured grids is still a very active area of research. On the Connection Machine systems we have recently implemented the so called spectral decomposition technique [12, 13, 14, 48, 54]. Fiedler showed that the second largest eigenvalue and the ordering of the associated eigenvector can be used for partitioning of a mesh.

Johan [25, 26] has used this technique for finite element computations on unstructured meshes. As model problems, Johan used a planar triangular mesh between an outer ellipse and an inner double ellipse and a nonplanar grid of tetrahedra between concentric cylinders. The planar grid had 8,307 nodes, 16,231 triangles, and 24,537 edges. The numbers of shared nodes and edges as a function of the number of partitions are given in Table 1. The grid for the concentric spheres consisted of 20,374 nodes, 107,416 tetrahedra, and 218,807 faces. Some of the data for the spectral decomposition of this mesh are summarized in Table 2.

The spectral decomposition technique is now being applied to large–scale finite element meshes with a million to several million elements. The results will be reported elsewhere.

3.3   Allocation of partitions

The consecutive, cyclic, and block–cyclic allocation schemes [28] select subsets
of data elements to be assigned to the same node. Compiler directives, such as
axis weight, SERIAL and ALIGN, address the issue of choosing the nodal array
shape.

Another data layout issue is the assignment of partitions to nodes. The network topology and the data reference pattern are two important characteristics
in this assignment. The nodes of the Connection Machine system CM–200 are
interconnected as a binary cube with up to 11 dimensions. A binary cube network of n dimensions has 2^n nodes. It is well-known that regular grids are
subgraphs of binary cubes and that binary–reflected Gray codes [52] generate
embeddings of arrays into binary cube networks that preserve adjacency [28].
The binary–reflected Gray code is efficient, both in preserving adjacency and in
node utilization, when the length of the axes of the data array is a power of two
[22]. For arbitrary data array axes' lengths, the Gray code may be combined
with other techniques to generate efficient embeddings [7, 24].

The binary–reflected Gray code embedding is the default embedding on the Connection Machine system CM–200 and is enforced by the compiler directive NEWS
for each axis. The standard binary encoding of each axis is obtained through
the compiler directive SEND. The binary encoding may be preferable for computations which require that elements differing in a single bit be operated upon
together, such as in the FFT. However, in this particular case, the code conversion can be integrated into the algorithm at no increase in the communication
time [36].

For unstructured grids, finding an optimal placement of the blocks is much less
apparent, even if data references are predominantly local in the physical grid as
in explicit methods for partial differential equations. Instead of attempting to
preserve locality of reference, minimizing the contention in the communication
system through randomized routing [65, 66] or randomized data allocation [49,
51] may be a viable strategy. In the Connection Machine Scientific Software
Library [60], CMSSL, we provide randomization of the data allocation as an
option, for instance, in sparse matrix–vector multiplication. The effectiveness of
a random allocation with respect to performance is evaluated on gather/scatter
operations discussed in Section 4.3.

3.4   Summary – data allocation

In summary, on the Connection Machine systems, consecutive data allocation is
used by the compilers to aggregate data for a node. In addition to the consecutive
allocation, High Performance Fortran will also support cyclic and block–cyclic
allocation. The address space is treated as a multidimensional address space with

as many axes as there are axes in the data array. The default shape of the local address space has local axes of approximately equal lengths. A binary–reflected Gray code encoding preserves adjacency in the index space when mapped to the binary cube network of the CM–2 and CM–200.

The shape of the local address space can be controlled through compiler directives. Such directives also allow for the choice of a binary axis encoding instead of the Gray code encoding for the CM–2 and CM–200. The CM–5 only supports binary encoding [62].

The spectral decomposition technique is provided as a means of partitioning unstructured grids for preservation of locality of reference for many computations on such grids. Randomization of the data allocation is supported as a means of reducing the contention in the communication system. Spectral decomposition and randomized allocation is offered in the form of library routines in the CMSSL. Randomized routing is used on the CM–5.

4 Communication primitives

The following is a list of communication primitives that we have found important in the programming of the Connection Machine systems.

- One–to–all reduction/copy
- All–to–all reduction/copy
- Gather/scatter
- One–to–all personalized communication
- All–to–all personalized communication
- Dimension(index) permutation
- Generalized shuffle permutations
- Scan/parallel prefix
- Lattice emulation
- Butterfly emulation
- Data manipulator network emulation (PM2I network emulation)
- Pyramid network emulation
- Bit–inversion
- Index reversal ($i \leftarrow N - -i$)

Below we will discuss the need for some of the communication primitives above and the techniques used to achieve high bandwidth utilization.

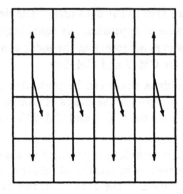

Figure 1: Broadcasting of a pivot row in LU decomposition.

4.1 Broadcast

Broadcast and reduction from a single source to subsets of nodes, holding an entire row or column, is critical for the efficiency of computations such as LU and QR factorization. In fact, many concurrent broadcast (and reduction) operations are desired in these computations as illustrated in Figure 1. Whether or not these broadcast operations imply communication that interfere, depends upon the network topology and how the index space is mapped to the nodes. On a binary cube network, entire subcubes are often assigned to a data array axis. In such a case, the broadcasts within the different columns in the index space do not interfere with each other, and the concurrent broadcast operation degenerates to a number of broadcasts within disjoint subsets of nodes. However, in other networks such a data mapping may not be feasible, and the simultaneous broadcast from several sources to distinct subsets of nodes may require a more complex routing for optimal bandwidth utilization.

Global broadcast and reduction is used, for instance, in the conjugate gradient method. But, even for the conjugate gradient method, several simultaneous broadcast operations may be required, since for massively parallel machines it is quite common that many computations of the same kind are performed concurrently, so called *multiple instance computation* [32].

Using a binomial tree to broadcast M elements from a node to all other nodes requires a time of nM with the communication restricted to one channel at a time, while the time is proportional to M with concurrent communication on all channels of every node, *all–port* communication. However, the lower bounds for the two cases are M and $\frac{M}{n}$, respectively [33]. Thus, the binomial tree algorithm is nonoptimal by a factor of n in both cases.

Multiple spanning trees rooted at the same node can be used to create lower bound algorithms [33]. The basic idea is: the source node splits its data set into $\frac{M}{n}$ disjoint subsets and sends each subset to a distinct neighbor. Then, each of these neighbor nodes broadcasts the data set it received to all other nodes (except the original source node) using spanning binomial trees. By a suitable

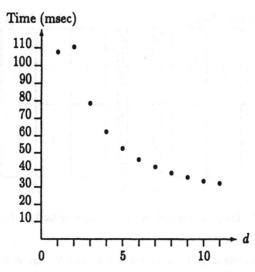

Figure 2: Time in msec for broadcast of 16k 32–bit data elements on Connection Machine system CM–200 as a function of number of cube dimensions.

construction of the trees, the n binomial trees are edge disjoint, and the full bandwidth of the binary n–cube is used effectively.

The multiple spanning binomial tree algorithm is used for broadcasting on the Connection Machine systems CM–2 and CM–200. The performance is illustrated in Figure 2 [30]. As expected, the time to broadcast a given size data set decreases with the number of nodes to which the set is broadcast.

4.2   All–to–all broadcast

Another important communication primitive is the simultaneous broadcast from each node in a set to every other node in the set, *all–to–all broadcast*. This communication is typical for so called direct N–body algorithms, but it is also required in many matrix algorithms. Here we will illustrate its use in matrix–vector multiplication.

With the processing nodes configured as a two–dimensional nodal array for the matrix, but as a one–dimensional nodal array for the vectors, both all–to–all broadcast and all–to–all reduction are required in evaluating the matrix vector product. Figure 3 illustrates the data allocation for both row major and column major ordering of the matrix. The data allocation shown in Figure 3 is typical on Connection Machine systems.

For a matrix of shape $P \times Q$ allocated to a two–dimensional nodal array in column major order, an all–to–all broadcast [18, 33, 55, 56] is required within the columns of the nodes for any shape of the nodal array and for any length of the matrix Q–axis.

After the all–to–all broadcast, each node performs a local matrix–vector multiplication. After this operation, each node contains a segment of the result vector y. The nodes in a row contain partial contributions to the same segment of y, while different rows of nodes contain contributions to different segments of y.

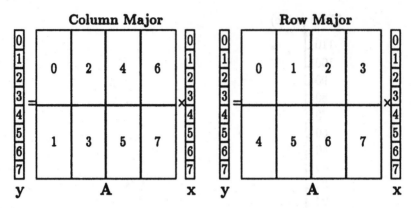

Figure 3: Data allocation on a rectangular nodal array.

No communication between rows of nodes is required for the computation of y. Communication within the rows of the nodes suffices.

The different segments of y can be computed by all–to–all reduction within processor rows, resulting in a row major ordering of y. But, the node labeling is in column major order, and a reordering from row to column major ordering is required in order to establish the final allocation of y. Thus, for a column major order of the matrix elements, matrix–vector multiplication can be expressed as:

> All–to–all broadcast of the input vector within columns of nodes
> Local matrix–vector multiplication
> All–to–all reduction within rows of nodes to accumulate
> partial contributions to the result vector
> Reordering of the result vector from row major to column major order.

All–to–all broadcast or reduction is required also when a one–dimensional nodal array configuration is used for the matrix [46].

In all–to–all broadcast, the lower bound for an n–cube where each node initially holds M elements is $M(N-1)$ for communication restricted to a single port at a time and $\frac{M(N-1)}{n}$ for all–port communication [33]. A simple yet optimal, all–port, algorithm for all–to–all broadcast uses n Hamiltonian paths for each node. For all–to–all broadcast, the Hamiltonian paths need not be edge–disjoint. Finding and constructing edge–disjoint cycles is a complex problem [1].

A Hamiltonian cycle can be constructed by moving across cube dimensions according to the transition sequence in a binary–reflected Gray code. Translating such a cycle to another source node by performing an exclusive–or operation on every node address by the source node index, assuming the first cycle has node zero as its source, creates $2^n = N$ paths. These paths cannot be edge–disjoint. But, it can be shown, that for all–to–all broadcast, there is no contention between data packets moving along the paths generated by a binary–reflected Gray code. Moreover, it can be shown that paths generated by rotating the address bits in the Gray code can be used without contention [33], thus providing n paths for each node. The initial data set M in each node is divided into n pack-

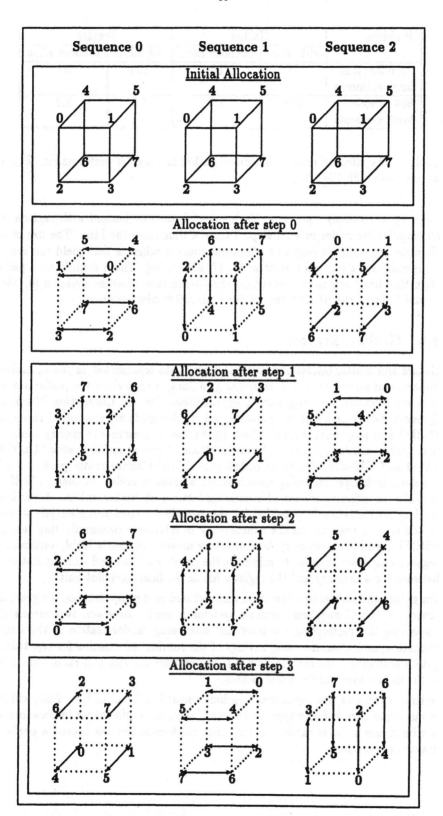

Figure 4: Three concurrent exchange sequences in a 3-cube.

Problem	Gather		Scatter	
	std alloc.	random alloc	std alloc.	random alloc
3200 20–node brick elements	75	50	124	55
864 8–node brick elements	5.6	3.7	7.2	3.4

Table 3: The effect of randomization on gather and scatter performance. Times in msec on an 8k CM–200.

ets of approximately equal size. Each subset is then exchanged with packets in all neighboring nodes in each step. Figure 4 illustrates the idea. The use of n Hamiltonian paths is only one of several routing schemes that yield the same complexity for all–to–all broadcast [3, 17, 33, 55, 56]. The n Hamiltonian path algorithm has been implemented on the Connection Machine systems [5, 46]. Figure 5 shows the performance of the CM–200 implementation.

4.3 Gather/Scatter

Gather and scatter operations on regular grid data represented as one or multidimensional arrays, as well as irregular grid data, is critical for the performance of many scientific and engineering applications. On the Connection Machine Systems, gather and scatter operations on regular grids are supported through PSHIFT (for polyshift) [19, 60], which allows the programmer to specify concurrent shift operations in one or both directions of one or multiple axes. On the CM–2 and CM–200 with Gray coded axes, PSHIFT concurrently performs all the data exchanges requiring communication between nodes. In effect, PSHIFT provides an effective means of emulating lattices on binary cubes. A further level of optimization is provided by the so called stencil compiler [4], which in addition to maximizing the concurrency in internode communication (using PSHIFT), avoids unnecessary local memory moves and uses a highly optimized register allocation in order to minimize the number of load and store operations between local memory and the register file in the floating–point unit.

For gather and scatter operations on unstructured grid computations, the general router on the Connection Machine systems is used. However, two means of improving the performance is provided, one being randomization of the data allocation, and a second being savings of the routing information for repetitive gather scatter operations. Table 3 [47] summarizes the effect of randomization of the data allocation for a few meshes.

In these examples, the performance enhancement is a factor of 1.5 – 2.25, which in our experience is fairly typical. In some cases, the performance improvement has been larger. It is rarely the case that randomization has caused a performance degradation.

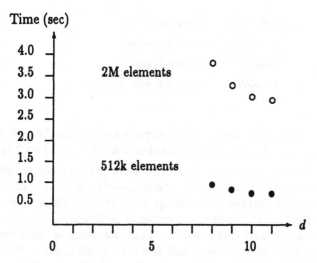

Figure 5: Time for physical all–to–all broadcast on a Connection Machine system CM–200. Array sizes are $2M = 2^{21}$ and $512K = 2^{19}$ 32–bit elements.

4.4 Personalized communication

In *one–to–all personalized communication* a node sends a unique piece of data to every other node. An example is matrix computations where a node holds an entire column, which may need to be redistributed evenly over all the nodes, as in some algorithms for matrix–vector multiplication [46]. In all–to–all personalized communication, each node sends unique information to all other nodes. Personalized communication is not limited to matrix transposition but encompasses operations such as bit–reversal, transposition or bit–reversal combined with a code change (such as the conversion between binary code and binary–reflected Gray code) and bit–inversion. We now illustrate the significance of personalized communication in computing the FFT on a multiprocessor.

In computing the FFT on distributed data, one possibility is to exchange data between nodes, and have one of the nodes in a pair compute the "top" and the other compute the "bottom" of the butterfly requiring data from the two nodes. This type of algorithm is currently used on the Connection Machine systems CM–2 and CM–200 [39]. When there are two or more elements per node, then an alternative is to perform an exchange of data between nodes such that each node in a pair computes one complete butterfly. The sequence of exchanges required for the FFT amounts to a shuffle, as illustrated below, where the | separates node address bits to the left and local memory address bits to the right:

Example 1.

Address	Index
$(54321|0)$	$(54321|0) = (54321|x_0)$
$(04321|5)$	$(x_0 a_4 a_3 a_2 a_1 | a_5)$
$(05321|4)$	$(a_4 x_0 a_3 a_2 a_1 | a_5)$

$$(05421|3) \qquad (a_4 a_3 x_0 a_2 a_1 | a_5)$$
$$(05431|2) \qquad (a_4 a_3 a_2 x_0 a_1 | a_5)$$
$$(05432|1) \qquad (a_4 a_3 a_2 a_1 x_0 | a_5)$$
$$(15432|0) \qquad (a_4 a_3 a_2 a_1 a_5 | x_0)$$

Thus, the end result of the sequence of exchanges is a shuffle on the node address field. Each step is equivalent to the transposition of a collection of 2×2 matrices.

In practice, for a one–dimensional transform, there are typically several local memory bits. For performance, under many models for the communication system, minimizing the number of exchange steps is desirable, i.e., instead of performing bisections as in the example above, it is desirable to perform multisections including all local memory bits. Thus, for instance, with two local memory bits four–sectioning is being used as shown in Example 1. With three local memory bits, eight–sectioning is used as shown in Example 3.

Example 2.

Address	Index
(65432|10)	$(65432\|10) = (65432\| \underbrace{x_1}_{j1} \ \underbrace{x_0}_{j0})$
(10432|65)	$(\underbrace{x_1 x_0 a_4 a_3 a_2}_{m} \| \underbrace{a_6 a_5}_{m})$
(10652|43)	$(\underbrace{a_4 a_3}_{m} \underbrace{x_1 x_0}_{m} \ \underbrace{a_2}_{n-k \cdot m} \| a_6 a_5)$ $\underbrace{}_{k \cdot m}$
(10654|23)	$(\underbrace{a_4 a_3 a_2}_{n-m} \ \underbrace{x_0}_{(k+1)m-n} \ \underbrace{x_1}_{n-k \cdot m} \| \underbrace{a_6 a_5}_{m})$ under x_0: $j0$, under x_1: $j1$
(23654|10)	$(\underbrace{a_4 a_3 a_2}_{n-m} \ \underbrace{a_6}_{(k+1)m-n} \ \underbrace{a_5}_{n-k \cdot m} \| \underbrace{x_0 x_1}_{m})$
(23654|10)	$(\underbrace{a_4 a_3 a_2}_{n-m} \ \underbrace{a_6}_{(k+1)m-n} \ \underbrace{a_5}_{n-k \cdot m} \| \underbrace{x_1 x_0}_{m})$

Example 3.

Address	Index
(6543|210)	(6543|210)
(2103|654)	$(\underbrace{x_2 x_1 x_0 a_3}_{m} \| \underbrace{a_6 a_5 a_4}_{m})$

$$(2106|354) \quad \left(\underbrace{a_3}_{n-m} \quad \underbrace{x_1 x_0}_{(k+1)m-n} \quad \underbrace{x_2}_{n-k\cdot m} \quad | \underbrace{a_6 a_5 a_4}_{m} \right)$$

$$\underbrace{}_{j0} \quad \underbrace{}_{j1}$$

$$(3546|210) \quad \left(\underbrace{a_3}_{n-m} \quad \underbrace{a_6 a_5}_{(k+1)m-n} \quad \underbrace{a_4}_{n-k\cdot m} \quad | \underbrace{x_1 x_0 x_2}_{m} \right)$$

$$(3546|210) \quad \left(\underbrace{a_3}_{n-m} \quad \underbrace{a_6 a_5}_{(k+1)m-n} \quad \underbrace{a_4}_{n-k\cdot m} \quad | \underbrace{x_2 x_1 x_0}_{m} \right)$$

Examples 2 and 3 were deliberately chosen such that the exchanges cannot simply be treated as digit exchanges with increased radix for the digit but must indeed be treated as exchanges with digits of different radices. Moreover, the last few exchange steps were made such that the final order represents an m-step shuffle on the nodal address bits, where m is the number of bits used to encode the first exchange. This node address ordering requires a local memory shuffle to restore the original local memory ordering. In practice, it may, in fact, be preferable to avoid the local memory reordering by performing the last exchange such that local memory is normally ordered, which would leave the node addresses in an order corresponding to two shuffles: one m-step shuffle on all n node address bits, one n mod m shuffle on the last m bits.

All the above illustrations are made for the case where the indices are encoded in a binary code. With the part of the data index assigned to the node address field encoded, for instance, in binary-reflected Gray code, the actual communication pattern must account for the fact that the butterfly computations are made on bits in binary encoding, while the data allocation uses Gray code. In [36] we show how the butterfly emulation based on multisectioning of Gray coded data on a binary cube can be performed in the same time as if the data had been binary coded.

In multidimensional FFT, all of local memory should be considered in performing the multisectioning. For details see [31].

The FFT example above makes use of a sequence of all-to-all personalized communications. Before briefly discussing some algorithms for this type of communication in binary cubes, we consider the communication required to restore the original index order for the FFT. In the case of the FFT, the bits in the encoding of the output indices are computed in reverse order. Thus, what is required to establish a normal index map in the frequency domain is an unshuffle with bit-reversal. Figure 6 [31] shows a particular example.

The lower bounds for all-to-all personalized communication with M data elements per node is $\frac{nMN}{2}$ for communication restricted to a single port per node and $\frac{MN}{2}$ for all-port communication [33]. The corresponding bounds for one-to-all personalized communication are $(N-1)M$ and $(N-1)M/n$, respectively. Balanced spanning trees [23] provide for optimal one-to-all and all-to-all personalized communication in communication systems allowing all-port communication. A balanced spanning tree has N/n nodes in each of the n subtrees

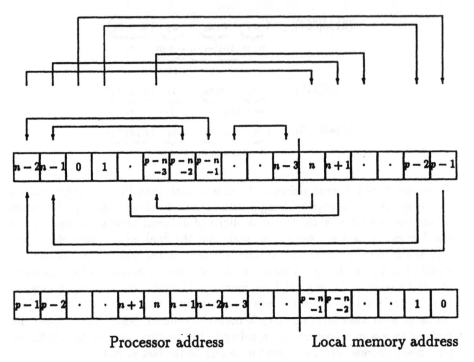

Processor address   Local memory address

Figure 6: Two step reordering after 4–section based radix-2 FFT. First step, bit–exchange between nodes; second step, bit–exchange between local memory and node addresses. $p \leq 2n - m$.

of the root. The use of n rotated spanning binomial trees rooted in each node also yields the desired complexity. Algorithms for both one–to–all and all–to–all personalized communication are discussed in [33]. In our FFT example above, several all–to–all personalized communications were performed in succession. In such a case, it may be of interest to minimize the time elements are in transition from source to destination in order to minimize pipeline delays, if the communication system allows successive all–to–all personalized communications on different nodal dimensions to be pipelined. Algorithms with a minimal transition time are presented in [35].

Bit–reversal with an equal number of dimensions assigned to the node address field and the local memory address field constitutes one form of all–to–all personalized communication. The performance on various sizes of the CM–2 is shown in Figure 7 [30]. As expected, the execution time is almost independent of the machine size for a fixed size data set MN. The increase in the execution time is largely due to the fact that local memory operations cannot be performed in parallel. Thus, there is a term proportional to n in addition to the constant term.

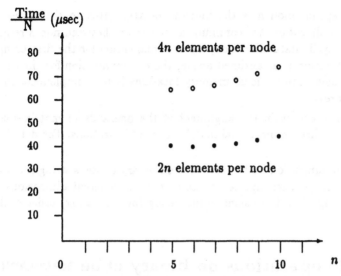

Figure 7: All-to-all personalized communication on the Connection Machine.

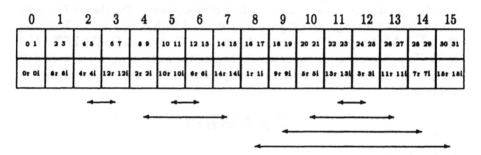

Figure 8: Postprocessing for real–to–complex FFT. Bit–inversion in subcubes.

4.5   Index reversal – bit–inversion

Index reversal is another important permutation used for instance in the computation of real–to–complex FFT. For this computation the standard algorithm requires that data with indices i and $N-i$, $0 \leq i < N$, be operated upon in a preprocessing or postprocessing step for the FFT [57, 59]. In binary–coded data, the index reversal required for the FFT corresponds to a two's–complement subtraction (bit complement plus one).

However, in the case of the real–to–complex FFT on a one–dimensional array with binary–coded data, the first step in one of the most common algorithms is to perform a complex–to–complex FFT on the array viewed as a half–size, one–dimensional, array of complex data points. The result is shown in Figure 8. The Figure also shows that the postprocessing, matching indices i and $N-i$, corresponds to bit–inversion in subcubes of the form $00\ldots01xx\ldots x$, with the inversion being performed on the bits denoted by x.

If there are more than one complex data point per node, then the communication requirements depend upon how the indices are aggregated to the nodes. In consecutive data allocation, the communication pattern between nodes remains the same. In a cyclic data allocation, the communication for the first complex local memory location is as outlined above; the communication for the second and all subsequent complex local memory locations is bit–complement on the entire node address.

Bit–inversion also occurs in the alignment of the operands in matrix–matrix multiplication on three–dimensional nodal array configurations. For details see [29].

Concurrent communication for bit–inversion on binary cubes is straightforward. For instance, multiple exchange sequences starting in different dimensions and progressing through the dimensions in increasing (or decreasing) order cyclicly can be used.

5   Shuffle operations on binary cube networks

In considering FFT computations through the use of multisectioning, we noticed that the effect on the original index space corresponds to a m–step shuffle, where m is the number of bits encoding the first digit exchange. For the FFT computation the various digit exchanges are interleaved with computation. Restoring the original index order corresponds to an unshuffle (except for the FFT which in itself implements a bit–reversal). Reshaping the nodal array for a given data array also represents a general shuffle operation. For instance, changing the allocation

$$\begin{pmatrix} a_3\, a_2\, m_2\, a_1\, a_0\, m_1\, m_0 \\ y_2 y_1\, y_0\, x_3 x_2 x_1\, x_0 \end{pmatrix}$$

to the allocation

$$\begin{pmatrix} m_2 m_1 m_0\, a_3\, a_2\, a_1\, a_0 \\ y_2\, y_1\, y_0\, x_3 x_2 x_1 x_0 \end{pmatrix},$$

where x_i and y_i denote bits encoding an x–axis and y–axis respectively, and a_i denotes nodal address bits and m_i local memory address bits, constitutes a generalized shuffle, or dimension permutation. The dimension permutation is: $a_3 \leftarrow a_1 \leftarrow m_1 \leftarrow a_2 \leftarrow a_0 \leftarrow m_0 \leftarrow m_2 \leftarrow a_3$. In this example, the reshaping resulted in a single cycle on the dimensions. In general, the reshaping may result in several cycles, just as the m–step shuffle in general can be decomposed into several cycles.

A shuffle can be implemented as a sequence of successive pairwise dimension exchanges starting in any position. In a binary cube, such exchanges imply communication in two cube dimensions for each step if both dimensions in an exchange are nodal address dimensions. However, it is also possible to use a fixed memory dimension for each exchange. If the first exchange is repeated as a last exchange, then the result is a shuffle on all bits but the fixed exchange dimension. For a shuffle on n bits, the first alternative requires $n - 1$ exchanges while the last requires $n + 1$ exchanges. Thus, at the expense of two additional exchanges, each exchange only involves one nodal address dimension. In [34] we present algorithms that are nonoptimal by at most two exchanges, regardless of the number of cube dimensions in the shuffle and data elements per node. The idea for the algorithms is to use multiple exchange sequences (embeddings), exploiting the fact that a shuffle can be performed as a sequence of exchanges starting at any bit and proceeding in order of decreasing dimensions cyclicly.

6 Summary

We have discussed some of the data allocation techniques used to preserve locality of reference on the Connection Machine systems, namely data aggregation, nodal array shape, unstructured grid partitioning, and placement of partitions among the nodes. We have also demonstrated the use of several communication primitives, discussed optimal implementations of these with respect to utilizing the communications bandwidth of binary n-cubes, and given a few results from their implementation on the Connection Machine systems CM-2 and CM-200. Scheduling the communications knowing the global communication needs has resulted in significant speedups for some communication patterns on the CM-2 and CM-200. For PSHIFT, a speedup of up to a factor of four has been observed, while for bit-reversal a speedup of close to two orders of magnitude has been observed in extreme cases. The choice of nodal array shape has been observed to affect the performance of matrix multiplication by more than one order of magnitude [45]. Randomization of the data allocation typically yields a performance improvement by a factor of 1.5 – 3 on the CM-2 and CM-200 for gather/scatter operations on irregular grids.

References

[1] B. Alspach, J.-C. Bermond, and D. Sotteau. Decomposition into cycles i: Hamilton decompositions. In G. Hahn et. al., editor, *Cycles and Graphs*, pages 9–18. Kluwer Academic Publishers, 1990.

[2] Christopher R. Anderson. An implementation of the fast multipole method without multipoles. *SIAM J. Sci. Stat. Comp.*, 13(4):923–947, July 1992.

[3] D. P. Bertsekas, C. Ozveren, G.D. Stamoulis, P. Tseng, and J.N. Tsitsiklis. Optimal communication algorithms for hypercubes. *Journal of Parallel and Distributed Computing*, 11:263–275, 1991.

[4] M. Bromley, Steve Heller, Tim McNerny, and Guy Steele. Fortran at ten Gigaflops: The Connection Machine convolution compiler. In *Proceedings of ACM SIGPLAN 1991 Conference on Programming Language Design and Implementation*. ACM Press, 1991.

[5] Jean-Philippe Brunet and S. Lennart Johnsson. All-to-all broadcast with applications on the Connection Machine. *International Journal of Supercomputer Applications*, 6(3):241–256, 1992.

[6] J. Carrier, L. Greengard, and V. Rokhlin. A fast adaptive multipole algorithm for particle simulations. *SIAM J. of Scientific and Statistical Computations*, 9(4):669–686, July 1988.

[7] M.Y. Chan. Embedding of grids into optimal hypercubes. *SIAM J. Computing*, 20(5):834–864, 1991.

[8] G. Dahlquist, Å. Björck, and N. Anderson. *Numerical Methods*. Series in Automatic Computation. Prentice Hall, Inc., Englewood Cliffs, NJ, 1974.

[9] William J. Dally. *A VLSI Architecture for Concurrent Data Structures*. PhD thesis, California Institute of Technology, 1986.

[10] William J. Dally. The J-Machine: A fine–grain concurrent computer. In *Proc. IFIP Congress*, pages 1147–1153. North-Holland, August 1989.

[11] Jack. J. Dongarra and Stanley C Eisenstat. Squeezing the most out of an algorithm in Cray Fortran. *ACM Trans. Math. Softw.*, 10(3):219–230, 1984.

[12] M. Fiedler. Algebraic connectivity of graphs. *Czechoslovak Mathematical Journal*, 23:298–305, 1973.

[13] M. Fiedler. Eigenvectors of acyclic matrices. *Czechoslovak Mathematical Journal*, 25:607–618, 1975.

[14] M. Fiedler. A property of eigenvectors of nonnegative symmetric matrices and its application to graph theory. *Czechoslovak Mathematical Journal*, 25:619–633, 1975.

[15] Charles M. Flaig and Charles L Seitz. Inter–computer message routing system with each computer having separate routing automata for each dimension of the netwrok, 1988. U.S. Patent 5,105,424.

[16] High Performance Fortran Forum. High performance fortran language specification, version 0.4. Technical report, Department of Computer Science, Rice University, November 1992.

[17] Geoffrey C. Fox and Wojtek Furmanski. Optimal communication algorithms on the hypercube. Technical Report CCCP-314, California Institute of Technology, July 1986.

[18] Geoffrey C. Fox, Mark A. Johnsson, Gregory A. Lyzenga, Steve W. Otto, John K. Salmon, and Wojtek Furmanski. *Solving Problems on Concurrent Processors*. Prentice-Hall, 1988.

[19] William George, Ralph G. Brickner, and S. Lennart Johnsson. Polyshift communications software for the Connection Machine systems CM-2 and CM-200. Technical report, Thinking Machines Corp., March 1992.

[20] Gene Golub and Charles vanLoan. *Matrix Computations*. The Johns Hopkins University Press, 1985.

[21] Leslie Greengard and Vladimir Rokhlin. A fast algorithm for particle simulations. *Journal of Computational Physics*, 73:325–348, 1987.

[22] I. Havel and J. Móravek. B-valuations of graphs. *Czech. Math. J.*, 22:338–351, 1972.

[23] Ching-Tien Ho and S. Lennart Johnsson. Spanning balanced trees in Boolean cubes. *SIAM Journal on Sci. Stat. Comp*, 10(4):607–630, July 1989.

[24] Ching-Tien Ho and S. Lennart Johnsson. Embedding meshes in Boolean cubes by graph decomposition. *J. of Parallel and Distributed Computing*, 8(4):325–339, April 1990.

[25] Zdenek Johan. *Data Parallel Finite Element Techniques for Large–Scale Computational Fluid Dynamics*. PhD thesis, Department of Mechanical Engineering, Stanford University, 1992.

[26] Zdenek Johan and Thomas J. R. Hughes. An efficient implementation of the spectral partitioning algorithm on the connection machine systems. In *International Conference on Computer Science and Control*. INRIA, 1992.

[27] S. Lennart Johnsson. Dense matrix operations on a torus and a Boolean cube. In *The National Computer Conference*, July 1985.

[28] S. Lennart Johnsson. Communication efficient basic linear algebra computations on hypercube architectures. *J. Parallel Distributed Computing*, 4(2):133–172, April 1987.

[29] S. Lennart Johnsson. Minimizing the communication time for matrix multiplication on multiprocessors. Technical Report TR-23-91, Harvard University, Division of Applied Sciences, September 1991. To appear in Parallel Computing.

[30] S. Lennart Johnsson. Performance modeling of distributed memory architectures. *J. Parallel and Distributed Computing*, 12(4):300–312, August 1991.

[31] S. Lennart Johnsson. Data ordering in multisection FFT. Technical report, Thinking Machines Corp., 1992. In preparation.

[32] S. Lennart Johnsson. *Compilation Techniques for Novel Architectures*, chapter *Language and Compiler Issues in Scalable High Performance Libraries*. Springer Verlag, 1993. Harvard University Technical Report TR-18-92.

[33] S. Lennart Johnsson and Ching-Tien Ho. Spanning graphs for optimum broadcasting and personalized communication in hypercubes. *IEEE Trans. Computers*, 38(9):1249–1268, September 1989.

[34] S. Lennart Johnsson and Ching-Tien Ho. Generalized shuffle permutations on Boolean cubes. *J. Parallel and Distributed Computing*, 16(1):1–14, 1992.

[35] S. Lennart Johnsson and Ching-Tien Ho. Optimal communication channel utilization for matrix transposition and related permutations on Boolean cubes. *Discrete Applied Mathematics*, 1992.

[36] S. Lennart Johnsson and Ching-Tien Ho. Boolean cube emulation of butterfly networks encoded by Gray code. *Journal of Parallel and Distributed Computing*, 1993. Department of Computer Science, Yale University, Technical Report, YALEU/DCS/RR-764, February, 1990.

[37] S. Lennart Johnsson, Ching-Tien Ho, Michel Jacquemin, and Alan Ruttenberg. Computing fast Fourier transforms on Boolean cubes and related networks. In *Advanced Algorithms and Architectures for Signal Processing II*, volume 826, pages 223–231. Society of Photo-Optical Instrumentation Engineers, 1987.

[38] S. Lennart Johnsson, Michel Jacquemin, and Robert L. Krawitz. Communication efficient multi-processor FFT. *Journal of Computational Physics*, 102(2):381–397, October 1992.

[39] S. Lennart Johnsson and Robert L. Krawitz. Cooley-Tukey FFT on the Connection Machine. *Parallel Computing*, 18(11):1201–1221, 1992.

[40] Monica S. Lam, Edward E. Rothenberg, and Michael E. Wolf. The cache performance and optimizations of blocked algorithms. In *The Sixth International Conference on Architectural Support for Programming Languages and Operating Systems*, pages 63–74. ACM Press, 1991.

[41] Guangye Li and Thomas F. Coleman. A parallel triangular solver for a distributed memory multiprocessor. *SIAM J. Sci. Statist. Comput.*, 9(3):485–502, 1988.

[42] Guangye Li and Thomas F. Coleman. A new method for solving triangular systems on a distributed memory message-passing multiprocessor. *SIAM J. Sci. Statist. Comput.*, 10(2):382–396, 1989.

[43] Woody Lichtenstein and S. Lennart Johnsson. Block cyclic dense linear algebra. *SIAM Journal of Scientific Computing*, 14(5), 1993. Thinking Machines Corp., Technical Report, TMC-215, December 1991.

[44] Christoffer Lutz, Steve Rabin, Charles L. Seitz, and Donald Speck. Design of the mosaic element. In *Proceedings, Conf. on Advanced research in VLSI*, pages 1–10. Artech House, 1984.

[45] Kapil K. Mathur and S. Lennart Johnsson. Multiplication of matrices of arbitrary shape on a Data Parallel Computer. Technical Report 216, Thinking Machines Corp., December 1991.

[46] Kapil K. Mathur and S. Lennart Johnsson. All-to-all communication. Technical Report 243, Thinking Machines Corp., December 1992.

[47] Kapil K. Mathur and S. Lennart Johnsson. Communication primitives for unstructured finite element simulations on data parallel architectures. *Computing Systems in Engineering*, 3(1 - 4):63–72, December 1992.

[48] Alex Pothen, Horst D. Simon, and Kang-Pu Liou. Partitioning sparse matrices with eigenvectors of graphs. *SIAM J. Matrix Anal. Appl.*, 11(3):430–452, 1990.

[49] Abhiram Ranade. How to emulate shared memory. In *Proceedings of the 28th Annual Symposium on the Foundations of Computer Science*, pages 185–194. IEEE Computer Society, October 1987.

[50] Abhiram Ranade and S. Lennart Johnsson. The communication efficiency of meshes, Boolean cubes, and cube connected cycles for wafer scale integration. In *1987 International Conf. on Parallel Processing*, pages 479–482. IEEE Computer Society, 1987.

[51] Abhiram G. Ranade, Sandeep N. Bhatt, and S. Lennart Johnsson. The Fluent abstract machine. In *Advanced Research in VLSI, Proceedings of the fifth MIT VLSI Conference*, pages 71–93. MIT Press, 1988.

[52] E.M. Reingold, J. Nievergelt, and N. Deo. *Combinatorial Algorithms*. Prentice-Hall, Englewood Cliffs. NJ, 1977.

[53] Arnold L. Rosenberg. Preserving proximity in arrays. *SIAM J. Computing*, 4:443–460, 1975.

[54] Horst D. Simon. Partitioning of unstructured problems for parallel processing. *Computing Systems in Engineering*, 2:135–148, 1991.

[55] Quentin F. Stout and Bruce Wagar. Intensive hypercube communication I: prearranged communication in link-bound machines. Technical Report CRL-TR-9-87, Computing Research Lab., Univ. of Michigan, Ann Arbor, MI, 1987.

[56] Quentin F. Stout and Bruce Wagar. Passing messages in link-bound hypercubes. In Michael T. Heath, editor, *Hypercube Multiprocessors 1987*. Society for Industrial and Applied Mathematics, Philadelphia, PA, 1987.

[57] Paul N. Swarztrauber. Symmetric FFTs. *Mathematics of Computation*, 47(175):323–346, July 1986.

[58] Paul N. Swarztrauber. Multiprocessor FFTs. *Parallel Computing*, 5:197–210, 1987.

[59] Clive Temperton. On the FACR(l) algorithm for the discrete Poisson equation. *J. of Computational Physics*, 34:314–329, 1980.

[60] Thinking Machines Corp. *CMSSL for Fortran*, 1990.

[61] Thinking Machines Corp. *CM-200 Technical Summary*, 1991.

[62] Thinking Machines Corp. *CM-5 Technical Summary*, 1991.

[63] Thinking Machines Corp. *CM Fortran optimization notes: slicewise model, version 1.0*, 1991.

[64] Charles Tong and Paul N. Swarztrauber. Ordered Fast Fourier transforms on a masively parallel hypercube multiprocessor. *Journal of Parallel and Distributed Computing*, 12(1):50–59, May 1991.

[65] Leslie Valiant. A scheme for fast parallel communication. *SIAM Journal on Computing*, 11:350–361, 1982.

[66] Leslie Valiant and G.J. Brebner. Universal schemes for parallel communication. In *Proc. of the 13th ACM Symposium on the Theory of Computation*, pages 263–277. ACM, 1981.

A Realizable Efficient Parallel Architecture

Burkhard Monien[1] * Reinhard Lüling[1] *, Falk Langhammer[2]

[1] Department of Computer Science, University of Paderborn, Germany
e-mail : bm@uni-paderborn.de, rl@uni-paderborn.de
[2] Parsytec Computer, Aachen, Germany, e-mail : falk@parsytec.de

Abstract. The near future will present large scale parallel computers, able to provide computing power of more than one TFlop per second. It is commonly agreed that these systems will be based on the model of asynchronous processors connected by a point to point network. There are a number of different network architectures presented in the past.

In this paper we present an architectural principle that combines efficiency, realizability for very large systems, and inherent reliability needed for such large parallel processing systems. The here presented *Fat Mesh of Clos network* principle can be scaled in many ways to fulfill the special requirements of a system design.

Two realizations of this principle are presented: One is based on static switches combined to form a fully reconfigurable system. This architecture has been realized for systems containing up to 320 processors.

The other realization uses dynamic routing switches. By combining wormhole routing with randomized and local adaptive routing this network provides large capacity and very short latency times. The efficiency of our principle is demonstrated by simulations.

Both realizations presented here are built and commercialized by Parsytec Computer.

1 Introduction

Over the last years parallel computing has received considerable attention of researchers in science and engineering. One of the main reasons for the growing interest lies in the difficulties to increase the performance of sequential computers due to technical and physical limitations. Furthermore, the availability of cheap mass fabricated microprocessors and communication switches makes it more economical to connect hundreds and thousands of these components than to build highly specialized sequential computers.

Theoretically, such a collection of processors working in parallel can achieve unbounded performance and is therefore suitable to solve problems of all areas of science and engineering. Among these are, for example, computational intensive problems like weather forecasting and computational fluid dynamics or real time problems like vision and speech recognition.

---

* This work was partly supported by the German Federal Department of Science and Technology (BMFT), PARAWAN project 413-5839-ITR 9007 BO and by the DFG Forschergruppe "Effiziente Nutzung massiv paralleler Systeme"

A number of different architectures for the construction of parallel computers have been proposed. Flynn [10] has given a classification based on the way data and instructions are processed. Conventional von Neumann architectures perform a single operation on one data set per computation step (SISD architecture). The architecture is called SIMD if in each step one instruction is performed on a number of data sets in parallel. This architecture has been realized in a number of *massively parallel computers* like the DAP, Connection Machine and MasPar MP-1 systems. All these systems consist of many very small processing elements (up to 65536 in the case of the Connection Machine) providing large performance for suitable applications.

MIMD-type architectures, which are at present most popular for the design of parallel computer systems, perform a number of different instructions on multiple data streams in one step. In comparison with the existing SIMD systems, the processors used for this architecture are usually much more powerful. In most cases, conventional microprocessors are used. Popular systems of this kind are Intel's Paragon and iWarp systems, NCubes, Alliant FX, the CM-5 of Thinking Machines Corp., the KSR1 of Kendall Square Research and Transputer networks.

The processors in a MIMD system communicate with each other either by one global memory, as in the case of the Alliant FX computer, or via message passing on an interconnection network. In case of a message passing parallel system (distributed memory system), the structure of the underlying network decisively effects the efficiency of any algorithm performed on such a system. A number of different network topologies have been suggested.

One of the most important ones is the hypercube. It is used in the Intel iPSC, the NCube and also for the Connection Machine. Other important networks are meshes, used for the Intel Paragon machine and multistage networks used for the Transputer system SC320, the CM-5 and the Meiko CS-2 machine.

At present, most of the realized systems contain less than 1000 processors, but there is an ongoing effort [14, 22] to build MIMD systems performing one TFlop per second. It is a well accepted fact that these large scale parallel computer systems based on today's and shortly forthcoming technologies can only be realized as asynchronous processor networks, working in MIMD fashion, connected by a point-to-point interconnection network.

Networks used for the realization of such large machines have to be optimized according to measures like efficiency, realizability and reliability. The efficiency of a communication network is equivalent to its ability to provide large throughput (number of delivered messages per time step) and small communication latency for any fixed user dependent communication pattern. This ability is important for the overall usability of the network. A further problem is this context is to be seen in the ability of a network to provide multiuser access in a most efficient and general way without effecting other users.

The efficiency is sometimes measured by its ability to realize given communication structures in an efficient way concerning edge dilation and congestion [19], and sometimes in terms of network capacity (maximal throughput) and latency times for globally randomized communication patterns [5]. For both measures network parameters like large bisection width, large number of edge disjoint paths between any two nodes and small network diameter, are of vital importance [20]. In this paper we will concentrate on the second measure. The efficiency can be further increased by using methods like randomized routing to avoid hot spots and by local or global adaptive routing to avoid local blockings.

Most characteristics of a communication network, increasing efficiency, decrease its realizability. Networks with small diameter, large bisection width and a large number of redundant paths, are hard to realize because of the complex wiring structure and the length of the used cables [3]. Another important factor for the realizability of a network is the cost efficiency of the network structure. The costs of the processors and the network should be balanced according to the targeted ratio between computation and communication efficiency. Thus, the network structure should optimize the ratio between network efficiency and number of used components.

So, there exists a trade-off between network efficiency and network realiability. A two-dimensional mesh and a multistage interconnection network are two counterparts. A mesh is very easy to realize, but has low efficiency. Multistage interconnection networks, on the other hand, provide large communication bandwith and low latency times but are very hard to realize.

A third important property of a communication network is its reliability, generally effected by the number of redundant paths which has already been found to be important for the efficiency. It is also effected by the number of different components used for the realization of the network, which we already found to be important for its realiazability.

Thus, when designing communication networks able to realize large scale parallel machines, one has to consider the trade-off between efficiency and realizability.

This paper aims at describing an architectural principle for the flexible realization of large scale processor networks taking the problems mentioned above into account. It is based on a Clos network of h stages with the top r stages resolved and the remaining $h - r$ stages connected by a number of independent grids. This so-called "Fat Mesh of Clos" combines high communication efficiency, by using randomized and local adaptivity routing fulfilling most of the requirements concerning realizability and reliability. Therefore, it can be regarded as a suitable network for realizing very large parallel computer systems.

We will describe two realizations of this concept. One is based on static routing chips connected to form a fully reconfigurable processor network able to realize any regular network of degree four [11]. The other one uses the presented principle to construct large scale parallel machines based on a dynamic routing switch. Both architectures are suitable for any processor with a constant number of communication links. We will present a realization of these systems for the Inmos Transputer processors.

2 Architecture

The architecture of switching networks can be classified by several criteria. Concerning the capabilities of the used switches, static and dynamic switching networks can be distinguished. In case of a static switch, the connections between input and output ports are arranged before the program execution and are fixed during the

---

[3] A formal definition of realizability is not available but as realizability is effected by the wiring structure of the network, the VLSI area complexity can partly serve as a parameter.

whole runtime. In this way, the switches are used to realize a fixed interconnected network.

Dynamic switching networks provide communication paths between any two processors of a distributed system. The outgoing link for an incoming message is chosen according to routing information which is statically provided by a routing table or by the message itself. There are some problems inherent in this approach. If the buffer space is bounded, which is the case for all switches realized so far, store and forward deadlocks can occur. This problem has been solved for a number of different well known networks by designing appropriate routing algorithms [8]. Randomized routing [25] is a very powerful technique to overcome hotspots. To reduce the latency time, techniques like wormhole and cut-through routing [8] were introduced and realized in different architectures [7, 13].

Dynamic switching networks allow communication between any two processors independent of the concrete hardware architecture. Nevertheless, the architecture plays a very important role for the efficiency of the system, since even if the routing scheme is deadlock free, it can lead to blockings, effecting the performance considerably. This effect is even augmented by wormhole routing, as a message can block a path of some length in the network. The structure of the physical network influences the probability of such blockings.

Another distinction criteria is the connection capability of the used switches. According to [3], one can distinguish single and double sided switches. The former have only one set of connections which are all treated equally. In such switches, any port can be connected to any other port. Since all of them can be both, source and destination of messages, the ports must be bidirectional. Double sided switches connect two different sets of ports. In this case, ports of one set (input ports) can only be connected to ports of the other one (output ports).

2.1 Basic Concept of the Architecture

Our architecture is based on single sided switches and on the Clos network [3, 4], whose origins come from the field of telephone research. A typical Clos network consists of three stages with $n = m \cdot k$ inputs and n outputs. It is built up by k $m \times m$ switches in the first and third stage and m $k \times k$ switches in the middle stage. If these switches are able to realize any connection of its input to its output ports, the complete network can realize any permutation and is called rearrangeable. This construction can easily be extended to larger numbers of stages.

Special members of the family of Clos networks are the Benes and complementary Benes networks. The former is constructed of a Clos network by setting $m = 2$ and $k = \frac{n}{2}$ and recursively decomposing the center stage until the complete network consists of 2×2 switches. The latter results from the recursive decomposition of a Clos network with $m = \frac{n}{2}$ and $k = 2$. Both constructions can also be extended to larger switches.

We define a Clos network of height h built up of single sided switches of equal size $2k$ by the following scheme :

- a single switch of size $2k$ connecting k links to processors is a Clos network of height 1.

– a Clos network of height h is built by connecting k Clos networks of height $h-1$ by k^{h-1} switches. Since each of the k subnetworks has k^{h-1} external links, k^{h-1} switches are used in level h in a way that the i–th external link of each subnetwork is connected to the i–th switch of level h.

At the top stage of a Clos network only half of the switches are necessary, since no links are used to connect to higher stages.
Figure 1 presents a Clos network of height 3 for $k = 4$ and processors connected by 4 links to the network. Networks of this kind have intensively been studied in the

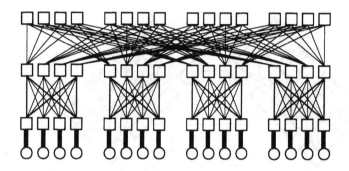

Figure 1. The Clos Network of height 3

past and are for example used as the basic communication network for the Parsytec SuperCluster SC320 [11], the CM-5 of Thinking Machines [17] (the fat tree is realized by a Clos network) and the Meiko CS-2 machine [18]. Due to the long wires used to connect the switches according to this scheme, these systems are hard to realize for larger processor numbers, as extremely advanced technology is needed, leading to high costs and less reliability. On the other hand it is hard to enlarge the network, since a slight enlargement can make a complete new network level necessary.

For reasons of realizability and reliability, we define the so-called *Fat Mesh of Clos* network. A Fat Mesh of Clos(h, r) is defined by substituting the r top stages of a complete Clos network of height h by a mesh structure. The deletion of the r top stages partitions the Clos network into k^r clusters, each consisting of a Clos network of height $h - r$. Such a network has k^{h-r-1} switches in its top stage with k external links each. For $1 \leq i \leq k^{h-r-1}$ the i-th switch of all clusters' top stages are connected by a mesh of dimension $\frac{k}{2}$ resulting in k^{h-r-1} independent meshes.
This network is much easier to realize than a complete Clos network, since the cluster structure can be built up of a moderate size Clos network which is realizable as a frame of the complete system. The different clusters are connected by a fat mesh which is also very easy to realize and which provides large communication capacity while the use of very short cables increases reliability and realizability.
The presented architecture can therefore be regarded as an extension of the fat tree presented in [17]. Inside each cluster we use the same network as for realizing the fat tree, while in our case a set of fat trees is connected via a fat mesh. The advantage of

fat meshes over higher dimensional networks like hypercubes with constant bisection width has already been shown in [5].

If not explicitly defined, we assume k to be 4 for the rest of this paper. This is a reasonable number, since eight-path switches are used in many parallel systems nowadays. Thus, the global structure is built of a number of independent two dimensional meshes. A Fat Mesh of Clos built of these this switches has a bisection width of $2^r \cdot 4^{h-r-1}$ if $r > 0$ and $\frac{1}{2}4^h$ if $r = 0$. Figure 2 presents a Fat Mesh of Clos(3,1). In this case the two-dimensional grids are degenerated to circles of length 4.

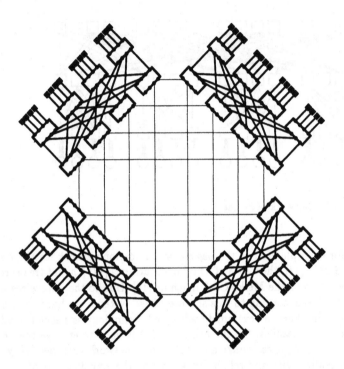

Figure 2. Fat Mesh of Clos(3,1)

For large k one can construct meshes of higher dimension as described above or use more links in one direction, increasing the performance considerably if localized adaptive routing schemes can be used. The advantages of such an architecture are not fully considered in this paper.

2.2 Efficiency of Fat Mesh of Clos Networks

To study the efficiency of the presented architecture we observe its behavior under the steady state model: Each processor generates a new packet with probability λ at each time step, sending it to a uniform randomly chosen processor. We will present latency times for different parameters λ and describe the maximal point of stability λ_{max} (maximal network capacity) for different networks. λ_{max} is defined to be the maximal injection rate which does not lead to backlogs. For any $\lambda > \lambda_{max}$ the latency time (time between generation and reception of a message at its destination) will grew in an unbounded way.

Since the results are strictly dependent on the concrete capabilities of the used switches, we make the following assumptions :

- Communication is done by wormhole routing
- A switch having $2k$ bidirectional links can store one flit of a message per ingoing link.
- Each message contains its destination in its first flit.
- The switch allows the generation of randomized headers from a given interval which are placed before the actual header and used as the new actual header.
- Headers can be deleted when passing through outgoing links
- Outgoing links can be grouped together such that a message which has to be routed via one of the outgoing links is adaptively send via an unblocked link of that group (local adaptive routing). This link is chosen in a round robin fashion. The positive effect of this strategy on the communication efficiency for different networks has already been investigated in [12].

All these features are realized in the Inmos C103/C104 routing chips belonging to the new T9000 processor family [13] and partly in some other switches, too.

To achieve maximal communication bandwidth and minimal latency times, we make extensive use of these properties. In detail, routing a message from processor a to processor b in a Fat Mesh of Clos(h, r) is done by :

- Sending the message to a random least common ancestor of a and b if both processors belong to the same Clos network, and then deterministically to the destination processor. We use randomized local adaptive routing to achieve maximal performance for the first routing phase.
- Sending the message to a random switch on the top stage of the Clos network in which the message starts routing on the mesh to the destination cluster and then deterministically to processor b. A deadlock free routing algorithm based on dimension ordering is used for routing on the mesh [8].

The analysis of the steady state model is extremely interesting, but also very difficult for wormhole routing. In [23] some results are given for hypercube and butterfly networks for the packet routing problem, assuming infinite buffer capacity per switch. The differences between this model and the one used here are considerable and don't allow the application of the results.

In [9] results for the steady state wormhole routing problem on the two-dimensional mesh are presented. It was shown that a nearly optimal injection rate can be reached and that messages are delivered with high probability in nearly optimal time.

Other results for the steady state model were mostly gained by simulations [5, 6, 12]. In the following we present first results for the maximal network capacity of the Fat Mesh of Clos network if uniformly randomized routing is used. To do this, we have to study the bottlenecks of the network.

Basically, there are two types of bottlenecks. One is induced by the bisection width of the mesh. Note that the bisection of the network Clos(h, r) with eight-path switches, i.e. $k = 4$, is equal to $2^r \cdot 4^{h-r-1}$ for $r > 0$. Following an argument from [15], chapter 1.7.2, this limits the expected maximal number of messages a processor can receive per step to $\frac{1}{L \cdot 2^r}$ if L is the number of flits per message. In the following we call this bound "bisec" (bisection bound).

The second type of bottlenecks is caused by the structure of the Clos network. We allow no buffers on the switch. Therefore, messages passing a switch can block each other. An approximation of the throughput of a Clos network taking these blockings into account can be computed for the circuit switching model, where a message going from the top stage to the processors on the bottom stage blocks a complete path in the network. We count the expected number of messages which can be routed to its destination per step according to this model. In the steady state packet routing model the number of messages arriving at their destinations will be larger, since messages having not reached the bottom stage are "stored" inside the network leading to a larger throughput in the next step.

For a switch on stage h' in a network of h stages having k incoming links from stage $h' + 1$ and k outgoing links to stage $h' - 1$, we can compute, see [15] chapter 3.4.9, the probability that at least one ingoing message has to be routed through a fixed outgoing link by

$$1 - \left(\frac{k-1}{k}\right)^k .$$

Since the number of incoming messages on stage h' is equivalent to the number of outgoing messages of stage $h' + 1$, we get the following recursive formula for the probability that at least one message has to be routed via a fixed outgoing link of a switch on stage h'.

$$P(h') = P(h' + 1) - \left(\frac{k-1}{k} \cdot P(h' + 1)\right)^k .$$

As $\frac{1}{L \cdot 2^r}$ is an upper bound for the injection rate not leading to backlogs, the probability that an incoming link on the top stage receives a message is bounded by $\frac{1}{2^r}$. We assume $P(h) = \frac{1}{2^r}$ to be the probability that there is a message entering an incoming channel of the Clos network's top stage from a neighbored cluster. Using the above formula we get an approximation of the number of messages which can be received by a processor per time step. In the following we will denote this bound by "csm" (circuit switching model).

Table 1 and 2 present the network capacity gained by simulating various Fat Mesh of Clos networks. The network capacity is equal to the maximal injection rate λ which does not cause any backlogs. It also shows the ratio between network capacity and bisection width in percent (λ/bisec). To compute the latency time which is defined to be the average number of time steps necessary for a message to reach its destination, we assume a globally synchronized system where in one time step, a flit can pass one routing chip. All results are computed for simple packet routing and for wormhole routing using 4 flits per message. This number was chosen, because the Inmos routing chips C103 and C104 use wormhole routing with 4 flits per message.

h	r	proc.	mesh	latency	λ	λ/bisec	bisec	csm	$\frac{\lambda \cdot 10^7}{A}$
3	0	64	1x1	10.91	0.50782	0.50782	1	0.43200	619.897
3	1	64	2x2	11.28	0.34427	0.68854	0.50	0.35392	896.536
3	2	64	4x4	11.70	0.16539	0.66156	0.25	0.22752	1722.812
4	0	256	1x1	11.48	0.43618	0.43618	1	0.36692	33.277
4	1	256	2x2	11.97	0.33307	0.66614	0.50	0.30965	54.211
4	2	256	4x4	13.09	0.17228	0.68912	0.25	0.20884	112.161
4	3	256	8x8	13.77	0.06997	0.55976	0.125	0.11926	182.213
5	0	1024	1x1	14.79	0.38770	0.38770	1	0.31945	1.848
5	1	1024	2x2	15.41	0.31665	0.63330	0.50	0.27552	3.221
5	2	1024	4x4	15.57	0.17264	0.69056	0.25	0.19304	7.025
5	3	1024	8x8	16.29	0.07889	0.63112	0.125	0.11403	12.840
5	4	1024	16x16	18.28	0.03285	0.52560	0.0625	0.06105	21.386
6	0	4096	1x1	19.26	0.34384	0.34384	1	0.28318	0.102
6	1	4096	2x2	23.58	0.25006	0.50012	0.50	0.24836	0.158
6	2	4096	4x4	25.23	0.16408	0.65632	0.25	0.17951	0.417
6	3	4096	8x8	27.40	0.08048	0.64384	0.125	0.10925	0.818
6	4	4096	16x16	28.59	0.03659	0.59040	0.0625	0.05967	1.488
6	5	4096	32x32	32.32	0.01501	0.48032	0.03125	0.03089	2.853

Table 1. Results for packet routing, $k = 4$

h	r	proc.	mesh	latency	λ	λ/bisec	bisec	csm	$\frac{\lambda \cdot 10^7}{A}$
3	0	64	1x1	24.51	0.14033	0.56132	0.25	0.10800	171.301
3	1	64	2x2	28.95	0.09940	0.79520	0.125	0.08848	258.854
3	2	64	4x4	31.46	0.04853	0.77648	0.0625	0.05688	505.521
4	0	256	1x1	19.62	0.11519	0.46076	0.25	0.09173	8.788
4	1	256	2x2	30.34	0.08822	0.70576	0.125	0.07741	14.358
4	2	256	4x4	37.61	0.04983	0.79728	0.0625	0.05221	32.441
4	3	256	8x8	40.38	0.02218	0.70976	0.03125	0.02982	57.760
5	0	1024	1x1	24.73	0.10172	0.40688	0.25	0.07987	0.485
5	1	1024	2x2	26.85	0.08109	0.64872	0.125	0.06888	0.824
5	2	1024	4x4	28.96	0.04436	0.70976	0.0625	0.04826	1.805
5	3	1024	8x8	41.30	0.02124	0.67968	0.03125	0.02851	3.457
5	4	1024	16x16	72.35	0.01091	0.69824	0.015625	0.01526	7.103
6	0	4096	1x1	28.75	0.08755	0.35020	0.25	0.07079	0.026
6	1	4096	2x2	31.19	0.07340	0.58720	0.125	0.06209	0.046
6	2	4096	4x4	37.89	0.04408	0.70528	0.0625	0.04488	0.121
6	3	4096	8x8	55.41	0.02127	0.67968	0.03125	0.02731	0.216
6	4	4096	16x16	74.35	0.00978	0.62591	0.015625	0.01492	0.397
6	5	4096	32x32	90.75	0.00468	0.59904	0.0078125	0.00772	0.761

Table 2. Results for wormhole routing, $k = 4$

The tables show, that the network capacity is slightly larger than csm if the number of resolved stages is low. If, on the other hand, the number of resolved stages is very high, leading to a large mesh, the network capacity is lower than csm. The first observation can be explained by the fact that we do not take into account that some messages don't pass through the top stage of the Clos network. As the number of these messages increases with the cluster size, csm becomes less exact for small r. The overestimation of the network capacity for larger r seems to be due to our taking the upper bound determined by the bisection width of the mesh for the probability of a message entering the top stage of a cluster.

If $r = h-1$, csm is slightly smaller than bisec. Note, that a Fat Mesh of $Clos(h, h-1)$ connects 4^{h-1} clos networks of height 1 (one switch) making additional blockings inside the switches possible.

The tables show that the bisection width of the pure Clos network is not reached by far. With the number of resolved stages growing, λ/bisec also increases, since the bisection bound of the mesh is closer to reality than the bisection width of the Clos network. For medium numbers of resolved stages λ/bisec is relatively high. In these cases many messages are entirely routed inside the Clos network, not effecting the mesh bisection bound. Therefore, λ/bisec becomes smaller if all stages are resolved. Comparing packet routing and wormhole routing, the network capacity is closer to the bisection width if wormhole routing is used. This can partly be explained by using a result of [9] for continuous routing on the mesh stating that routing on a two dimensional mesh containing n processors does not lead to backlogs if each processor generates messages with probability $\frac{c}{L\sqrt{n}+2n}$ for a constant c.

In general, we observed that the global bottleneck of the Fat Mesh of Clos network, determining the overall throughput of the network, changes with the number of resolved stages. For very small r, the overall bottleneck is a result of the Clos bottleneck. For larger r the bisection width of the mesh determines the maximal number of packets a processor can receive per time step.

Table 1 and 2 present the latency time for the maximal network capacity λ. It should be noticed that the latency time is very sensitive to the injection rate if it is near to the network capacity making an exact estimation difficult. A better understanding of the network latency can be gained by regarding it as a function of the injection rate. Figure 3 presents results for different injection rates, using packet routing. There is an extremely large increase in the latency time if λ is close to the network capacity.

To realize the Fat Mesh of Clos as the basic communication network of a parallel computer, one has to optimize the ratio between efficiency and costs of the used components. The costs of the network are most decisively effected by the number of used switches, communication cables, the length of the cables, and the wiring complexity. Other parameters as cooling, power consumption are in general independent of the concrete network architecture and are therefore of minor interest.

The number of switches (#*switch*) used for the realization of a Fat Mesh of $Clos(h, r)$ can easily be computed as :

$$\#switch = \begin{cases} 4^{h-1} \cdot (h-r) & \text{if } r > 0 \\ 4^{h-1} \cdot (h - \frac{1}{2}) & \text{if } r = 0 \end{cases}$$

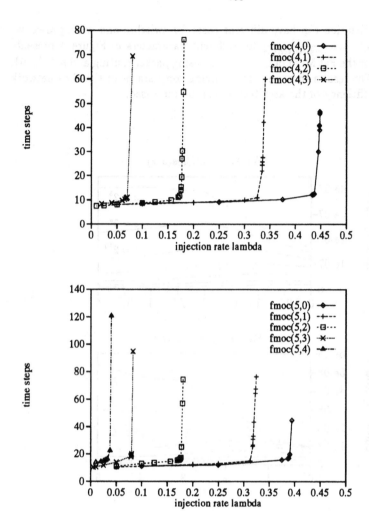

Figure 3. Latency for 256 and 1024 processors, $k = 4$

A detailed analysis of the wiring costs depends very much on the used technology [14]. We use the VLSI area complexity (A) as a measure for the wiring complexity. For the Fat Mesh of Clos(h, r) we get the following values :

$$A = \begin{cases} 60 \cdot 4^{2h-r-2} & \text{if } r > 0 \\ 32 \cdot 4^{2h-2} & \text{if } r = 0 \end{cases}$$

If we compare the number of used switches and the network capacity, the pure Clos network makes most efficient use of the switches, whereas the pure mesh is more efficient, measuring the ratio of efficiency and area complexity. (see table 1 and 2).

As a concrete realization can have different costs for switches and wiring area, we present efficiency/costs$=\frac{\lambda}{c\cdot\#switch+A}$ for different parameters c. Figure 4 presents efficiency/costs for the Fat Mesh of Clos network using packet routing and $h \in \{5, 6\}$, $c = 2^8, \ldots, 2^{14}$. The results show that by resolving some stages of the Clos network the overall cost efficiency of the architecture can be increased.

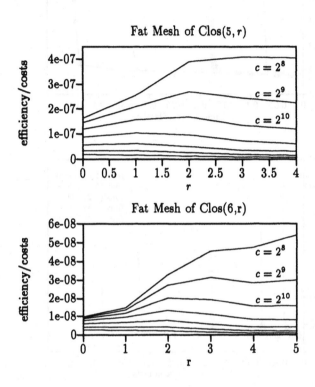

Figure 4. efficiency/costs for Mesh of Clos networks, $k = 4$

It is also interesting to study the efficiency of this network for local communication patterns which are more common in practice than globally randomized patterns. We have done so by embedding a two dimensional mesh of processes into the architecture in an obvious way. Per time step we generated a message with a fixed probability that maximizes the total throughput. This message is send to a random processor having distance i to the generating node on the embedded mesh with probability $e^{-i\cdot\alpha}$. Table 3 presents the network capacity for 4 flit wormhole routing and different parameters α.

We can observe that there is only a very small performance decrease if the number of resolved stages increases. This is especially true for entirely local communication patterns. Since for many applications (e.g. numerical simulation methods like finite

h	r	$\alpha = 1.0$	$\alpha = 0.5$	$\alpha = 0.1$
3	0	0.15072	0.13758	0.09332
3	1	0.14574	0.12253	0.07462
3	2	0.06631	0.05529	0.04149
4	0	0.14997	0.13635	0.06284
4	1	0.14801	0.13309	0.06286
4	2	0.10854	0.07729	0.04490
4	3	0.04111	0.03111	0.02131
5	0	0.14912	0.13585	0.09268
5	1	0.10092	0.13509	0.08734
5	2	0.10663	0.11054	0.05433
5	3	0.07104	0.05179	0.02501
5	4	0.02350	0.01546	0.01058
6	0	0.14863	0.13530	0.09924
6	1	0.14867	0.13541	0.09743
6	2	0.14783	0.13058	0.06843
6	3	0.12340	0.08588	0.03283
6	4	0.04827	0.03042	0.01147
6	5	0.01526	0.00985	0.00458

Table 3. Results for local communication patterns, $k = 4$

element method) most of the communication is local on regular network structures (e.g. meshes), these results show that the presented principle leads to very small performance decreases compared to the complete Clos network, while factors like realizability increase dramatically for a decomposed Clos network.

3   A Realization of the Architecture Using Static Routing Chips

In this chapter we describe a parallel computer system realized by Parsytec Computer which is built of static single sided switches with 96 links. We use the T800 Transputer, a microprocessor integrating a floating point unit, 4 KByte of memory and 4 serial links. The system is presently realized for up to 320 processors. Due to the large switches, it is possible to use a pure Clos network. The following figure presents the complete architecture including the connections to the external environment.

To map a user application containing n nodes, which is always a regular graph of degree 4, onto the machine, this network has to be partitioned into $\lfloor \frac{n}{16} \rfloor$ subgraphs of size 16 with at most 32 external edges each.

It is easy to prove that a partition using 36 external edges can always be constructed. In fact, for every natural number m, every regular graph of degree 4 can be partitioned into clusters of size m with at most $2m + 4$ external edges per cluster [11]. We

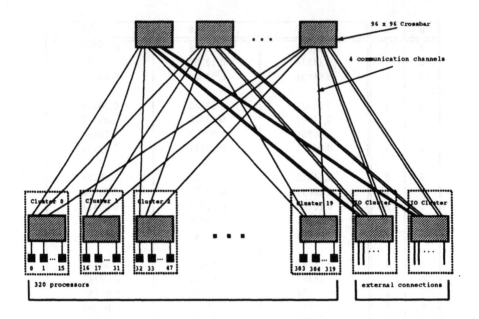

Figure 5. Architecture of the SC320

carried out quite a number of experiments with 4-regular graphs of 320 nodes and always found a partition into clusters of size 16 with at most 32 external edges each. We use a distributed simulated annealing algorithm to partition the network. This algorithm is able to separate all given graphs arising in practice (up to 320 nodes) very quickly, as they have a huge number of short cycles.

To map the 32 external edges onto the switches of the top stage we treat the clusters of the bottom stage as a regular network of degree 32. This graph is partitioned into 8 graphs of degree 4. The question of partitioning a regular network of degree $2d$ into d networks of degree 2 has already been studied in 1891 by Petersen [21], who proved that such a partition exists. The algorithm he presented is based on the construction of an Euler circle and an alternating coloring of the edges. This algorithm works in linear time for networks whose degree is a power of two, as in our case. General algorithms have been presented by various authors. For an overview see [11].

Since the used switch allows a new configuration of single links without changing the general structure when allocating a set of clusters to a user, the whole system has very good multiuser qualities. If a user allocates $16 \cdot k + x$, $1 \leq x \leq 15$ processors, a fraction of one cluster has to be used. We use a best fit strategy to choose this cluster.

By now, two systems containing up to 320 processors have been installed and have worked for nearly two years. Practical experiences with up to 24 user entries for the system show that the number of blocked processors due to non-available external connections for clusters which are shared between different users is very small (about 2 to 5 percent).

4 Realization of the Architecture Using Dynamic Routing Switches

The advent of the Inmos C103/C104 single sided routing chips makes it possible to construct large scale parallel computer systems providing large communication bandwidth (100 MBit/sec per link and direction) and low latency routing (use of randomized and local adaptive wormhole routing, 0.5 μsec setup time). In the following we will describe the architecture of the Parsytec GC system using the 8-path C103 routing switch. The system will provide, in its largest configuration a sustained performance of more than 200 Gigaflops per second [14]. It uses redundancy (one spare processor per 16 processors) and a general modular design based on the principle defined by the Fat Mesh of Clos. For a dettailed description of the used technologies see [14].

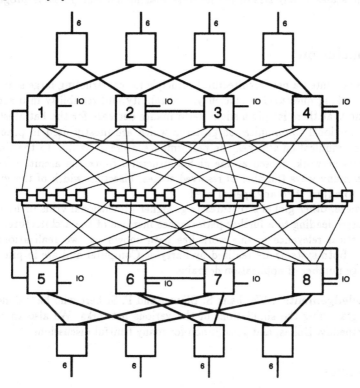

Figure 6. Construction of a cluster using C103 switches

The general structure of the GC machine is a three-dimensional Fat Mesh of Clos with 16 processors per cluster connected by a two-stage Clos network. The clusters are connected by 8 links in each direction of the three-dimensional space, making 48 external links necessary. The concrete architecture of this cluster is shown in figure 6. It slightly differs from the original Mesh of Clos definition, which is due to the fact that a Clos network would require more than two stages if 48 external links per cluster should be provided and 16 processors connected. Our architecture guarantees that there are four distinct paths between every two processors, leading to an increased communication bandwidth for various communication patterns.

The internal architecture of each cluster allows the direct embedding of grid and hypercube structures without any edge dilation or congestion of the communication channels into the cluster. Since the overall structure is a three-dimensional mesh, the architecture can be used for the efficient realization of most of the mesh-type structures appearing in scientific computing. All required networks are automatically embedded into the architecture, providing the user with a so-called virtual network topology, since all concrete hardware details are hidden from the user application. The embedding is done by a parallel algorithm running on the network itself (every processors x computes the processes mapped onto x). Therefore, the embedding algorithm scales to any size of the network making efficient portable programming possible.

5 Conclusion

We have presented a new architectural principle for constructing large scale parallel systems, taking questions of efficiency, realizability and reliability into account. It was found that there is only a slight performance decrease for the Fat Mesh of Clos network for local communication patterns which are mostly used in practice. For global communication schemes the performance decrease is due to the limitations of the grid network, chosen as the global structure. Since the architecture can be scaled in many ways (number of resolved stages, bisection width of the grid), it is possible to adjust it to any special need.

Furthermore, other global structures (e.g. higher dimensional grids or hypercubes) can be used, leading to a further performance increase of the architecture.

The practical relevance of this work has been shown by two realizations of this principle. Both systems are realized by Parsytec Computer and are in practical use for a large number of application domains.

Acknowledgements : We thank S. Blömer and P. Siebert who have done a great job, programming the simulations of the various networks. We also thank Seshu Madhavapeddy, Dallas, and Jens Simon for many fruitful discussions.

References

1. V. E. Benes, Mathematical Theory of Connecting Networks and Telephone Traffic, New York, Academic Press, 1965
2. B. Bollobás, Extremal Graph Theory, Academic Press 1978
3. G. Broomell, J. R. Heath, Classification, Categories and Historical Development of Circuit Switching Technologies, Computing Surveys, vol. 15, no. 2, June 1983
4. C. Clos, A study of non blocking switching networks, Bell System Technical Journal, March 1953, pp. 407-424
5. W. Dally, Performance Analysis of k ary n cube interconnection networks, IEEE Trans. Computers, 39, 1990, pp. 775-785

6. W. Dally, Fine grain message passing concurrent computers, 3rd Conf. on Hypercube Concurrent Computers and Applications, ACM Press, 1988, pp. 2-12

7. W. J. Dally, C. L. Seitz, The Torus Routing Chip, Distributed Computing, 1986, no. 1, pp. 187-196

8. W. J. Dally, C. L. Seitz, Deadlock-Free Message Routing in Multiprocessor Interconnection Networks, IEEE Transactions on Computers, vol. C-36 1987, no. 5, pp. 547-553

9. S. Felperin, P. Raghavan, E. Upfal, A Theory of Wormhole Routing in Parallel Computers, ACM Symposium on Foundations of Computer Science, 1992, pp. 563-572

10. M. J. Flynn, Very high-speed computing systems, Proceedings of the IEEE 54,12, Dec. 1966, pp. 1901-1909

11. R. Funke, R. Lüling, B. Monien, F. Lücking, H. Blanke-Bohne, An optimized reoncfigurable architecture for transputer networks, Proc. of the 25th Hawaii Int. Conf. on System Sciences (HICSS) 1992, vol. 1, pp. 237-245

12. H. Hofestädt, A. Klein, E. Reyzl, Performance Benefits from Locally Adaptive Interval Routing in Dynamically Switched Interconnection Networks, Proc. of 2nd European Distributed Memory Computing Conference, Lecture Notes in Computer Science 487, pp. 193-202

13. Inmos, The T9000 Transputer Products Overview Manual, First Edition 1991

14. F. Langhammer, F. Wray, Supercomputing and Transputers, ACM Int. Conf. on Supercomputing, 1992, pp. 114-129

15. F. T. Leighton, Introduction to Parallel Algorithms and Architectures, Arrays, Trees, Hypercubes, Morgan Kaufmann Publishers, 1992

16. F. T. Leighton, B. M. Maggs, A. G. Ranade, S. B. Rao, Randomized Routing and Sorting on Fixed-Connection Networks Internal Report

17. C. E. Leiserson et.al., The Network Architecture of the Connection Machine CM-5, ACM Symposium on Parallel Algorithms and Architectures, 1992, pp. 272-285

18. Meiko CS-2, product announcment at Supercomputing 92, Minneapolis, Parallelogram, November 1992, pp. 10-11

19. B. Monien, H. Sudborough, Embedding one Interconnection Network in Another, Computing Suppl. 7, 1990, pp. 257-282

20. B. Monien, R. Feldmann, R. Klasing, R. Lüling, Parallel Architectures: Design and Efficient Use, Symposium on Theoretical Aspects of Computer Science (STACS) 1993, Lecture Notes in Computer Science

21. J. Petersen, Die Theorie regulärer Graphen, Acta Math. 15 1891, pp. 193-220

22. J. Rattner, The New Age of Supercomputing, 2nd European Conf. on Distributed Memory Computing 1991, Lecture Notes in Computer Science 487, pp. 1-6

23. G. D. Stamoulis, J. N. Tsitsiklis, The Efficiency of Greedy Routing in Hypercubes and Butterflies, ACM Symposium on Parallel Algorithms and Architectures, 1991, pp. 248-259

24. J. D. Ullman, Computational Aspects of VLSI, Computer Science Press, Inc. 1984

25. L. G. Valiant, G. J. Brebner, Universal schemes for parallel communication Proc. of ACM STOC 1981, pp. 263-277

26. L. G. Valiant, General Purpose Parallel Architectures, in : J. van Leeuwen, Handbook of Theoretical Computer Science, vol. A, chapter 18, pp. 943-971, Elsevier Publishers, 1990

27. J. van Leeuwen, R. B. Tan, Interval Routing, The Computer Journal, vol. 30, no. 4, 1987, pp. 298-307

28. J. S. Ward, J. B. G. Roberts, J. G. Harp, Design of a Configurable Multi-Transputer Machine, Esprit P1085 Working Paper 1, August 1985

Hardware Support for Collective Communication Operations

Larry Rudolph*

Department of Computer Science
The Hebrew University
Jerusalem 91904 Israel
email: rudolph@cs.huji.ac.il

Abstract. We describe the design of a communications board that supports collective communications operations of parallel programs. Each cluster of processors are interconnected by a bus and connected to the communications board. The communications boards are, in turn, connected to a low latency, high bandwidth, slow configuration time crossbar network. The design is geared towards low-end (inexpensive) parallel computer architectures.

Such an architecture is motivated by recent advances in parallel programming models and in particular by the "loosely synchronous" style of parallel programming. Subgroups of processors alternatively perform local work with collective communication operations. This allows time to reconfigure the large crossbar and enables communication between processors without interrupts. The important broadcast, scatter, gather, and transpose operations can be efficiently supported.

1   Introduction

Recent advances in parallel programming models encourage corresponding advances in parallel processing architectures. In particular, the "loosely synchronous" model of parallel programming ([4]) and more recent proposals for collective communications libraries ([3]) have very specific interprocessor communication demands. We believe that systems with a moderate number of processors interconnected by a few bus clusters can be modified easily to support these demands.

The basic model of computation assumes an MIMD type of control and more specifically an SPMD (single program multiple data) model. Each processor has a local memory and some interprocessor connection links. In the loosely synchronous model, processors alternate between phases of local computation and global communications. All processors participate in a the global communication. This programming style is attractive because is simplifies the coordination of complex communications between different processors and it is representative of many supercomputer application programs. Experience parallelizing many applications reveals that often the majority of time is spent in performing local work while the majority of coding effort and debugging is involved with the communications. The idea is to provide

* This work has been supported in part by a US-Israel BSF Grant #88-45 and France-Israel BSF Grant #3310

direct software and hardware support for the frequently used communication operations such as shift, broadcast, scatter/gather, transpose, reduction, and barrier synchronization.

The loosely synchronous model encourages polling over interrupts. Since each processor will eventually make a call to the communication routine. When it invokes a communication routine, the processor can then check for incoming messages and perform any intermediate routing that is needed thereby obviating the need to interrupt the processor whenever a message arrives. The model was first developed for the early hypercube architectures in which the processors themselves had to forward messages that required several "hops." Newer architectures employ special routing chips to perform this function. However, the model has been found to be a quite useful programming paradigm.

Of course, there are several drawbacks. First, the model assumes that all processors participate in the global communication operation, whether or not they have any information to send or receive. This was needed for the early architectures. But, in many applications, the processors can be partitioned into groups corresponding to the structure of the application and where each group has a different communication pattern. Second, each communication operation is usually executed very many times. That is, there is some inner loop the alternates between local work and a particular communication operation. The setup of the communication operation is time consuming and in many situations need be performed just once at the beginning.

A set of collective communication operations and their semantics that address the above two weaknesses has been introduced by Bala et al. [3]. The result offers a parallel programming style with a potential for scalable, efficient and portable implementations over a wide range of machines. We follow their terminology and use the term collective communication operation to emphasize that the loosely synchronous model may apply independently within a group of processors and that not all processors need participate in each communication operation.

Parallel processors come in many shapes and forms. A survey of over 300 parallel processors that have been built over the years shows that a majority of these architectures employ a bus as the major interconnection scheme and use fewer than 32 processors of moderate strength [5]. A bus-based system, however, cannot provide the interconnectivity demands. At any time, only one processor can place information on the bus. A circular shift operation among p processors requires p bus operations. We propose to augment the popular and economical bus architecture with a special communications board that can support the collective communication operations. The board is essentially a crossbar with a memory buffer placed at each cross point.

In the rest of this paper, the collective communication operations are reviewed. Then, our architectural design is presented that supports for these operations. Section 4 explains ways in which the architecture can be scaled to support larger numbers of processors. Section 5 discusses the implications of the extensions.

2 Collective Communication Operations

In this section we give a brief overview of the communication requirements of collective communication operations. Processors or processes are organized into groups; a process may belong to more than one group. Groups can be formed "top-down" in systems supporting dynamic process creation or "bottom-up" by partitioning an existing group into several disjoint subgroups. ¿From time to time, all the processes within a subgroup participate in a collective communication. All the processes in the group must participate.

The following is a (partial) list of possible collective communication operations. In each one, all the processors in a group must participate in the call. We assume that there are p processors in the group and in general, messages are of size n words.

- Broadcast – One of the processors in the group is identified as the originator of the broadcast and the rest of the processors are receivers. The originator sends a message that is received by all the other $p - 1$ processors.
- Scatter – Like the broadcast operation, the scatter operation identifies a unique processor as the originator and the rest as receivers. However, the data to be sent to be sent (scattered among the processors) is divided into p equal parts and processor i receives part i. That is, the n data words to be scattered can be viewed as a two dimensional array of size $p \times \frac{n}{p}$ and is scattered over the processors in the group with each processor getting a different row.
- Gather – The gather operation is the inverse of the scatter. One processor is identified as the receiver. Each processor sends a row and the receiver assembles these rows into a two dimensional array.
- Transpose – The transpose operation can be viewed as Scatter and Gather operations performed by all p processors. Each processor can be considered to contain a column of a two dimensional, $p \times p$ matrix. Each matrix entry consists of n words. For each i, processor i is the originator of a scatter operation and it is also the target of a gather operation. The two dimensional matrix is transposed among the processors in the group.
- Shift – Unlike the above operations, all processors are both senders and receivers in the shift operation. Associated with each processor is a unique target processor. Each processor sends a message to its target and receives a message from its predecessor.
- Reduce – In the reduce operation, a binary associative function, f, is supplied, and each processor provides an input, x_i. Again, one processor is identified as the target and it will receive f applied to all the inputs. In particular, summing and max are two popular reduce operations.
- Partition – Given a group of processors, the partition operation subdivides them into subgroups based on a key. Each processor provides a key and all those processors with identical keys are placed in the same subgroup.

In many current implementations, these operations are supported on fixed topology, message passing architectures, such as hypercube or mesh. For each group, a topology is mapped onto the underlying topology.

3 Hardware Implementation

We propose to extend the very popular bus-based parallel processing systems with a special purpose communications board in order to support the special needs of collective communication operations (Figure 1). The design takes advantage of the inherent polling nature of this model. Since each processor ensures that it will execute the collective communication call, there is no need to interrupt the processor when data for it is ready. Hence, the usual overhead requirements of message-passing architectures can be reduced. Data is moved from the sending processor to a memory buffer. It is then fetched from the memory buffer to the receiving processor when that processor executes a receive. A slightly more complex control logic will allow data to be routed directly to the receiver, if the receive is already waiting for the data.

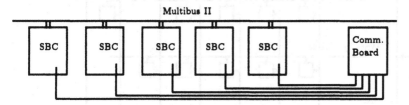

Fig. 1. An overview of the simple system. Each processor board is a Single Board Computer (SBC). Processors are interconnected by a bus; the bus can support both message passing and remote access to the memory associated with each processor, i.e. distributed, shared memory. The Intel Multibus II our method of achieving this goal. In addition, each processor is directly connected to the special purpose communications board.

We first discuss the architecture of a very small system in which all the memory buffers can fit on a single board and all processors reside in a single bus. The memory buffers are small, each consists of a single chip.

3.1 Basic System Configuration

We propose a set of p^2 memory buffers arranged as a two dimensional array. Memory buffer (i,j) can be written to by processor i and read from by processor j. That is, each processor can write to all those memory buffers in its row and read from all those in its column (see Figure 2).

The following describes how each of the communication primitives can be supported:

– Broadcast – The originator stores a copy of the message to be broadcast in all the memory buffers in its row. Special bus logic supports can support the simultaneous storing of each word into all the buffers along a row. After the message has been placed in all the buffers, a flag in the shared memory is set. All the other processors read there corresponding memory buffer in the originators row.

Communications Board Design

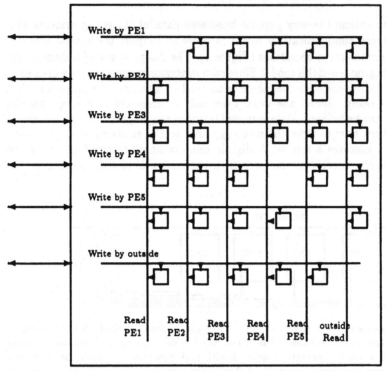

Fig. 2. An example communications board. Here, there are six bidirectional connections to the board: 5 processors and one outside connection to another communications board (for scalable design). Each processor can store (write) into any memory buffer along its row and fetch (read) from any memory buffer along its column.

- Scatter – The originator, say processor i, writes slice j of its array into memory buffer i,j. Receiver j reads this memory buffer.

- Gather – Each processor in the group writes its piece into the memory buffer of the column corresponding to the destination processor. The destination processor reads all the memory buffers from its column.

- Transpose – This operation is essentially a scatter by all the processors followed by a gather by all the processors. Thus, its implementation is straight forward.

- Shift – If processor i is to send its data to processor j, then it writes to memory buffer i,j and reads from buffer k,i if it is to receive a message from processor k.

- Reduce – If the number of processor in the group is small, then it best to broadcast the values to all the processors and have each processor compute the appropriate prefix. For larger subgroups binary tree schemes can be used.

3.2 Scaling to Higher Dimensions

A variation of the scheme enables the support of a larger number of processors. A system supporting P processors, consists of B bus subsystems or clusters, with p processors per bus; $B = P/p$. We assume that each communications board can support $k > p$ write lines, k read lines, and k^2 memory buffers. The $g = k - p$ remaining lines are connected to other communication boards. See Figure 3.

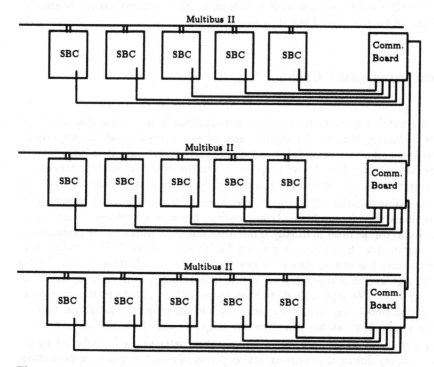

Fig. 3. A prototype system will consists of 15 processors: 5 PEs per bus cluster and three bus clusters. Each communications board supports 7 lines; 5 for the processors within the cluster and 2 for connections to the other clusters.

If $g \geq B - 1$, then it is simple to interconnect the whole system in two steps. Each communications board is connected to all the processors in its bus cluster as well as to all the other communication boards. The special board-to-board lines act like the processor read and write lines.

We assume that the number of processors per board is a power of 2, $p = 2^m$. Thus the low-order m bits of the processor id. specify the processor number within a cluster and the high order bits specify the cluster. We explain how to read and write between any two processors; extensions to the communication operations should be straightforward.

Suppose that processor $i = i_1 2^m + i_0$ wishes to send a message to processor $j = j_1 2^m + j_0$. Processor i writes to memory buffer j_1 in its row on the local communications board (row i_0 in communications board i_1). Processor j reads from memory buffer i_1 in its column j_0 on its local communications board j_1. This causes data from communications board i_1 to be moved to communications board j_1 and placed in the memory buffer j_0 along row i_1. The data for j can then be moved to processor j.

There is an interesting tradeoff as to when to move data between communications boards. One the one hand, it can "pushed" over whenever the memory buffer begins to get full. On the other hand, it can be pulled over whenever any processor on one communications board requires some data from another communications board. All data destined for that board can then be pulled.

4 Interconnection Cache

When the number of extra lines per communications board is less than the total number of clusters, then the full system cannot be connected in just two hops and a more complex scheme is needed. Instead of using a complex, expensive, high latency network between the boards, we propose to use the notion of an interconnection cache as introduced and studied in a slightly different context by Schenfeld ([7, 6]).

It is possible to build a low latency, high bandwidth interconnection network for large numbers of nodes, such as a large crossbar, however, it requires a long configuration time. Unlike most multistaged interconnection networks whose performance can be captured with just the parameters for latency and bandwidth, such a low-latency network has two notions of latency. There is the usual latency caused by the delay through switches and gates. In addition, there is the time required to configure the network. We make this distinction since with certain technologies, a large configuration time is required to set each switch in the proper configuration thereby enabling a very short latency time when messages actually traverse the network.

Our idea is exploit the fact that communication patterns are fixed for a long period of time, say during the entire execution period of an inner, loosely synchronous, loop. This observation has been used by optimizing compilers to place expensive data structure initializations outside a loop. In Bala et al. [3] it is argued that one may setup the configuration for a collective communication operation and then invoke it many times. Most of the The cost of a large initial overhead can be easily amortized by the many invocations. Similarly, this fact can be used to configure part of the network associated with the group of processors that is about to begin a new communication pattern.

A second feature of this two stage network configuration is that many standard topologies can be efficiently embedded in such a structure ([7, 1]). For example, suppose that all the processors are arranged according to a two dimensional mesh. Suppose the p processors in a cluster form a connected subarray of the mesh. Then, there need to be $4\sqrt{p}$ connections to processors in other clusters. But these neighboring processors will all be concentrated in four other clusters, and so only 4 outside links are needed. If there are only p^2 processors, then a better arrangement would be to place a column of processors into a cluster and only two intercluster links will be needed.

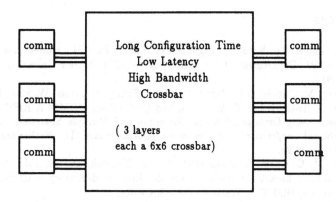

Fig. 4. In a larger system, each communications board will have several connections to other communications boards. These connections will be via a slowly changing cross-bar network. The collective communication model expects that each major configuration will be used a large number of times. Hence a long setup time can be tolerated.

5 Conclusion

We have proposed a simple extension to a bus based parallel processing system or a modification to a small parallel processor with a crossbar interconnection network. The main idea is to place memory buffers at each crosspoint. Such a structure efficiently supports many of the communication demands of the loosely synchronous model of parallel programming with collective communication operations.

Our design is quite close to that of the OMP machine built at USC [2]. The main difference is that we are motivated from the need to support the collective communication operations. This has several implications as to the lower level design options. Each PE will not be running a heavy operating system. In addition our machine will be of significantly smaller scale, use of i80486 processors instead of i80860 and our shared memory modules will be of significantly smaller size so that they can all fit on one board. In addition, the OMP project propose to scale their design by using larger dimensional crossbar which effectively means putting a switch at each processor to the appropriate dimension. Our extension is more like a multistaged network with the ability to move the data through the network on a demand basis.

References

1. A. Barak and R. Ben-Natan, "Assignment of Tasks to Parallel Architectures," Technical Report 92-01, Department of Computer Science, The Hebrew University, Jerusalem, Israel, 1992.
2. K. Hwang, M. Dubois, D.K. Panda, S. Rao, S. Shang, A. Uresin, W. Mao, H. Nair, M. Lytwyn, F. Hsieh, J. Liu, S. Mehrotra, and C.M. Cheng, "OMP: A RISC-based Multiprocessor using Orthogonal-Access Memories and Multiple Spanning Buses," *1990 International Conference on Supercomputing*, Amsterdam, The Netherlands, September 1990, pp. 7-22.
3. V. Bala, M. C. Chen, S. Kipnis, C-Y. Lin, L. Rudolph, and M. Snir, "A high-level communication library for massively parallel distributed-memory machines," *Internal Memorandum*, IBM T. J. Watson Research Center.
4. G. Fox, M. Johnson, G. Lyzenga, S. Otto, J. Salmon, and D. Walker, *Solving Problems on Concurrent Processors, Volume I: General Techniques and Regular Problems*, Prentice-Hall, Englewood Cliffs, New Jersey, 1988.
5. G. Lerman and L. Rudolph, *Parallel Processors: Will They Ever Meet? A Three Decade Survey of Parallel Computers*,
6. L. Rudolph and E. Shenfeld, "Interconnection Cache for Large Interconnection Networks," Manuscript, Department of Computer Science, Hebrew University, Jerusalem, Israel, 1992.
7. E. Shenfeld, "A Parallel Architecture for a Digital Optical Computer," Ph.D. Thesis, Department of Computer Science, The Hebrew University, Jerusalem, Israel, 1992.

Programmable Active Memories:
a Performance Assessment

P. Bertin, D. Roncin, J. Vuillemin
Digital Equipment Corporation
Paris Research Laboratory
85 Av. Victor Hugo
92563 Rueil Malmaison Cedex, France.

October 19, 1992

Abstract

We present some quantitative performance measurements for the computing power of Programmable Active Memories (PAM), as introduced by [BRV 89]. Based on Field Programmable Gate Array (FPGA) technology, the PAM is a universal hardware co-processor closely coupled to a standard host computer. The PAM can speed up many critical software applications running on the host, by executing part of the computations through a specific hardware design. The performance measurements presented are based on two PAM architectures and ten specific applications, drawn from arithmetics, algebra, geometry, physics, biology, audio and video. Each of these PAM designs proves as fast as any reported hardware or super-computer for the corresponding application. In cases where we could bring some genuine algorithmic innovation into the design process, the PAM has proved an order of magnitude faster than any previously existing system (see [SBV 91] and [S 92]).

1 PAM concept

Like any RAM memory module, a PAM is attached to the system bus of a host computer. The processor can write into, and read from the PAM. Unlike a RAM, the PAM processes data between write and read instructions. The specific processing is determined by the content of its *configuration memory*. The host can change the PAM configuration by *downloading* a new design, within a few milliseconds.

We speed up a specific software application running on the host, by executing its *critical inner-loop* through an appropriate hardware design downloaded into the PAM. Ten examples of such designs and applications are presented below. Equipped with these ten designs, our PAM&Host system is ready to be compared with more conventional solutions (specific hardware, super-computer software) designed for processing the application.

Due to the great variety of the operations required by each application, quantitative performance comparison between existing computer architectures is a challenging art (see [HP 90]). Traditional measurement units include Gips (billion of instructions per second, i.e. 1000 MIPS), *Gops* (billion of fixed-point arithmetic operations/sec) and *Gflops* (billion of floating-point operations/sec). None of these measures is particularly well-defined (which instructions? how many bits?) or relevant for every application. They are particularly ill-adapted to comparing the performance of hardware algorithms. Even the most appropriate *Gbops* measure (billion of boolean operations/sec) fails to capture the important notions of data movement and global routing, which are invariably a major consideration in hardware design. To proceed, we are led to pragmatically quote the measures which are most appropriate to each application, with a systematic *Gbops* estimate so as to provide a common reference point.

2 Two PAM architectures

Our assessment is based on two PAM architectures realized at DEC's Paris Research Lab., $DECPeRLe_0$ (see [BRV 89]) and $DECPeRLe_1$ (see [BRV 92])

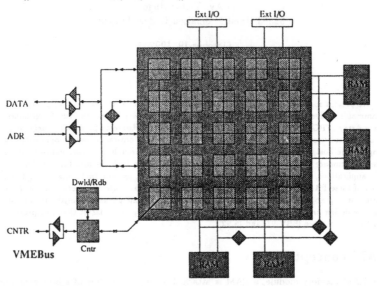

which we refer to as P_0 (figure above) and P_1 (see [BRV 92]) in the following. Each PAM is made of a large configurable array of PABs[1], a variable clock generator, download logic, host bus interface logic, and local RAM acting as a cache. For the purpose of evaluating Xilinx [X 87] based designs such as ours, it is convenient to define the Programmable Active Bit (PAB) as in [BRV 89]: a PAB consists of a universal 4 inputs combinatorial gate and a synchronous flip-flop. Our two PAM architectures P_0 and P_1 have the following vital statistics:

PAM	part	number	PABs	F_{max} (MHz)	Power (Gbops)	RAM (MB)	Host bus (MBs)
P_0	$XC3020$	25	3.2K	25	80	0.5	8
P_1	$XC3090$	23	14K	40	588	4	100

This chart exhibits the three most important architectural parameters conditioning which application benefits most from a PAM speed-up:

---

[1] Elementary configurable logic gates, here-after called Programmable Active Bits (Pab)

- The number of PABs (3.2K for P_0 and 14K for P_1), together with the application-dependent maximal clock frequency (25 MHz and 40 MHz) at which we can reliably operate. The product of these two numbers is the maximum theoretical computing power of the PAM, expressed in Gbops (80Gbops for P_0 and 588Gbops for P_1).

- The host bus bandwidth: 8 MB/s for P_0 through a VME bus, and 100 MB/s for P_1 through the *TURBOchannel* [TC 91].

- The size of the local (fast) RAM: 0.5 MB for P_0 and 4 MB for P_1.

3 Ten PAM applications

The following applications were chosen to span a wide range of current leading edge computational challenges. In each case, we provide a brief description of the design, the names of the implementors, and a performance comparison with similar reported work. In each case, the following simple paradigm has been applied:

compile the inner loop in PAM hardware, and let software handle the rest!

In what follows, we let $(a \div b)$ represent the quotient and $(a \cdot| \cdot b)$ the remainder in the integer division.

3.1 Long multiplication

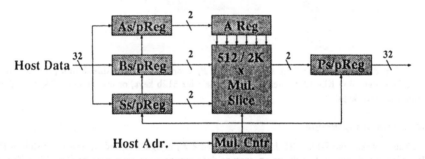

We have programmed both PAMs into long multipliers ($n = 512$ bits for P_0, and $n = 2K$ bits for P_1) computing $P = A \times B + S$, with A a n-bits multiplier, and B, S arbitrary size multiplicands and summands (see [L 76], [BRV 89] and [SBV 91]). These multipliers are interfaced with an arbitrary-precision arithmetic package *BigNum* (see [SVH 89]) so that any program based on that software takes advantage of the PAM without modification, by simply relinking with a modified BigNum library. This respectively speeds up raw multiplication by a factor up to 24 (P_0) and 30 (P_1) for long operands, as compared to the host workstation. For example, P_0 equipped with this design computes RSA encryption/decryption at 1500 bits per second for arbitrary 512-bit keys (see [RSA 79]); this is about 10 times faster than our best software version on the same host.

The P_1 implementation produces product bits at 66 Mbits/s, which makes it faster than *any* known machine for which we could obtain benchmark measures. It is at least 16 times faster than the best reported figures for a Cray II or a Cyber 170/750 by [BW 89]. The multiplier can be used to directly compute a 50 coefficients (16-bits) polynomial convolution (FIR filter) at 16 times *audio real time* (2 × 24 bits samples at 48 kHz).

3.2 RSA cryptography

To further investigate the tradeoffs which are possible in our hybrid hardware/software system we focused on the RSA cryptosystem (see [RSA 79]), which can be cast entirely in terms of long multiplications. Starting from the above general-purpose multiplier, M. Shand from DEC-PRL implemented a series of hardware/software systems spanning two orders of magnitude in performance. The latest version is based on an original hardware design for computing modular products at the rate of two bits per cycle [SV 92]. The system uses three differently programmed P_0 boards, all operating in parallel with the host (see [SBV 91]). At 200 kbit/s decoding speed, this is faster than *any* currently existing 512 bits RSA implementation, in *any* technology, as of February 1990. A recent survey by [Br 90] grants the previous speed record for 512 bits keys RSA decryption to a VLSI from AT&T, at 19 kbits/sec.

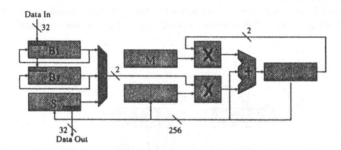

M. Shand has ported the RSA system to one P_1 board; at 30MHz, this design provides either two independent 350 Kbs RSA encryption channels for 512b keys, or one 90Kbs RSA encryption channel for 1Kb keys.

3.3 Data compression

M. Skubiszewski from DEC-PRL has implemented a P_0 design to speed up the algorithm of [ZL 77], which is well known to achieve an average data compression ratio varying from 2 for English (or French, or Polish ...) plain text to 3 for C (or Lisp, or Pascal ...) source code.

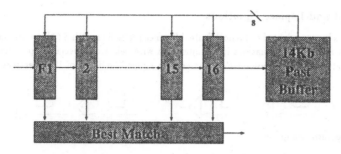

The design is a massively parallel method which computes 64 byte comparisons on each (70 ns) cycle; it matches the next 16 bytes in the file to be compressed against the last 4k bytes seen (stored in the local RAM), in order to detect the longest substring previously seen. While this design performs a respectable 1 Gops (8 bits integer comparison), it ends-up in a disappointing factor two speed-up, when compared to optimized software such as Unix's *compress*. Indeed, such optimized software avoids most of the comparisons performed in the hardware, by detecting early that they are irrelevant to the final output. A more elaborate hardware design is needed to genuinely speed up this particular algorithm.

3.4 String matching

Given an alphabet $A = (a_1, \ldots, a_n)$, a probability $(S_{ij})_{i,j=1\ldots n}$ of substitution of a_i by a_j, and a probability $(I_i)_{i=1\ldots n}$ (resp. $(D_i)_{i=1\ldots n}$) of insertion (resp. deletion) of a_i, one can use a classical dynamic programming algorithm to compute a probability of transformation of w_1 into w_2; this defines a *distance* between any two words w_1 and w_2 over A.

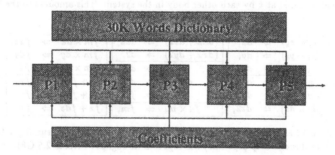

D. Lavenier from IRISA (Rennes, France) has implemented this algorithm with a P_0 design which computes the distance between an input word and all 30K words in a dictionary; it reports the k words found in the dictionary which are closest to the input. The system processes 200K words/sec: this is faster than a solution previously implemented at CNET using 12 Transputers; it has only half of the performance obtained by a system previously developed at IRISA, based on 28 custom VLSI chips and 2 PC boards.

Applications of this algorithm include automated mail sorting using OCR scanners, on-the-fly keyboard spelling corrections, and DNA sequence matching (see [L 87]).

3.5 Heat and Laplace equations

[V 92] shows how to adapt the classical finite difference method (see [FLS 63]) to compute solutions of the Heat and Laplace equations in n dimensions with help from special purpose hardware. An implementation of the method on P_1 operates with a pipe-line depth of 128 operators:

Each operator computes:

$$\mathcal{O}(v_0, v_1) = \begin{cases} v_0, & \text{when } v_0 \cdot | \cdot 2 = 1, \\ 2(v_0 \div 4 + v_1 \div 4 + (v_0 \cdot | \cdot 4) \div 2), & \text{otherwise,} \end{cases} \tag{1}$$

all with 24b fixed-point data format. At 20 MHz, this amounts to 5 Gops (24b adds, tests and shifts); it is easy to show (see [V 92]) that fixed-point gives the same results as floating-point operations for this specific problems; the achieved performance thus exceeds those reported in [McB 88] and [McB&al 91] for solving the same problem with super-computers. A sequential computer needs to execute 25 billion instructions per second (25 Gips), to reproduce the same computation.

The heat and Laplace equations have many applications in mechanics, circuit technology, fluid dynamics, electrostatics, optics, finance $\cdots$

3.6 Newton's mechanics

J. Vuillemin has specified a P_1 design for computing the evolution of a n-body system, using Newton's equations. The design computes the gravitational field acting on body k by summing the individual fields induced at k by each other body in the system. This amounts to the following 18 operations:

$$
\begin{array}{|lll|lll|lll|}
\hline
(x_i - x_k) & \Rightarrow & dx, & (dx2 + dz2) & \Rightarrow & dxz, & fm \times dx & \Rightarrow & fdx, \\
(y_i - y_k) & \Rightarrow & dy, & (dxz + dy2) & \Rightarrow & d2, & fm \times dy & \Rightarrow & fdy, \\
(z_i - z_k) & \Rightarrow & dz, & \sqrt{d2} & \Rightarrow & d, & fm \times dz & \Rightarrow & fdz, \\
(dx \times dx) & \Rightarrow & dx2, & d \times d2 & \Rightarrow & d3, & fx + fdx & \Rightarrow & fx, \\
(dy \times dy) & \Rightarrow & dy2, & \frac{1}{d3} & \Rightarrow & fd, & fy + fdy & \Rightarrow & fy, \\
(dz \times dz) & \Rightarrow & dz2, & fd \times m_i & \Rightarrow & fm, & fz + fdz & \Rightarrow & fz. \\
\hline
\end{array}
\tag{2}
$$

Positions and forces are represented as 20 bits floating-point numbers. Assuming a 40ns internal cycle (achievable through deep pipe-line) the expected throughput exceeds 2.5 GFlops (this design has not been tested by printing time).

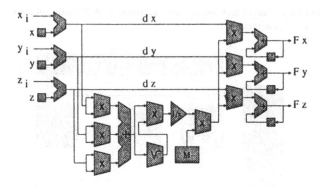

3.7 Binary 2D convolution

B. Chen and J. Vuillemin have implemented a 7×7 binary 2D convolver on P_0, for performing erosion, dilation and matching on black and white images, as defined in [S 82].

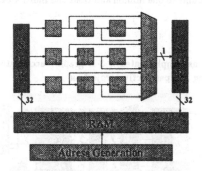

The convolver runs at 25 MHz, generating one pixel each 40ns; it completes a single convolution pass over one 512×512 image in 10 milliseconds; this allows for up to 4 successive operations (erosion, dilation, or matching) at video rate. Reproducing this performance through optimized software would require a 200 Mips computer.

3.8 Boltzmann machine

M. Skubiszewski has implemented two successive versions of a hardware emulator for binary neural networks, based on the *Boltzmann machine* model (see [S 90] and [S 92]).

The Boltzmann Machine is a probabilistic algorithm which minimizes quadratic forms over binary variables, i.e. expressions of the form

$$E(\vec{N}) = \sum_{i=0}^{n-1} \sum_{j=0}^{i} w_{i,j} N_i N_j \tag{3}$$

where $\vec{N} = (N_0, \ldots, N_{n-1})$ is a vector of binary variables and $(w_{i,j})_{0 \leq i,j < n}$ is a fixed matrix of *weights*. It is typically used to find approximate solutions to $\mathcal{NP}$-hard problems, such as graph partitioning or circuit placement.

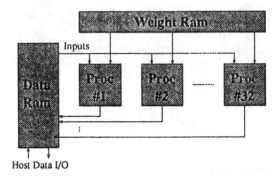

Host Data I/O

The latest realization, on P_1, can solve problems with up to 1400 variables, using 16-bit weights, for a total computing power of 500 *megasynapses per second* (the megasynapse is the traditional unit used in this field, it amounts to one million additions and multiplications, or one million terms of (??)).

3.9   3D Geometry

H. Touati from DEC-PRL has implemented a 3-D graphic accelerator for P_1, which supports translation, rotation, clipping and perspective projection.

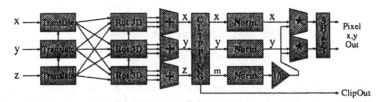

At 25MHz, it has a peak performance of 1.56 million points per second, using 16 bit fixed point coordinates for the input and output, and up to 32 bits for the intermediate results. It takes a 300 Mips processor to achieve the same throughput.

3.10   Discrete cosine transform

This design (by J. Vuillemin and D. Martineau on P_1) compresses video *in real time* through multi-dimensional fast discrete cosine transform. The fDCT implements the following network:

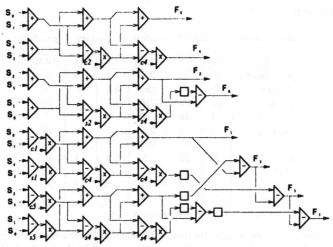

The overall design computes 48 fixed-point (32 bits outputs) operations (add, substract, multiply and shift) on each 40ns cycle, for a total of 1.4 Gops. To match this performance through software would require a 15 Gips microprocessor.

4 Conclusion

The following chart summarizes the practical PAM performance achieved by each of our ten designs:

Design	Kab	MHz	Gbops	Gops	Gips	PAM
Multiplier	8	33	264	0.8	2.6	P_1
RSA	8	32	256	0.5	4	P_1
DCT	10	25	250	1.4	15	P_1
Newton	10	25	250	2.5†	5	P_1
Laplace	10	20	200	7.5	20	P_1
Boltzmann	8	25	200	1	1.5	P_1
3D Geometry	3	25	75	0.5	0.7	P_1
Ziv Lempel	3	15	45	1	2	P_0
String	3	10	30	0.15	0.3	P_0
2D convolution	1	25	25		1	P_0

†These are Gflops, with 20 bit floating-point numbers.

The applications are ranked according to the most reliable performance measure, namely the *Gbops*. As a comparative measure of resource utilisation in such systems, the following charts the maximum theoretical performance of generic PAM hardware (in *Gbops*) obtained by multiplying the maximal clock frequency (in MHz) by the area (in PABs):

PAM	Area	1MHz	20MHz	50MHz
XC3020	128	0.1	2.5	6.4
XC3090	640	0.6	12.8	32
P_0	3.2K	3.2	64	
P_1	14K	14	280	700

Three years of PAM design lead us to believe the following:

1. For each of the chosen application, we have shown that the level of performance achieved with the PAM is comparable to the best figures reported using super-computers or custom silicon circuits.

   Our applications have been carefully selected for having a clearly identified (PAM implementable) inner-loop, which accounts for a vast percentage of the software run-time. For such low level processing, the PAM proves more cost effective than any super-computer.

   Due to their software complexity, many current super-computers applications still remain outside the possibilities of current PAM technology.

2. Each mentioned PAM design was implemented and tested within one or two months, starting from the delivery of the specification software. This is roughly equivalent to the time it takes to implement a *highly optimized* software version of the same system with a super-computer; both are technically challenging, yet remain an order of magnitude faster than the time it takes to cast a system into silicon.

3. The cost of P_1 is comparable to that of a high-end workstation. This is orders of magnitude lower than the cost of a super-computer. Based on figures from [McB 88], we find that the price (in $ per operation per second) of solving the Heat and Laplace equations is 100 times higher with super-computers than with the PAM.

4. Another field of applications, not covered by any existing super-computer, is open to PAM technology: high-bandwith interfaces to the external world, with a *fully programmable real-time* capability. The P_1 PAM has a 256b wide connector, capable to deliver up to 6.4 Gbit/s of external bandwidth. It is a "simple matter of hardware programming" to interface directly with any electrically-compatible external device, by programming its communication protocol into the PAM itself. Applications for this capability are numerous, including high-bandwidth networks, audio & video input or output devices, ...

5 Bibliography

BRV 89 P. Bertin, D.Roncin and J. Vuillemin: *Introduction to Programmable Active Memories* Systolic Array Processors, J. McCanny, J. McWhirter, E. Swartzlander Jr. editors, pp 300-309, Prentice Hall, (1989). Also available as PRL report 3, Digital Equipment Corp., Paris Research Laboratory, 85, Av. Victor Hugo. 92563 Rueil-Malmaison Cedex, France, (1989).

BRV 92 P. Bertin, D. Roncin, J. Vuillemin: *Programmable Active memories: the Coming of Age* PRL report in preparation, Digital Equipment Corp., Paris Research Laboratory, 85, Av. Victor Hugo. 92563 Rueil-Malmaison Cedex, France, (1992).

Br 90 E.F. Brickell: *A Survey of Hardware Implementations of RSA* Proceedings of Crypto '89, Lecture Notes in Computer Science, Springer-Verlag, (1990).

BW 89 D. A. Buell, R. L. Ward, A Multiprecise Integer Arithmetic Package The journal of Supercomputing 3, pp. 89-107; Kluwer Academic Publishers, Boston 1989.

FLS 63 R.P. Feynman, R.B. Leighton, M. Sands: *The Feynman lectures on PHYSICS*, 3 volumes, Addison-Wesley, (1963).

GK 89 J.P. Gray, T. Kean: *Configurable Hardware: Two Case Studies of Micro-grain Computation* Systolic Array Processors, J. McCanny, J. McWhirter, E. Swartzlander Jr. editors, pp. 310-319, Prentice Hall, (1989).

HP 90 J.L. Hennessy, D.A. Patterson: *Computer Architecture: A Quantitative Approach,* Morgan Kaufmann Publishers, Inc. (1990).

L 76 R.F. Lyon: *Two's complement pipeline multipliers* IEEE Trans. Comm., COM-24:418-425, (1976).

L 87 D.P. Lopresti: *P-NAC: A Systolic Array for Comparing Nucleic Acid Sequences* Computer Magazine 20(7):98-99, (1987).

McB 88 O.A. McBryan. Connection Machine Application Performance. In *Scientific Applications of the Connection Machine,* World Scientific, pp 94-114 (1989).

McB&al 91 O.A. McBryan, P.O. Frederickson, J. Linden, A. Schüller, K. Solchenbach, K. Stüben, C-A. Thole, U. Trottenberg. Multigrid Methods on Parallel Computers - A Survey of Recent Developments. *Impact of Computing in Science and Engineering,* Academic Press, Vol. 3(1), pages 1-75 (1991).

RSA 79 R.L. Rivest, A. Shamir, L. Adleman: *Public key cryptography* CACM 21, 120-126, 1979.

S 82 J.P. Serrat: *Image Analysis and Mathematical Morphology* Academic Press, New York, (1982).

SVH 89 B. Serpette, J. Vuillemin, J.C. Hervé: *BigNum: A Portable Efficient Package for Arbitrary-Precision Arithmetic* PRL report 2, Digital Equipment Corp., Paris Research Laboratory, 85, Av. Victor Hugo. 92563 Rueil-Malmaison Cedex, France (1989).

S 90 M. Skubiszewski: *A hardware Emulator for Binary Neural Networks* Proceedings of the International Neural Network Conference, vol. 2, pp. 555-558, Paris, (1990)

SBV 91 M. Shand, P. Bertin and J. Vuillemin: *Hardware Speedups in Long Integer Multiplication*, Computer Architecture News, 19(1):106-114, (1991)

SV 92 M. Shand, and J. Vuillemin: *A Hardware Implementation for fast RSA Cryptography.* to appear, (1992)

S 92 M. Skubiszewski: *An Exact Hardware Implementation of the Boltzmann Machine*, PRL report in preparation, Digital Equipment Corp., Paris Research Laboratory, 85, Av. Victor Hugo. 92563 Rueil-Malmaison Cedex, France, (1992).

TC 91 Digital Equipment Corp.: *TURBOchannel Hardware Specification*, DEC document EK-369AA-OD-007A, (1991)

V 92 : J.E. Vuillemin: *Contribution à la résolution numérique des équations de Laplace et de la chaleur*, PRL report 16, Digital Equipment Corp., Paris Research Laboratory, 85, Av. Victor Hugo. 92563 Rueil-Malmaison Cedex, France, (1992).

X 87 Xilinx, Inc. : *The Programmable Gate Array Data Book* Product Briefs, Xilinx, Inc., (1987).

ZL 77 J. Ziv, A. Lempel: *A Universal Algorithm for Sequential Data Compression* IEEE transactions on information theory, IT-23(3):337-343, (1977).

The Role of Randomness in the Design of Interconnection Networks

Tom Leighton
Mathematics Department and
Laboratory for Computer Science
Massachusetts Institute of Technology
Cambridge, Massachusetts 02139

Bruce Maggs
NEC Research Institute
4 Independence Way
Princeton, New Jersey 08540

October 16, 1991

Abstract

It has recently been discovered that randomly-wired interconnection networks outperform traditional well-structured networks in several notable respects. Among other things, randomly-wired networks have been found to be exceptionally fault-tolerant and well-suited for both packet-routing and circuit-switching applications. In this paper, we survey the recent research on interconnection networks, highlighting the discovery of randomness as a useful and powerful design tool.

1 Introduction

Networks derived from hypercubes form the architectural basis of many parallel computers, including machines such as the BBN Butterfly, the Connection Machine, the IBM RP3 and GF11, the Intel iPSC, and the NCUBE. The butterfly, in particular, is quite popular, and has been demonstrated to perform reasonably well in practice. An example of an N-input butterfly ($N = 8$) with depth $\log N = 3$ is shown in Figure 1. The nodes in this graph represent switches, and the edges represent wires. In a typical application,

level

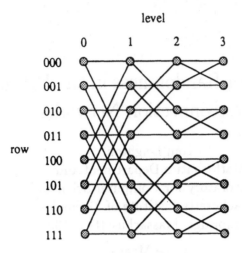

Figure 1: An 8-input butterfly network.

a network such as that shown in Figure 1 is used to transport messages (generally consisting of data) from the switches on level 0, called the *inputs*, to those on level $\log N$, called the *outputs*. The inputs and outputs of the network are typically connected to the processors and the blocks of memory in a parallel computer. When a processor in the computer needs some data from the memory, a message requesting the data is sent through the network from the processor to the appropriate block of memory and the data is then passed back through the network to the processor.

The standard message routing algorithm for a butterfly is quite simple. Each message simply follows the unique path of length $\log N$ from its source input to its destination output. One problem with this algorithm (and hence the network) is that if some switch or edge along the unique path from input i to output j (say) becomes congested or fails, then communication between input i and output j will be disrupted.

1.1 Dilated butterflies

Because message congestion is a common occurrence in real networks, the wires in butterfly networks are typically *dilated*, so that each wire is replaced by a *channel* consisting of 2 or more wires. In a d-dilated butterfly, each channel consists of d wires. Because it is harder to congest a channel than it is to congest a single wire in a butterfly, dilated butterflies are better routing networks than simple butterflies [7, 10, 17].

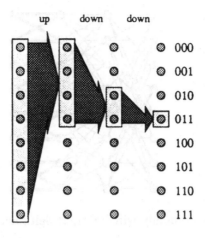

Figure 2: The logical path from any input to output 011.

1.2 Delta networks

Butterfly and dilated butterfly networks belong to a larger class of networks called *delta* networks [9]. The switches on each level of a delta network can be partitioned into *blocks*. All of the switches on level 0 belong to the same block. On level 1, there are two blocks, one consisting of the switches that are in the upper $N/2$ rows, and the other consisting of the switches that are in the lower $N/2$ rows. In general, the switches in a block B of size M on level l have neighbors in two blocks, B_{upper} and B_{lower}, on level $l + 1$. The upper block, B_{upper}, contains the switches on level $l + 1$ that are in the same rows as the upper $M/2$ switches of B. The lower block, B_{lower}, consists of the switches that are in the same rows as the lower $M/2$ switches of B. The edges from B to B_{upper} are called the *up* edges, and those from B to B_{lower} are called the *down* edges. The three blocks, B, B_{upper}, and B_{lower}, and the edges between them are collectively called a *splitter*. The switches in B are called the *splitter inputs*, and those in B_{upper} and B_{lower} are called the *splitter outputs*.

In a delta network, each input and output are connected by a single logical (up-down) path through the blocks of the network. For example, Figure 2 shows the logical path from any input to output 011. In a butterfly, this logical path specifies a unique path through the network, since only one up and one down edge emanate from each switch. In general, however, each switch may have several up and down edges, say d of each, and each step of the logical path can be taken on any one of d edges.

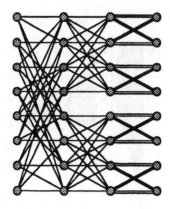

Figure 3: A randomly-wired 8-input delta network with $d = 2$.

1.3 Randomly-wired delta networks and expansion

Dilated butterflies have remained the network of choice for many parallel machines. Recent work, however, suggests that this may change in the near future. In fact, it now appears as though randomly-wired delta networks are superior to dilated butterflies for many message routing applications. (A *randomly-wired delta network* is a delta network where the up edges and the down edges within each splitter are chosen at random subject to the constraint that each splitter input is incident to d up edges and d down edges and each splitter output is incident to $2d$ edges. A randomly-wired 8-input delta network with $d = 2$ is shown in Figure 3.)

The crucial property that randomly-wired delta networks are likely to possess is known as *expansion*. In particular, an M-input splitter is said to have (α, β)-*expansion* if any set of $k \leq \alpha M$ inputs is connected to at least βk up outputs and βk down outputs, where $\beta > 1$, $\alpha \beta < 1/2$, and α and β are fixed constants. Figure 4 shows a splitter with expansion (α, β). Splitters with expansion are good for routing since one must block βk splitter outputs in order to block k splitter inputs. In classical networks such as the butterfly, the reverse is true: it is possible to block $2k$ inputs by blocking only k outputs. When this effect is compounded over several levels, the effect is dramatic. In classical networks such as the butterfly, a single fault can block 2^l switches l levels back, whereas in a *delta network with expansion* (i.e., a delta network consisting of splitters having expansion), it takes β^l faults to block a single switch l levels back.

Splitters with expansion can be constructed deterministically, but for

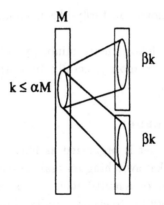

Figure 4: An M-input splitter with expansion property (α, β).

$d \geq 3$, randomized wirings typically provide the best possible expansion. In fact, the expansion in each splitter of a randomly-wired delta network with $2d \times 2d$ switches will be close to $d - 1$ with high probability.

1.4   History and terminology

Randomly-wired delta networks and delta networks with expansion have been studied by several researchers. In 1974, Bassalygo and Pinsker [4] used delta networks with expansion to construct the first nonblocking network of size $O(N \log N)$ and depth $O(\log N)$. (Nonblocking networks will be defined later in this paper.) In 1980, Fahlman [6] proposed a related randomly-wired network called the Hashnet. More recently, Upfal [18] studied delta networks with expansion (which he called *multibutterflies* – a term that was attributed to Ron Fagin) and provided a simple deterministic algorithm for routing any permutation of N messages in $O(\log N)$ steps on an N-input network. (In fact, Upfal's algorithm can be pipelined to route $\log N$ permutations in $O(\log N)$ steps.) Leighton and Maggs [15] then proved that a delta network with expansion is an efficient routing network even when many of the switches are faulty. In addition, Arora, Leighton, and Maggs [3] developed a circuit-switching algorithm for a related network and showed that it can be used to establish connections in a nonblocking fashion. Most recently, DeHon, Knight, and Minsky [5] designed a 64-processor switching network using a randomly-wired delta network for processor-to-memory communications. In addition, there have been some recent experimental studies [8, 14] that provide further evidence that randomly-wired delta networks outperform traditional butterfly-like networks in several important respects.

In this paper, we will follow the terminology of [18] and refer to a delta network with expansion (or, more generally, to a randomly-wired delta network) as a multibutterfly.

1.5 Outline of the paper

The remainder of this paper is organized as follows. Section 2 describes a simple algorithm for packet-switching on multibutterfly networks. An algorithm for circuit-switching on a multibutterfly is presented in Section 3. Section 4 describes a strategy for tolerating faults. Finally, Section 5 sketches an algorithm for establishing connections in a randomly-wired nonblocking network.

A list of references is inlcuded at the end of the paper. In particular, we refer the reader to the recent text by Leighton [12] for a comprehensive discussion of routing algorithms on traditional butterfly-like networks, and to [3, 13, 15, 18] for more information on the theory of randomly-wired delta networks, delta networks with expansion, multibutterflies, and related networks. For more information on experimental work concerning these networks, we refer the reader to [8, 14]. For more information on implementations of these networks, we refer the reader to [5].

2 Packet switching

In a one-to-one packet routing problem, each input sends a packet to a distinct output. The goal of the routing algorithm is to deliver the packets to their destinations as quickly as possible, subject to the constraint that at each time step, each edge can transmit at most one packet. There may also be restrictions on the number of packets that can be queued at any one switch.

In 1989, Upfal [18] proved that an N-input d-butterfly with expansion (α, β) can solve any one-to-one packet routing problem in $O(\log N)$ steps using a simple greedy algorithm. Moreover, he showed that by using pipelining, $O(\log N)$ problems can also be routed in $O(\log N)$ steps. The result is important because the only other known deterministic on-line linear-hardware $O(\log N)$-step packet routing algorithm [11] requires the use of the AKS sorting circuit [2] (which is more complicated and has larger constant factors).

2.1 The algorithm

Upfal's algorithm starts by partitioning the packets into *waves* so that at most one packet in each wave is destined for any set of L contiguous outputs. One way to do this is to group packets into the same wave if they are in the same permutation and their destinations are congruent modulo L. If there are P permutations to be routed, this results in the formation of at most PL waves. In general, we will set $L = \frac{1}{2\alpha}$ since then will we be guaranteed that at most $\frac{M}{2L} = \alpha M$ packets in any wave will ever pass through the up (or down) edges of any M-input splitter of the multibutterfly (for any M). This will allow us to apply the (α, β) expansion property to the set of inputs of any splitter occupied by the packets of a single wave at any time. (E.g., if k inputs of a splitter contain packets of a single wave that want to traverse up edges, then these inputs are connected to at least βk up outputs.) This is because packets going through the $\frac{M}{2}$ up (or $\frac{M}{2}$ down) splitter outputs can only be destined for the descendant set of $\frac{M}{2}$ contiguous multibutterfly outputs.

The routing of the packets proceeds in stages, each stage consisting of an even and odd phase, and each phase consisting of $2d$ steps. In even phases, packets are sent from even levels to the next (odd) level, and in odd phases, packets are sent from the odd levels to the next (even) level. The edges connecting levels are colored in $2d$ colors so that each node is incident to one edge of each color. In each phase, we process the colors in sequence, one step per color. For each color, we move a packet forward along an edge with that color if there is a packet in the switch at the tail of the edge that wants to go in that direction (up or down) and if there is no packet in the switch at the head of the edge. Alternatively, if there is a packet in the switch at the head of the edge and if it is in a later wave than the packet at the tail of the edge, then the two packets are swapped, so that the packet in the earlier wave moves forward. Note that every switch processes and/or contains at most one packet at any step.

The following theorem summarizes the performance of Upfal's algorithm.

Theorem 2.1 ([15, 18]) *On an N-input multibutterfly with expansion (α, β), Upfal's algorithm routes P permutations in $O(P + \log N)$ steps.*

3   Circuit switching

In a one-to-one circuit-switching problem, each input wishes to establish a connection (path) to a distinct output. The connections must not intersect at any switch or edge. The goal of the circuit switching algorithm is to find the connections as quickly as possible.

In 1990, Arora, Leighton, and Maggs discovered an $O(\log N)$-bit-step algorithm for circuit switching on multibutterfly networks. This algorithm is described in what follows. The only previously known $O(\log N)$-bit-step algorithms for circuit switching relied on the AKS sorting circuit [2], or used randomness on the hypercube [1]. (Recently, Leighton and Plaxton have developed an $O(\log N)$-bit-step randomized sorting algorithm for the butterfly [16].)

3.1   Unique neighbors

The circuit-switching algorithm requires the splitters in the multibutterfly to have a special unique-neighbors property. An M-input splitter is said to have the (α, δ) *unique neighbor property* if in every subset X of $k \leq \alpha M$ inputs, there are δk nodes in X which have an up-output neighbor that is not adjacent to any other node in X, and there are δk nodes in X which have a down-output neighbor that is not adjacent to any other node in X. It is relatively easy to prove [3] that any any splitter with (α, β) expansion has the (α, δ) unique-neighbors property where $\delta = 2\beta/d - 1$, provided that $\beta > d/2$. Randomly-wired multibutterflies are known to have expansion (α, β) where $\beta > d/2$ [15, 18] with high probability. Explicit constructions of such splitters are not known, however.

3.2   The algorithm

In order for the algorithm to succeed, the number of paths passing through each M-input splitter must be at most αM. Thus, in an N-input network, we only make connections between the N/L inputs and outputs in rows that are multiples of L, where L is some fixed constant greater than $1/\alpha$.

There is a simple algorithm for extending paths from one level to the next in an M-input splitter with the (α, δ) unique-neighbors property. The basic idea is that those paths at switches with unique neighbors can be extended without worrying about blocking any of the other paths. Paths are extended by repeating steps of the following type. First, every unextended path sends out a proposal to his neighbors among the splitter outputs in the desired direction (up or down). Next, every output that receives precisely one proposal sends back its acceptance to that proposal. Finally, every unextended path that receives an acceptance advances to one of its accepting outputs. In each step, the fraction of unextended paths drops by a factor of $(1 - \delta)$. Thus, after $O(\log M)$ phases, all of the paths are extended. By applying this algorithm one level at a time, it is possible to establish paths from the inputs to the outputs of an N-input multibutterfly with the (α, δ) unique-neighbors property in $O(\log^2 N)$ bit-steps.

A more sophisticated algorithm is needed to construct the paths in $O(\log N)$ bit-steps. Given a set of paths that need to be extended at an M-input splitter, the algorithm does not wait $O(\log M)$ time for every path to be extended before it begins the extension at the next level. Instead, it executes path extension steps until the number of unextended paths falls to some fraction, ρ, of its original value, where ρ is fixed constant that depends on d. Then the path extension process can start at the next level. The danger is that the paths left behind may find themselves blocked by the time they reach the next level. To ensure that this doesn't happen, stalled paths send out *place-holders* to all of their neighbors at the next level, and henceforth the neighbors with place-holders participate in path extension at the next level, as if they were paths. Of course, the neighbors holding place-holders must in general extend in both the upper and the lower output portions of the splitter, since they don't know yet which path will ultimately use them. Notice that a place-holder not only reserves a spot that may be used by a path at a future time, but also helps to chart out the path by continuing to extend ahead.

In order to prevent place-holders from multiplying too rapidly and clogging the system – since if the fraction of inputs of a splitter which are trying to extend rises above α, the path extension algorithm ceases to work – we need to ensure that as stalled paths get extended, they send *cancellation signals* to the placeholding nodes ahead of them to tell them they are not needed anymore. When a placeholding node gets cancellations from all the nodes who had requested it to hold their place, it ceases its attempts to extend. It also sends cancellations to any nodes ahead of it that may be holding a place for it.

The $O(\log N)$-step algorithm alternates between two types of phases. First, paths extension steps are executed until the fraction of unextended paths in each splitter drops by a factor of ρ. In this phase, each path is restricted to extend forward by at most one level. We refer to the first wave of paths and placeholders to arrive at a level as the *wavefront*. The wavefront moves forward by one level during each phase. If a path or placeholder in the wavefront isn't extended, then at the end of the phase it sends placeholders to all of its neighbors. In the second phase, cancellations are passed through the network. They travel a distance of C, where C is some fixed constant that depends on ρ and d.

The performance of the circuit-switching algorithm is summarized in the following theorem.

Theorem 3.1 ([3]) *On an N-input multibutterfly with expansion (α, β), $\beta > d/2$, the algorithm solves any one-to-one circuit-switching problem in $O(\log N)$ bit steps.*

4 Fault tolerance

In 1989, Leighton and Maggs [15] showed that multibutterfly networks are highly fault tolerant. In particular, they proved that no matter how an adversary chooses k switches to fail, there will be at least $N - O(k)$ inputs and $N - O(k)$ outputs between which permutations can be routed in $O(\log N)$ steps. Note that this is the best that could be hoped for in general, since the adversary can choose to make $\Omega(k)$ inputs and $\Omega(k)$ outputs faulty. In addition, they showed that $O(N^{3/4} \log N)$ random switch faults could be tolerated with high probability without isolating any inputs or outputs. Thus, the multibutterfly is the first bounded-degree network known to be able to sustain large numbers of faults with minimal degradation in performance.

4.1 The strategy

The strategy for tolerating worst-case faults consists of two stages, erasure of outputs and fault-propagation. The strategy for tolerating random faults consists solely of fault-propagation.

Each splitter in the multibutterfly is examined in the erasure stage. If more than an ε fraction of the splitter inputs are faulty, where $\varepsilon = 2\alpha(\beta' - 1)$ and $\beta' = \beta - \lfloor \frac{d}{2} \rfloor$ then the splitter as well as all descendant switches and outputs are erased from the network. The erasure of an M-input splitter causes the removal of M multibutterfly outputs, and accounts for at least εM faults. Hence, at most $\frac{k}{\varepsilon} = \frac{kL}{\beta' - 1} = O(k)$ multibutterfly outputs are removed by this process.

Next, working from level $\log N$ back to level 0, each switch is examined in the fault-propagation stage to see if at least half of its upper outputs lead to faulty switches that have not been erased, or if at least half of its lower outputs lead to faulty switches that have not been erased. If so, then the switch is declared faulty (but not erased). It is not difficult to prove [15] that at most $\frac{k}{\beta'-1}$ additional switches are declared faulty at each level by this process. Hence, at most $O(k)$ multibutterfly inputs will be faulty (declared or otherwise).

We now erase all the remaining faulty switches. This leaves a network with $N - O(k)$ inputs and $N - O(k)$ outputs. Moreover, every input in every splitter is linked to $\lceil \frac{d}{2} \rceil$ functioning upper outputs (if the descendant multibutterfly outputs exist) and $\lceil \frac{d}{2} \rceil$ functioning lower outputs (if the corresponding multibutterfly outputs exist). Hence every splitter has an (α, β') expansion property. Thus, we can apply Theorems 2.1 and 3.1 with β replaced by β' to show that the network can solve packet-switching and circuit-switching problems on the working inputs and outputs in $O(\log N)$ steps.

5   Nonblocking networks

In a *nonblocking network*, inputs are connected to outputs with node-disjoint paths, as they were in Section 3. The inputs, however, are not all required to make their requests for connections at the same time. Inputs may wait to make their requests, and may later break connections and request new ones. The main invariant obeyed by a nonblocking network is that any unused input–output pair can be connected by a path through unused switches, no matter what paths have previously been established. The 6-terminal graph shown in Figure 5 is an example of a nonblocking network. In particular, if Bob is talking to Alice and Ted is talking to Carol, then Pat can still call Vanna.

The existence of a bounded-degree strict-sense nonblocking network with size $O(N \log N)$ and depth $O(\log N)$ was first proved by Bassalygo and Pinsker [4] in 1974. Unfortunately, there has not been much progress on the problem of setting the switches so as to realize the connection paths since then. Until recently, no algorithm was known that could cope with simultaneous requests for connections in any $O(N \log N)$-size nonblocking network.

In 1990, Arora, Leighton, and Maggs discovered an $O(N \log N)$-switch

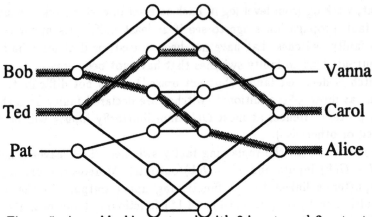

Figure 5: A nonblocking network with 3 inputs and 3 outputs.

nonblocking network for which each path connection can be made on-line in $O(\log N)$ bit-steps. The algorithms work even if many calls are made at once — every call still gets through in $O(\log N)$ bit-steps, no matter what calls were made previously and no matter what calls are currently active, provided that no two inputs try to access the same output at the same time.

5.1 Multi-Benes networks

The nonblocking network is called a *multi-Benes network*. A multi-Benes network is constructed by combining expanders and the Benes network in much the same way that expanders and butterflies are combined to form a multibutterfly. As shown in Figure 6, a multi-Benes network is essentially a reversed multibutterfly followed by a multibutterfly.

As in the circuit-switching algorithm, the network must be lightly loaded by some fixed constant factor L, where $L > 1/\alpha$. Since the other inputs and outputs are not used, the first and last $\lg L$ levels of the network can be removed, and the N/L inputs and outputs can each be connected directly to their L descendants and ancestors on levels $\lg L$ and $2\lg N - \lg L$, respectively.

The basic idea is to treat the switches through which paths have already been established as if they were faulty and to apply the fault propagation techniques from Section 4 to the network. In particular, we define a node to be *busy* if there is a path currently routing through it, and we recursively define a node to be *blocked* according to the following rule. Working backwards from level $2\lg N - \lg L - 1$ to level $\lg N$, a switch is declared blocked

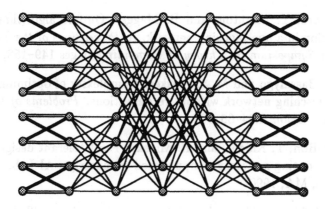

Figure 6: An 8-input 2-multi-Benes network.

if more than $2\beta - d - 1$ of its up (or down) neighbors on level $l + 1$ are busy or blocked. From level $\lg N - 1$ to level $\lg L$, a switch is declared blocked if more than $4\beta - d - 2$ of its $2d$ neighbors on level $l + 1$ are busy or blocked. A switch that is neither busy nor blocked is said to be *working*.

Two important properties can be proved about the network switches. First, for $\beta > 2d/3 + 2/3$ and $L > 1/2\alpha(3\beta - 2d - 2)$, at most a 2α fraction of the switches in any block are declared to be blocked. Thus, all of the unused inputs are working. As a consequence, no matter what paths have already been established, any unused input can reach any unused output. Second, for $\beta > d/2$, the network of working switches has a $(\alpha, 1/d)$ unique-neighbor property. As a consequence, the circuit-switching algorithm from Section 3 can be used to establish new paths, even if many requests for connections are made simultaneously.

References

[1] W. Aiello, T. Leighton, B. Maggs, and M. Newman. Fast algorithms for bit-serial routing on a hypercube. In *Proceedings of the 1990 ACM Symposium on Parallel Algorithms and Architectures*, pages 55–64, July 1990.

[2] M. Ajtai, J. Komlos, and E. Szemeredi. Sorting in $c \log n$ parallel steps. *Combinatorica*, 3:1–19, 1983.

[3] S. Arora, T. Leighton, and B. Maggs. On-line algorithms for path selection in a non-blocking network. In *Proceedings of the 22nd Annual ACM Symposium on Theory of Computing*, pages 149–158, May 1990.

[4] L. A. Bassalygo and M. S. Pinsker. Complexity of optimum nonblocking switching network without reconnections. *Problems of Information Transmission*, 9:64–66, 1974.

[5] A. DeHon, T. Knight, and H. Minsky. Fault-tolerant design for multistage routing networks. Unpublished manuscript, AI Lab, MIT, Cambridge, MA, 1990.

[6] S. E. Fahlman. The hashnet interconnection scheme. Technical Report CMU–CS–80–125, Department of Computer Science, Carnegie–Mellon University, Pittsburgh, PA, June 1980.

[7] R. R. Koch. Increasing the size of a network by a constant factor can increase performance by more than a constant factor. In *Proceedings of the 29th Annual Symposium on Foundations of Computer Science*, pages 221–230. IEEE, October 1988.

[8] S. Konstantinidou and E. Upfal. Experimental Comparison of Multistage Networks. Manuscript in Preparation, IBM Almaden Research Center, Almaden, CA, October 1991.

[9] C. P. Kruskal and M. Snir. A unified theory of interconnection network structure. *Theoretical Computer Science*, 48:75–94, 1986.

[10] C. P. Kruskal and M. Snir. The performance of multistage interconnection networks for multiprocessors. *IEEE Transactions on Computers*, C–32(12):1091–1098, December.

[11] F. T. Leighton. Tight bounds on the complexity of parallel sorting. *IEEE Transactions on Computers*, C–34(4):344–354, April 1985.

[12] F. T. Leighton. *Introduction to Parallel Algorithms and Architectures: Arrays, Trees, Hypercubes*. Morgan Kaufmann Publishers, San Mateo, CA, 1992.

[13] T. Leighton, C. Leiserson, and M. Klugerman. Theory of Parallel and VLSI Computation: Lecture Notes. MIT/LCS/RSS 10, January, 1991.

[14] T. Leighton, D. Lisinski, and B. Maggs. Empirical analysis of randomly-wired multistage networks. *Proceedings of the IEEE International Conference on Computer Design*, September 1990, pp. 380-385.

[15] T. Leighton and B. Maggs. Expanders might be practical: Fast algorithms for routing around faults in multibutterflies. In *Proceedings of the 30th Annual Symposium on Foundations of Computer Science*, pages 384–389. IEEE, October 1989.

[16] T. Leighton and G. Plaxton. A (fairly) simple circuit that (usually) sorts. In *Proceedings of the 31st Annual Symposium on Foundations of Computer Science*, pages 264–274. IEEE, October 1990.

[17] R. D. Rettberg, W. R. Crowther, P. P. Carvey, and R. S. Tomlinson. The monarch parallel processor hardware design. *Computer*, 23(4):18–30, April 1990.

[18] E. Upfal. An $O(\log N)$ deterministic packet routing scheme. In *Proceedings of the 21st Annual ACM Symposium on Theory of Computing*, pages 241–250, May 1989.

Chaos Router: Finally, A Practical Adaptive Router?[1]

[Extended Abstract]

Lawrence Snyder
University of Washington

Abstract: The Chaos router is compared with several contemporary adaptive router designs as well as with the state-of-the-art oblivious router used in contemporary parallel machines. The Chaos router is argued to approximate the oblivious router for raw performance and to be superior (as indicated in simulation studies) at high traffic loads and nonuniform loads.

Introduction

In recent years many adaptive routers have been proposed in an attempt to exploit the intuitively appealing idea that adaptively routing packets around congested regions of a network makes more sense than waiting for the congestion to clear. But to this day, there is no published performance data on any physically realized adaptive packet router. Among the possible reasons are that the few adaptive routers that have been built, e.g. Denelcor for the HEP and Thinking Machines for the CM-2, CM5, have been built by companies reluctant to published data on their designs, that the state-of-the-art oblivious routers used in most contemporary machines are sufficient because the machines are small and processors attached to the network are slow at injecting packets, and that many of the adaptive designs are actually impractical in one or more ways. In this paper the conclusions of a feasibility study of the Chaos router are presented. The study compared the Chaos router to other proposals as well as comparing it to the reigning champion, the oblivious router.

Router Designs

The context for the study is network routing for communication in parallel computers. Postulate a set of components (processors and/or memories) each connected to a communication coprocessor (also called a network interface), which injects messages into the network and receives messages ejected by the network. The N node network is assumed to be in the family of k-ary d-cube graphs, though most of the material applies to the "usual" graphs of network routing having multiple minimal paths between nonadjacent points. Each node in the network is connected to its neighbors in the graph by bidirectional channels. Additionally, each node is connected to the communication coprocessor of the component by

---

[1]Supported in part by NSF MIP-9013274, ONR N00014-91-J-1007, and NSF MIP-9213469.

two unidirectional links, the injection channel and the ejection channel, which are hereafter treated as a single channel. Thus, a node with graph degree d has $d+1$ channels. Finally, packets are expected to be small — say a quad word — with a header at the front giving the destination. The routers considered will be virtual cut through [Kermani & Kleinrock 79], though using wormhole routing [Dally & Seitz 87] would not materially change the results.

The state-of-the-art router found in most parallel computers today is an *oblivious* router, also known as a *dimension order* router. In such a router, the path taken between any source and destination is completely determined by the [source, destination] pair, i.e. the route is oblivious to the congestion in the network. Seitz's mesh routing chip, used in the Caltech Mosaic, Intel DELTA, Stanford DASH, MIT Alewife as well as being the ancestor of the router in the Intel Paragon, is an example of an oblivious router. The term was coined by Borodin and Hopcroft [Borodin & Hopcroft 85] who proved (constructively) that oblivious routers in bounded degree networks must have worstcase delivery time of $\Omega(\sqrt{N})$, a result that has recently been improved [Krizanc, Kaklamanis & Tsantilas 90]. It is not clear whether this worstcase performance has any practical significance. It is clear that because oblivious routers are extremely simple they can be made extremely fast in a physical implementation. This speed, especially relative to the processor's message injection rate, makes up somewhat for the lack of adaptivity. Finally, deadlock prevention, i.e. assuring that packets do not get "jammed," unable to advance, is straight forward for oblivious routers provided the k-ary d-cube does not have "wrap around," i.e. toroidal, connections and the routing is performed in dimension order. If the network is toroidal, virtual channels can prevent deadlock [Dally & Seitz 86], but with reduced performance [Bolding 92].

Among adaptive routers, there are two classifications. *Minimal adaptive* routers adapt to network congestion within the constraint that packets use only shortest (minimal distance) paths between source and destination. *Nonminimal adaptive* routers are not so restricted and packets can bypass congestion by using any path, even if it (at points) routes the packet further from its destination. When a router sends a packet away from its destination, it is said to *deroute*, or misroute, the message. In addition to preventing against deadlock, nonminimal adaptive routers must also prevent livelock, a condition in which packets continually circulate in the network but are not delivered. (Since packets cannot deroute in a minimal adaptive router, they do not need livelock protection.)

Minimal adaptive routers have been studied intensively in recent years [Konstantinidou 90, Felperin *et al.* 91, Cypher & Gravano 92]. Deadlock prevention is assured by ordering resources, such as buffer space, to assure that its use is cycle free. Though these routers perform well in simulation studies and have several desirable properties, unpublished studies [Konstantinidou 88] presently being confirmed at Washington indicate that minimal adaptive routers do not perform quite as well as nonminimal adaptive routers. An intuitive explanation might be: Packets in adaptive routers "discover" congestion when all forward paths are blocked. For minimal adaptive routers this is "too late," since the minimum distance constraint forces the packet to wait, adding to the congestion. Nonminimal adaptive routers, however, can "back up" and possibly bypass the congestion.

Nonminimal adaptive routers have also been studied extensively. Within this broad class there is a subset, corresponding to one "end" of the design space, known as *deflection* routers [Fang & Szymanski 91, Maxemchuk 89], or hot potato routers [Smith 81] or desperation routers [Smitley 89]. In a deflection router, packets arrive at a node simultaneously on incoming channels, are matched up with outgoing channels and are sent out simultaneously on the next step. If there are collisions, i.e. multiple packets require the same output channel, then the matching cannot be perfect and some of the packets are derouted, or *deflected*. Livelock protection, though ignored in some proposals, is nevertheless necessary. The solution used in the HEP [Smith 81] and other designs [Smitley 89] is to include in each packet a field for recording "battlescars." When a collision occurs, the losing packet, the one that is derouted, has its battlescar count increased. Battlescars can also be used in the matching step, for example, by giving priority to that packet with the highest battlescar. When the battlescar overflows the packet is sent directly to its destination on a predetermined "Eulerian" path without any further deflection. With two physical implementations, it would seem that deflection routing is the most widely implemented of the nonminimal adaptive routing techniques.

Packets in deflection routers are logically one flit[2] in length, because the headers must arrive at a node simultaneously to be routed; physically they should be short to assure satisfactory channel utilization since the virtual cut through technique cannot be used. The nonminimal alternatives to deflection routers, which might be called *continuous nonminimal routers*, make routing decisions whenever packets arrive at node and can thus exploit multiflit packets and virtual cut through techniques. The most fundamental difference is how they solve the livelock problem.

The priority type of continuous nonminimal adaptive router uses a timestamp in the header to resolve conflicts between packets competing for the same channel [Ngai & Seitz 89]. The technique, which is related to battlescars, compares the timestamps and gives priority to the older packet. This solves the livelock problem, provided the timestamps are distinct, because packets eventually age enough relative to the other network traffic to be routed directly to their destinations.

The Chaos router is a continuous nonminimal adaptive router that solves the livelock problem through randomization [Konstantinidou & Snyder 90]. When a packet arrives at a node in a Chaotic router there are three possibilities:

- There is a productive channel[3] free, and the packet cuts through to it directly.

- No productive channel is available, but there is space in the small local buffer, so the

---

[2]A flit or FLow control unIT is the smallest unit on which flow control can be performed; i.e. the smallest unit which must be transferred across a channel uninterrupted.

[3]A channel is productive if taking it moves a packet closer to its destination.

packet waits for a free productive channel.

- Neither a productive channel nor buffer space is available, so a waiting packet is randomly selected and derouted, making space for the arriving packet.

The random selection of a waiting packet is a sufficient condition to assure probabilistic livelock freedom. A router is said to be *probabilistically livelock free* if the probability a packet remains in the network for t seconds goes to 0 as t increases [Konstantinidou & Snyder 90]. Though probabilisitic livelock freedom is a weaker condition than deterministic livelock freedom, it is equivalent in practice since the deterministic bound on delivery from, say a priority router, is enormous.

In summary, the nonminimal adaptive routers presented all use a different approach to solve livelock — battlescars for deflection routers, timestamps for priority routers and randomization for Chaotic routers.[4] All nonminimal adaptive routers can implicitly solve the deadlock problem simply by derouting packets. Though conceptually straightforward, the implementation seems to require for the continuous class a technique such as the "packet exchange" protocol [Ngai & Seitz 89] that assures that packets can always move between routers.

Logical Comparisons

In order to assess the progress in routing research and to understand what router should be used in the next generation parallel computers, it is necessary to compare the proposals from a practical point of view. In this section the routers just introduced will be compared.

The oblivious router is the state-of-the-art in parallel computers, so it is the default choice and thus the "one to beat." The oblivious router's strength is that it is simple and therefore fast. This speed must be preserved in routers that offer other features, since crucial regions of the performance space, e.g. light load, may not benefit from the features, e.g. adaptivity. Thus, speed comparable to the oblivious router is essential.

The oblivious router's competition comes from nonminimal adaptive routers since they perform better than minimal adaptive alternatives. Though direct comparisons can be made between oblivious and the continuous nonminimal class, fair comparisons with deflection routers are difficult because of their one flit per packet property. A single flit/packet implies channels wide enough to handle the entire packet, a requirement that is very unrealistic for present day technology. Pin limitations and wiring constraints prevent designers from

---

[4]Notice that chaotic techniques can be used in deflection routing by randomizing during the match, e.g. by randomizing the assignment of "losing" packets to channels or using a greedy assignment that begins with a random incoming channel. Indeed, such a deflection router is simply a restricted chaotic router where the number of packets of local storage is 0 and there is one flit/packet.

using such wide channels and necessitate multiflit packets.[5] Once the number of flits/packet exceeds about four, experiments indicate that deflection is consistently inferior to other routing schemes. Therefore, deflection must be set aside because of unrealistic technology requirements.

The priority router can be eliminated by simple comparison with the chaotic router, since their principal difference is how livelock is handled. The priority router is strictly more complex than a chaotic router because determining which among colliding packets is oldest adds a significant complication to the critical path of the routing logic. The chaotic router does not need to make such decisions, giving it lower node latency and better overall performance [Konstantinidou 91]. It follows that if a continuous nonminimal adpative router is to compete with the oblivious router, it must be the Chaotic design.

Not only is the Chaotic router simpler, and therefore potentially faster, than the priority router, its critical path is essentially as simple as the oblivious router. The difference is between making the oblivious decision, i.e. "continue in this dimension or turn," and the adaptive decision, i.e. "which productive dimensions are free." Based on our initial implementation for a k-ary, 2-cube, i.e. mesh and torus networks, it can be estimated that the ratio between chaotic and oblivious critical path delays will be close to even. This reduction of complexity suggests that a Chaotic router could provide the benefits of adaptivity without seriously degrading the performance for those load profiles where the oblivious router does well.

One final word on topology. Oblivious routers prefer the mesh to the torus for two-dimension routing. As mentioned above dimension order routing on a mesh is deadlock free, while it is not on the torus. Though there are solutions for making oblivious routing deadlock free on a torus, the performance is unsatisfactory. Contrariwise, nonminimal adaptive routers have difficulty with the mesh because the alternative routes tend to cross the mesh, making the center a hot spot [Bolding & Snyder 92]. See Figure 1. Moreover the sides and corners of a mesh bias the benefit of derouting for some nodes in some directions. The torus is much preferred because it is node symmetric (the network "looks" the same from any position) and has better bisection bandwidth and diameter. Simulations confirm that the Chaos router does better on the torus than on the mesh, and it is better than the oblivious router on either topology even when they are normalized to the same bisection bandwidth [Bolding & Snyder 92]. Therefore the torus will be the standard 2D topology.

---

[5]There is another aspect illustrated by the deflection router to be used in the forthcoming Tera Computer. Although the channel width problem was solved by replicating the router, the network, a 3D torus, had to be reduced to degree 4 (by removing X direction and Y direction wires in alternating planes) in order to make the routing decision within the 2.5 ns clock tick, even using chaotic rather than battlescar livelock protection.

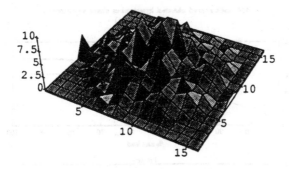

Figure 1: Average injection delay for a 256-node mesh.

Simulated Comparisons

Though reason might be a useful tool in reducing the total number of comparisons that must be made when assessing routers, it eventually becomes necessary to simulate the behavior of the finalists. The accompanying figures are a sampling of numerous simulation experiments comparing oblivious and Chaotic routers.

Simulations for 64, 256 and 1024 node torus and hypercube graphs were conducted [Bolding & Snyder 92], though only representative 256 node results are presented here. The C-based simulator has a granularity of a single flit transmitted per cycle. Routing decisions are assumed to be made in a single cycle. All machines use virtual cut-through.

Continuously injected traffic was simulated with statistics gathered after every epoch in which all nodes injected at least 50 packets. Average throughput and average latency were computed for each epoch with convergence defined to be a standard deviation in both statistics of less than 3% for the five most recent intervals. The presented results are typically averages of from three to five runs. Reported throughput is normalized to the capacity of the network's bisection bandwidth. Latency is the difference between the time the message entered and left the network, which does not include source queuing time.

Figures 2-3 show representative simulation experiments comparing the Chaos router with an oblivious router. The "4X hot spot" traffic is synthesized by selecting ten nodes at random to be four times more likely to be the destination of a packet than other nodes in the network. This traffic is intended to model a situation in which nodes contain frequently referenced data such as synchronization variables.

This sampling of results indicates a decided advantage for the Chaos router over the oblivious router in both throughput and latency. Though it appears that at extremely high loads the

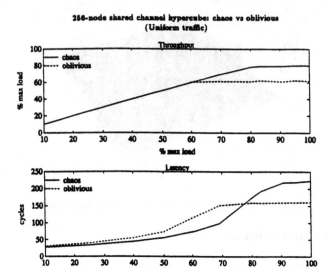

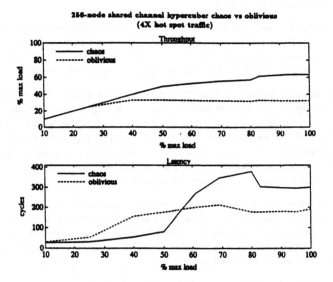

Figure 2: 256 node hypercube results.

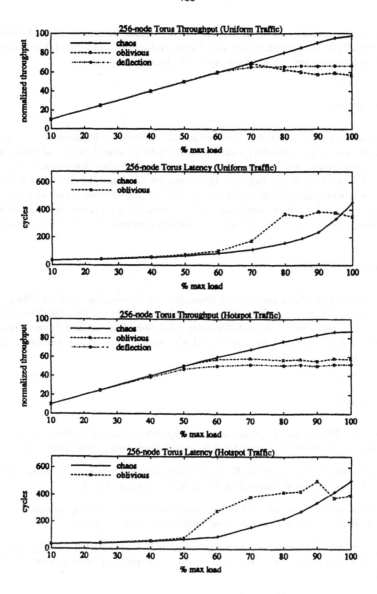

Figure 3: 256 node torus results.

latency of the oblivious router is superior to the chaotic router, there is at this point a great disparity in the number of messages the two routers are delivering (as indicated by the throughput curves) and so the advantage is an illusion.

Conclusions

After considering adaptive alternatives to the state-of-the-art oblivious router, it would seem that the Chaos router offers the greatest promise, both because it has the advantages of non-minimal adaptiveness and because it is sufficiently simple to admit fast implementations. The key to the simplicity is the fact that Chaos routers eliminate the livelock protection that complicates other nonminimal approaches by randomizing when messages must be derouted. The only penalty for this randomization is that the router is no longer deterministically live-lock free, but rather is probabilistically livelock free, a property that is practically equivalent.

Acknowledgment

The co-inventor of Chaos routing was Smaragda Konstantinidou. Kevin Bolding and Sen-ching "Samson" Cheung performed the simulations. Bolding has lead the design effort with Carl Ebeling and graduate students Sung-eun Choi, Soha Hassoun and Robert Wille, as well as Cheung. It is a pleasure to have worked with each of these fine researchers and to offer sincere thanks.

References

K. Bolding [1992], Nonuniformities introduced by virtual channel deadlock prevention, Technical Report TR 92-07-07, Computer Science and Engineering, University of Washington.

K. Bolding and L. Snyder [1992], Mesh and torus chaotic routing, *Proceedinsgs Brown/MIT Conference on Advanced Research in VLSI*, MIT Press, pp. 333–347.

A. Borodin and J. Hopcroft [1985], Routing, merging and sorting on parallel models of computation, *Journal of Computer and Systems Sciences*, 30:130–145.

R. Cypher and L. Gravano [1992], Adaptive, Deadlock-Free Packet Routing in Torus Networks with Minimal Storage, *Proceedings of International Conference on Parallel Processing*, 3:204–211.

W. Dally and C. Seitz [1986], The torus routing chip, *Journal of Distributed Computing*, Vol. 1, No. 3.

W. Dally and C. Seitz [1987], Deadlock-free message routing in multiprocessor interconnection networks, *IEEE Transactions on Computers*, C-36(5):547–553.

C. Fang and T. Szymanski [1991], An analysis of deflection routing in multi-dimensional regular mesh networks, *Proceedings IEEE INFOCOM '91*, pp. 859–868.

S. Felperin, G. Pifarre, L. Gravano and J. Sanz [1991], Fully adaptive, minimal deadlock-free routing in hypercubes, meshes and other networks, *Proceedings ACM Symposium on Parallel Algorithms and Architectures*, pp. 278–291.

P. Kermani and L. Kleinrock [1979], Virtual cut-through: A new computer communication switching technique, *Computer Networks*, 3:267–286.

S. Konstantinidou [1988], personal communication.

S. Konstantinidou [1990], Adaptive, minimal routing in hypercubes, *Proceedings MIT Conference on Advanced Research in VLSI*, pp. 139–153.

S. Konstantinidou and L. Snyder [1990], The chaos router: A practical application of randomization in network routing, *Proceedings ACM Symposium on Parallel Algorithms and Architectures*, pp. 21–30.

S. Konstantinidou [1991] Deterministic and chaotic routing in multicomputers, PhD Dissertation, University of Washington.

S. Konstantinidou and L. Snyder [1991], The chaos router: Architecture and performance, *Proceedings International Symposium on Computer Architecture*, IEEE pp. 212–222.

D. Krizanc, C. Kaklamanis and A. Tsantilas [1990], Tight bounds for oblivious routing in the hypercube, *Proceedings ACM Symposium on Parallel Algorithms and Architectures*, pp. 31–36.

N. Maxemchuk [1989] Comparison of deflection and store-and- forward techniques in the manhattan street and shuffle- exchange networks, *Proceedings of IEEE INFOCOM '89*, pp. 800–809.

J. Ngai and C. Seitz [1989], A framework for adaptive routing in multicomputer networks, *Proceedings of Symposium on Parallel Algorithms and Architectures*, pp. 1–9.

B. Smith [1981], Architecture and application of the HEP multiprocessor computer system, *Proceedings of SPIE*, pp. 241–248.

D. Smitley [1989], Design tradeoffs for a high speed network node. Technical Report SRC-TR-89-007, Supercomputing Research Center, Bowie MD.

An Experimental Study of Wormhole Routing in Parallel Computers

Sergio Felperin[1], Prabhakar Raghavan[2] and Eli Upfal[3]

[1] IBM Almaden Research Center, San Jose, California 95120, USA.
[2] IBM T.J. Watson Research Center, Yorktown Hts., New York 10598, USA.
[3] IBM Almaden Research Center, San Jose, California 95120, USA, and
The Weizmann Institute of Science, Rehovot 76100, Israel.

Abstract. A trend in multicomputer architecture is to use *wormhole routing*. In wormhole routing a message is transmitted as a contiguous stream of bits, physically occupying a sequence of nodes/edges in the network. Thus, a message resembles a worm burrowing through the network. In this paper we report the results of studies of simple wormhole routing algorithms for butterfly and mesh-connected networks.

1 Overview

Considerable theoretical and practical work on routing in parallel computers has dwelt on *packet routing:* messages are conveyed as packets, an entire packet can reside at a node of the network, and a packet is sent from the queue of one node to the queue of another node until it reaches its destination [2, 14, 18, 19, 20, 21]. While packet routing is very efficient asymptotically, this efficiency is often compromised by the overhead required by the packet routing mechanism; especially in maintaining queues in the intermediate nodes, and breaking long messages into small packets and then reconstructing the original messages when the pieces reach their destination (possibly out of order). Therefore, the current trend in multicomputer architecture is to use substantially simpler routing mechanisms, in particular *wormhole routing* [3, 6, 7, 8, 12, 17, 16]. A message is transmitted as a contiguous stream of bits, physically occupying a sequence of nodes/edges in the network. There are no queues in the intermediate nodes, and a node can only hold a (typically small) fraction of a message. The routing strategy is oblivious, keeping the overhead in the intermediate nodes minimal. When the head of a message reaches a node, the nodes reads the first few bits in the message's header, and uses them to direct the head of the message to the next node on its path. The rest of the message follows the head of the message as it moves, requiring no more intervention by the intermediate node. Thus a message resembles a worm burrowing through the network, giving rise to the name for this style of routing. In this paper we mention previous theoretical work on the analysis of wormhole routing, and then proceed to describe our experimental work using simple algorithms for butterfly and mesh-connected networks of processors. We compare our experimental results with the theorems.

Parallel machines that use variants of wormhole routing include the Intel Delta-machine, Intel iPSC/2, Intel Sigma, Symult S14, MIT J-machine, MIT April, and others. Previous research on wormhole routing focuses on simulations that study the extent to which a network can be loaded (as a fraction of the available bandwidth) before it gets clogged [5, 7, 15]. Other research has addressed the issue of *deadlock*, since in wormhole routing it is possible for a set of messages to mutually block each others' path [9]. On a two-dimensional mesh, for instance, it is known that if every message first travels along its row to the column of its destination, then turns into the column (call this the *one-bend path*), there is no deadlock.

To keep implementations simple and also to avoid deadlock, system designers have emphasized simple routing strategies (such as the one-bend path for the mesh). Our theorems and simulations both study the average-case behavior of such simple strategies when the input is drawn from a probability distribution.

1.1 Graph-theoretic model

Our network model incorporates the features that make wormhole routing practically interesting (such as small buffer size), and precludes algorithms that inject coordinating tokens in addition to messages By restricting ourselves to bounded-degree networks, we do not require nodes to handle an unbounded number of messages at any time step as some previous algorithms do.

We model a network by a graph; adjacent nodes are connected by two unidirectional links, one in each direction. We assume that each link has at its output a buffer that can hold one *flit* [7], or flow control unit — a message is composed of one or more flits. The length of a message is the number of flits that comprise the message. Only one flit of one message may pass through a link at any time step. Once the head of a message enters a link, all other flits of that message must pass through it before any other message can use that link. In each time step, the head of a flit may advance along the next link on its path, if that link is free. Otherwise it remains in the buffer at the output of the last link it traversed. If the head does advance, every flit in that message can advance along the next link from its current position. A message is said to be delivered when its tail arrives at its destination; we are interested in the number of steps that elapse before a message is delivered. Each node can buffer only a small constant number of flits, independent of message length.

Caveat: There is a great deal of confusion between the case we are dealing with, and the model of *virtual cut-through*. The latter resembles wormhole routing superficially, but differs in one crucial aspect: in virtual cut-through, the buffers at nodes can hold a constant number of *messages*, rather than a constant number of *flits*. Thus in virtual cut-through the buffer size at a node is proportional to the worm length.

2 Wormhole Routing on the Butterfly

In this section we study wormhole routing on a butterfly when each message independently chooses a random destination. Consider a butterfly network consisting of layers numbered $0, 1 \cdots \log N$ of N nodes each. The nodes at layer 0 are *sources*, while those at layer $\log N$ are *destinations*. Each source has a message of length L, and is bound for a random destination.

Consider the following simple delayed greedy algorithm: Fix a constant ℓ. Message i first chooses an integer d_i in $[0, \ell - 1]$. For a fixed positive constant c, the message waits $d_i \cdot cL \log N$ steps at its source before starting to travel (by the unique path in the butterfly) to its destination. In [10] we prove the following result on the performance of this algorithm.

Theorem 1. *Let $\ell = 10 \min\{L, \log N\}$. There is a constant c such that at the end of $10c\ell L \log N$ steps, every message has reached its destination with high probability.*

This result can be extended in two ways: (1) if message lengths are different and are chosen from a "well-behaved" distribution with expectation $\bar{L}$, then a message of length L_i is delivered in time $O(L_i + \log N + \bar{L} \log N \min\{\bar{L}, \log N\})$ with high probability; (2) when message lengths are arbitrarily chosen by an adversary, we give a batching scheme that ensures that a message of length L_i is delivered in time $O(L_i \log N \min\{L_i, \log N\})$ with high probability. All the above results for random destinations can be extended to worst-case permutations using Valiant's scheme.

We now give detailed results of simulations for our delayed greedy algorithm, aiming at answering two questions: (1) Is the above analysis tight? (2) Do initial delays improve the experimental performance of wormhole routing?

Let T_s be the time the message spends in the queue of its source before it is injected to the network, and T_l be the time it spends in the network while being routed. The latency of a packet in our simulations is defined to be the sum $T_s + T_l$. Note that the routing time is at least $3 \log N + L + 1$ (see section 4). Each point in the graphs represents the average of 30 independent runs.

Figure 1 gives the average latency for a 4096-input butterfly as a function of random delays ranging from 0 to 20 and for packet sizes ranging from 15 to 50 flits. A random delay of X steps (in the figures) means that each message is independently delayed for a number of steps uniform in $[0, X]$. The results show that random delays do not increase the average latency and that small random delays improve the routing time.

Figures 2 to 6 give the maximum delay for messages with 10 to 50 flits, random delays ranging from 0 to 15, for butterflies of 256 to 16384 inputs. Again random delay improves the routing performance.

We use interpolations to study how well the message latency suggested by the data fits the bound in our theorem. We have fitted the experimental data for maximum latency as a linear function of the network depth $\log N$, the message length L, the maximum random delay D and the product $L \log N$. The fitting function obtained was:

$$T_{\max}(N, L, D) = 0.68 \, L \log N + 0.19 \, L - 0.38 \, D + 2.89 \log N + 9.2$$

The function $T_{\max}(N, L, 15)$ is shown in Figure 7.

3 Wormhole Routing on a Mesh

In this section we study the following delayed greedy algorithm using one-bend paths for N-nodes two-dimensional mesh: Source i chooses an integer d_i independently and uniformly in the range $[0, ..., D-1]$. For a fixed constant b, the message M_i originating at source i then waits for $d_i(b^2 L \log^2 N + bL \log N + 2\sqrt{N})$ steps before traveling greedily by the one-bend path to its destination (traveling along its row first and then along the destination column). This algorithm has been analyzed in [10] for the case $D = \frac{2\sqrt{N}}{\log N}$.

Theorem 2. *[10] The above delayed greedy algorithm delivers all messages in $O(L\sqrt{N} \log N + N/\log N)$ steps with high probability.*

Clearly the above bound is weak when $L \ll \sqrt{N}/\log^2 N$, because the rate at which we launch messages is too low (think of the case $L = 1$).

We run simulations to study the performance of the above algorithm for shorter messages, and the contributions of the initial delays to the performance of the algorithm.

In our simulations each processor has 4 input buffers and 4 output buffers, one for each of the 4 directions.

Recall that we denote the time a packet spends in the queue before entering the network by T_s, and the routing time in the network by T_l. Note that the queueing time represents the sum of two random variables: (1) the random delay imposed by the algorithm and (2) the time a message waits in the queue after the random delay until the link it needs to path is free. Figure 8 shows two sets of 5 curves each. The first set, in the lower part of the figure, represents the expected queueing time $\overline{T_s}$ as a function of network size for random delays 0,25,50,75 and 100, with messages of 10 flits each. The second set, shown in the upper part of the figure, represents the average $\overline{T} = \overline{T_s} + \overline{T_l}$ as a function of network size, for the same random delays and message size. Network size varies from $25 \times 25 = 625$ to $125 \times 125 = 15625$ nodes. The figure shows that increasing $\overline{T_s}$ is almost compensated by a corresponding decrease in $\overline{T_l}$, as expected.

This effect is enhanced when we consider longer messages. Figure 9 shows the same sets of curves as Figure 8 but for messages of 100 flits. Note that the differences among the various T shown is almost negligible, and that for the larger random delays, the corresponding $\overline{T_s}$ become almost equal. Figures 10, 11, and 12 show $T_{\max}$ as a function of network size for different random delays.

The figures presented in this Section suggest that both the $\overline{T}$ and $T_{\max}$ match their theoretical bounds of $O(L\sqrt{N})$ for the various random delays and network sizes. The following is a fitting of the experimental data as a linear function of message length L, mesh side $\sqrt{N}$, maximum random delay D, and the product $L\sqrt{N}$:

$$T_{\max}(N, L, D) = 0.93 \, L \, \sqrt{N} + 1.40 \, L - 0.90 \, \sqrt{N} + 0.19 \, D + 54.09$$
$$\overline{T_s}(N, L, D) = 0.36 \, L \, \sqrt{N} - 0.21 \, L - 0.49 \, \sqrt{N} + 0.05 \, D + 40.51$$

4 The Simulator.

The simulator used is a C-program that we have developed, running on a IBM RS/6000 under the AIX operating system. Pseudo-random numbers are generated using the pseudo-random number algorithm shown in [13], modified to handle several pseudo-random streams simultaneously.

Each node has *input* buffers, one for each input link, *ouput* buffers, one for each output link and a mechanism to connect inputs to outputs. Each of these buffers can store two flits belonging to the same message. Input nodes in the butterfly and all nodes in the mesh have an *injection* queue, that can hold a whole message. Nodes that can receive messages have a *delivery* queue.

Time is computed in *cycles*. In a single cycle, a node can perform the following operations:

1. To set any number of connections from input to output buffers in the node, provided that the input has the head of a message and the output is not being used by any other message. The input buffers are handled in a round-robin fashion to guarantee fairness.
2. To clear connections between input and output buffers in the node, once the tail of a message has passed through them.
3. To pass one flit from each input buffer to an output buffer in the node connected to it in previous cycle, if the output buffer is not full.
4. To pass a flit from an output buffer of one node to the input buffer of a node connected to it, provided that the input buffer can store it. If the flit is the head of a message, the tail of the previous message must have left the input buffer.

Note that in our model a flit needs *at least* 3 steps to go from an input to an output buffer of a node. One step for entering the input buffer, one step for setting the connection to the output buffer, and the third step to pass through that connection.

References

1. B. Aiello, F.T. Leighton, B. Maggs, and M. Newman. Fast algorithms for bit-serial routing on a hypercube. In *Second Annual ACM Symposium on Parallel Algorithms and Architectures*, pages 55–64. ACM Press, 1990.
2. R. Aleliunas. Randomized parallel communication. In *ACM-SIGOPS Symposium on Principles of Distributed Systems*, pages 60–72, 1982.
3. W.C. Athas. Physically compact, high performance multicomputers. In *Sixth MIT Conference on Advanced Research in VLSI*, pages 302–313. MIT Press, 1990.
4. H. Chernoff. A measure of asymptotic efficiency for tests of a hypothesis based on the sum of observations. *Annals of Math. Stat.*, 23:493–509, 1952.
5. W. Dally. Performance analysis of k ary n cube interconnection networks. *IEEE Trans. Computers*, 39:775–785, 1990.
6. W. Dally and C.L. Seitz. Deadlock free message routing in multiprocessor interconnection networks. *IEEE Trans. Computers*, 36:547–553, 1987.
7. W.J. Dally. Fine grain message passing concurrent computers. In *Third Conference on Hypercube Concurrent Computers and Applications*, pages 2–12. ACM Press, 1988.
8. W.J. Dally. Virtual channel flow control. In *Seventeenth Annual International Symposium on Computer Architecture*, pages 60–68. ACM Press, 1990.
9. J. Duato. On the design of deadlock free adaptive routing algorithms for multicomputers: theoretical aspects. In *Second European Conference on Distributed Memory Computing*, pages 234–243. Springer Verlag LNCS 487, 1991.
10. S. Felperin, P. Raghavan, and E. Upfal. A theory of wormhole routing in parallel computers. In *33th Annual Symposium on Foundations of Computer Science*, 1992, to appear.

11. F.T. Leighton. Average case analysis of greedy routing algorithms on arrays. In *Second Annual ACM Symposium on Parallel Algorithms and Architectures*, pages 2–10. ACM Press, 1990.

12. M. Noakes and W.J. Dally. System design of the j machine. In *Sixth MIT Conference on Advanced Research in VLSI*, pages 179–194. MIT Press, 1990.

13. W.H. Press, *Numerical Recipes in C: The Art of Scientific Computing*, Cambridge University Press, 1988.

14. A. Ranade. How to emulate shared memory. In *Proceedings of the 28th Annual IEEE Symposium on Foundations of Computer Science*, pages 185–194, 1987.

15. D.S. Reeves, E.F. Gehringer, and A. Chandiramani. Adaptive routing and deadlock recovery: a simulation study. In *Fourth Conference on Hypercube Concurrent Computers and Applications*, pages 331–337. Golden Gate Enterprises, 1989.

16. C.L. Seitz, W.C. Athas, C.M. Flaig, A.J. Martin, J. Seizovic, C.S. Steele, and W.K. Su. The architecture and programming of the Ametek Series 2010 multicomputer. In *Third Conference on Hypercube Concurrent Computers and Applications*, pages 33–36. ACM Press, 1988.

17. R.J. Smith II. Experimental system kit hardware. In *Fourth Conference on Hypercube Concurrent Computers and Applications*, pages 713–725. Golden Gate Enterprises, 1989.

18. E. Upfal. Efficient schemes for parallel communication. *Journal of the ACM*, 31:507–517, 1984.

19. Eli Upfal. An $O(\log N)$ deterministic packet routing scheme. In *21st ACM Annual Symposium on Theory of Computing*, pages 241–250, 1989.

20. L. G. Valiant and G. J. Brebner. Universal schemes for parallel communication. In *Proceedings of the Thirteenth Annual ACM Symposium on Theory of Computing*, pages 263–277, Milwaukee, Wisconsin, May 1981.

21. L.G. Valiant. A scheme for fast parallel communication. *SIAM Journal on Computing*, 11(2):350–361, 1982.

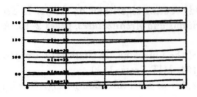

Figure 1: Average Latency vs. Random Delay for the 4096-input butterfly

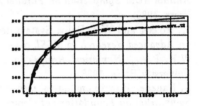

Figure 3: Maximum Latency vs. Number of Inputs in the butterfly— 20 flits messages

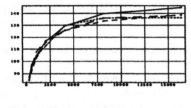

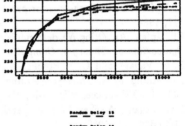

Figure 2: Maximum Latency vs. Number of Inputs in the butterfly— 10 flits messages

Figure 4: Maximum Latency vs. Number of Inputs in the butterfly— 30 flits messages

163

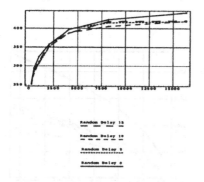

Random Delay 15

Random Delay 10

Random Delay 5

Random Delay 0

Figure 5: Maximum Latency vs. Number of Inputs in the butterfly— 40 flits messages

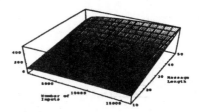

Figure 7: Fitting of Maximum Latency vs of Number of Inputs and Message Length in the butterfly. Random Delay = 15

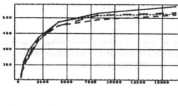

Random Delay 15

Random Delay 10

Random Delay 5

Random Delay 0

Figure 6: Maximum Latency vs. Number of Inputs in the butterfly— 50 flits messages

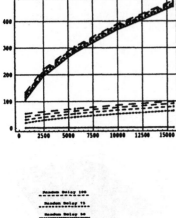

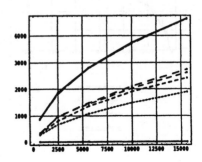

Figure 8: Average Latency and average Source Queuing as a function of network size for various random delays in the mesh — 10 flits messages

Figure 9: Average Latency and average Source Queuing as a function of network size for various random delays in the mesh — 100 flits messages

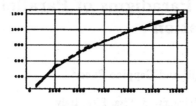

Figure 10: Maximum Latency as a function of network size for various random delays in the mesh — 10 flits messages

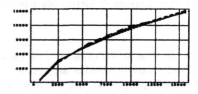

Figure 12: Maximum Latency as a function of network size for various random delays in the mesh — 100 flits messages

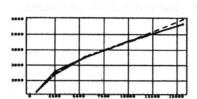

Figure 11: Maximum Latency as a function of network size for various random delays in the mesh — 50 flits messages

Three non Conventional Paradigms of Parallel Computation*

Fabrizio Luccio[1], Linda Pagli[1] and Geppino Pucci[2]

[1] Dipartimento di Informatica, Università di Pisa, Pisa, Italy
[2] Dipartimento di Elettronica e Informatica, Università di Padova, Padova, Italy

Abstract. We consider three paradigms of computation where the benefits of a parallel solution are greater than usual. Paradigm 1 works on a time-varying input data set, whose size increases with time. In paradigm 2 the data set is fixed, but the processors may fail at any time with a given constant probability. In paradigm 3, the execution of a single operation may require more than one processor, for security or reliability reasons. We discuss the organization of PRAM algorithms for these paradigms, and prove new bounds on parallel speed-up.

1 Introduction

The theory of parallel algorithms has a well known body, developed on the PRAM model [5]. Some folklore principles are at the base of this theory, in particular the ones that express upper and lower bounds on the processing time. Let Π be a problem of size N, and let $T^s(N)$ be the time required by the best known sequential algorithm A^s to solve Π. Any parallel algorithm A^p that solves Π with a number P of PRAM processors requires time $T^p(P, N)$ such that:

$$T^p(P, N) \geq \frac{T^s(N)}{P}. \tag{1}$$

Relation (1) expresses a renowned lower bound on parallel speed-up. The quantity $W(P, N) = T^p(P, N) \cdot P$ is called the *work* of A^p. If the operations of a parallel algorithm with P' processors are rescheduled into another algorithm with $P < P'$ processors, we have:

$$T^p(P, N) \leq \frac{W(P', N)}{P} + T^p(P', N), \tag{2}$$

that expresses Brent's principle on scaling.

Non conventional studies on parallel speed-up have been reported for example in [2], [11] and [7]. In particular, it has been shown that the above relations do not hold for specific classes of problems, if expressed in absolute terms [2], or in asymptotic terms [7]. This paper is aimed to provide a critical contribution to this area. In particular, we consider three algorithmic paradigms where the power of parallel computation is exploited to the extent that inequalities (1) and (2) may be violated, and discuss the organization and analysis of algorithms for these paradigms. We

* This work has been supported by MURST of Italy under a research grant.

have:

Paradigm 1. *The input data set varies dynamically.* The problem size N is defined as a non decreasing function of time. Intuitively an algorithm performs better than usual for increasing P, because the the processing time decreases and the problem size to be considered is smaller.

Paradigm 2. *The processors can fail with constant probability.* Again a parallel computation may become much faster with increasing P, because the number of non faulty processors decreases with time.

Paradigm 3. *A single operation may require $k > 1$ processors to be executed.* This situation may occur for security or reliability reasons. Trivially, the problem cannot be solved with less than k processors.

2   Computing with time-increasing data (Paradigm 1)

Let Π be a problem of size $N = n + f(n, t)$, where $f(n, t)$ is a non decreasing function of the initial size n and time t, $f(n, 0) = 0$. An algorithm A for Π terminates when all the data currently arrived have been treated, that is, the paradigm applies when a condition of consistency is required on a current set of data before an answer can be supplied.

The variability of N occurs for *on-line* problems, where it is assumed that an action has to be taken for each new datum before another datum arrives; and for *real-time* problems, where the time required by any of the above actions is upper bounded by a constant [9]. We study the impact of the variability of N on the design and complexity of algorithms, without imposing the above limitations. New data can be accumulated without being treated immediately, and the time needed to treat them is an arbitrary function of t. Moreover, our approach does not fall in the theory of queueing systems because the data arrival times are known deterministically and no fixed queueing discipline is imposed for their future use.

Many problems in Applied Physics work on variable data which obey to relations similar to the one given above for N, often in differential or integral form. For example the vacuum is made in a chamber while an imperfect valve lets a certain amount of air to enter again. The process terminates when a given condition is met (e.g., the pressure reaches a given value); at this point the valve is tapped and a different experiment can be initiated. In the theory of computing, interesting problems in Paradigm 1 are the ones that admit a sequential *data-accumulative* algorithm A^s (shortly *d-algorithm*). A^s is built for time-increasing data, but its time complexity $T^s(N)$ is the same, in order of magnitude, of the best algorithm working on the N data as if they were all available at time $t = 0$. One such problem admits an optimal parallel solution with P processors if there is a parallel algorithm A^p (*pd-algorithm*) working on time-increasing data, whose complexity is $T^p(P, N) = O\left(\frac{T^s(N)}{P}\right)$. For simplicity, we restrict our study to problems of the class $\mathcal{P}$ admitting a d-algorithm and a pd-algorithm, such that, for c and c_p constant:

$$N = n + knt, \tag{3}$$

$$t = T^s(N) = c(n + knt)^\alpha, \alpha \geq 1, \tag{4}$$

$$t_p = T^p(P, N) = \frac{c_p(n + knt_p)^\alpha}{P}, \text{ with } P \text{ constant or } P = n^\delta, \delta \le \alpha. \qquad (5)$$

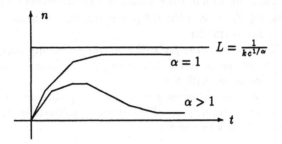

Figure 1

Figure 1 shows the plot of (4). For $\alpha = 1$ the algorithm terminates iff $n < \frac{1}{kc^{1/\alpha}}$, while the working time may become arbitrarily large for n approaching $\frac{1}{kc^{1/\alpha}}$. For $a > 1$ the behaviour is less favourable, because the amount of new data increases rapidly with t. For $P = $ constant, function (5) has a plot in n, t_p like the one of figure 1, with $L = \frac{(Pc/c_p)^{1/\alpha}}{kc^{1/\alpha}}$. For $P = n^\delta, \delta < \alpha$, the plot is the same, with $L = \frac{P^{1/(\alpha-\delta)}}{c_p^{1/(\alpha-\delta)}k^{\alpha/(\alpha-\delta)}}$. For $P = n^\alpha$, relation (5) becomes $t_p = c_p(1 + kt_p)^\alpha$, that is t_p is constant for proper values of c_p, k and α (this is consistent with the fact that the parallel algorithm is optimal and the sequential algorithm has complexity n^α). Note that relations (3) and (4) have been formulated under the hypothesis that the new knt data are loaded into memory without increasing the time complexity of the algorithm. It can be easily shown that this can be attained for $\alpha \ge 1$ as posed in (4).

The lower bound (1) on parallel speed-up does not apply to the problems solvable in Paradigm 1, where the benefits of a parallel solution may be stronger and more intrigued than usual. In general we can prove that:

Proposition 1. *For problems obeying relation (3), (4) and (5) we have* $\frac{T^*(N)}{P \cdot T^p(P,N)} > \frac{c}{c_p}$. *Furthermore, for $\alpha = 1$ the ratio* $\frac{T^*(N)}{P \cdot T^p(P,N)}$ *tends to ∞ for n tending to $\frac{1}{ck}$.*

Proposition 1 violates relation (1) for $c = c_p$, or for $\alpha = 1$ and n close to $\frac{1}{ck}$. For complexity functions different from (5), Proposition 1 must be reformulated (e.g., $P = \frac{n}{\log n}$ and $t_p = c_p \log n$, see below).

Another bound that does not apply in the framework of Paradigm 1 is the one expressed in Brent's principle (2). For brevity we restrict our discussion to the subfamily of pd-algorithms obeying relation (5) with $\alpha = 1$. Let A' be the fastest known such algorithm with P' processors. A' requires time

$$t_p' = \frac{c_p'(n + knt_p')}{P'}. \qquad (6)$$

For $P < P'$ consider a new algorithm A obtained from A' by rescheduling the operations of A'. Algorithm A requires time $t_p \ge t_p'$, hence $N = n + knt_p \ge n + knt_p' = N'$. However, to build A on N data, we have to reschedule A' on the same amount N of data, which in turn requires that A' be executed for a proper initial value n''

such that $N'' = n'' + kn''t_p'' = N = n + knt_p$, with $t_p'' = \frac{c_p'(n''+kn''t_p'')}{P'}$. We have:

$$t_p'' = \frac{c_p'(n + knt_p)}{P'}. \tag{7}$$

Let X'' denote the total number of operations performed by A' on N'', and let $W''(P', N'') = t_p'' \cdot P'$ be the corresponding work. Algorithm A is obtained by rescheduling the X'' operations of A'. As in the derivation of Brent's principle we obtain:

$$t_p \leq \frac{X''}{P} + t_p'' \leq \frac{W''(P', N'')}{P} + t_p'' = \pi t_p'', \text{ with } \pi = \frac{P' + P}{P}. \tag{8}$$

From relations (7) and (8), we easily derive a new formulation of Brent's principle:

Proposition 2. *A pd-algorithm obeying relation (5) with $\alpha = 1$, constant c_p', and P' processors, can be rescheduled for $P \leq P'$ processors and n initial data in time $T^p(P, N) \leq \frac{c_p'\pi n}{P' - kc_p'\pi n}$, with $\pi = \frac{P'+P}{P}$.*

Note that P, P' are in general functions of the problem size. Hence, when A' is rescheduled on n'' data, we have to enter $P' = P'(n'')$ in the bound Proposition 2. Since relation (6) can be rewritten as $t_p' = \frac{c_p'n}{P' - kc_p'n}$, the upper bound of the proposition can be interpreted as the time needed by the original algorithm A' working on πn initial data. This time can be made arbitrarily large for proper values of n, while t_p' stays limited, thereby making relation (2) non significant. Proposition 2 can be extended to different complexity functions with foreseeable results. An example is shown in the next section.

Let us now consider a *census* problem with time-varying data, solved under Paradigm 1. The computation is completed when all data currently arrived have been processed, independently of other data that may arrive at later times.

Problem 1 *Given a set I of integers, of size $N = n + knt$, compute the sum S of all the elements in I.*

Problem 1 occurs in an idealized banking operation, where the balance S of all movements in an account must be computed before a withdraw is honored. Note that the number of movements is given by an initial value n, plus an increment proportional to time and n. When S has been found, the algorithm terminates, and a different operation (e.g, a paying procedure) is initiated. For $n < \frac{1}{kc}$ this problem can be solved with a sequential linear time d-algorithm consisting of a scan, according to relation (4) with $\alpha = 1$. As well known, it can be solved in parallel on the initial n data with $P = \frac{n}{\log n}$ processors in time $O(\log n)$. For time-varying data we have:

Proposition 3. *Problem 1 admits a pd-algorithm with $P = \frac{n}{\log n}$ and $t_p \leq c_p \log n$.*

The algorithm is as follows:

1) subdivide the initial set of n data in P sections $I_1, \ldots, I_P$, of $\log n$ elements each; each processor computes the sum in I_i sequentially in time $c \log n$;
2) during step 1, $ckn \log n$ new data arrive. Assuming that $n \leq \frac{1}{ck}$, we have $ckn \log n \leq \log n$, then, we still have to compute the sum of $\leq \frac{n}{\log n} + \log n$ elements. This sum is computed in a binary tree fashion in time $c \log n$;

3) during step 2, $ckn \log n \leq \log n$ new data arrive. We can compute the sum of these data, plus the result of step 2, in time $c \log \log n$. The computation is iterated on the $\log \log n$, $\log \log \log n, \ldots, 1$ data arrived in the previous steps.

We have $t_p = c(\log n + \log n + \log \log n + \ldots) \leq c_p \log n$.

In the above algorithm, we have assumed an upper bound $\frac{1}{ck}$ on n. Since this value coincides with the asymptote of the sequential case, we can make a fair estimate of the parallel speed-up. Proposition 1 can be reformulated for $N = n + knt$ and $P = \frac{n}{\log n}$, to state that the ratio $\frac{t}{P t_p}$ tends to ∞ for n tending to $\frac{1}{ck}$, hence, the above is a pd-algorithm. In fact, we have $t = \frac{cn}{1-ckn}$ and $t_p \leq c_p \log n$, hence $\frac{t}{P t_p} \geq \frac{c}{c_p(1-ckn)}$. Proposition 2 can also be adapted to Problem 1, showing that Brent's principle can be violated in absolute and asymptotic terms.

3 Computing with faulty processors (Paradigm 2)

The new paradigm of parallel computation considered here is based on the assumption that the PRAM processors may fail. Upon occurrence of a failure, a processor stops permanently. Therefore, the algorithm must be organized in such a way that, for any processor failure, all the pending operations can still be executed.

To make a PRAM program robust, a common target is *graceful degradation*, that is, the computation is correctly carried to an end as long as at least one processor survives [4, 6, 8]. For this purpose, the operations must be dynamically assigned to the processors still alive, with some unavoidable replication. The goal is then the minimization of the total number of operations performed, while no bound can be posed on the total running time.

Our paradigm is completely different. Assuming a known probability distribution of the processor failures, we are able to set an upper bound on the running time, with a given probability of successful termination. Indeed, bounding the running time is a common requirement in algorithm design, and is crucial in real-time systems (see section 2) and in other practical contexts. Our result is obtained at the expense of an increase of the total number of operations, due to the need of their replication over the original *fault intolerant* algorithm (i.e., a standard algorithm designed for non failing processors). As anticipated in section 1, the bounds on parallel speed-up must be revised. In particular, the scaling bound of relation (2) is modified in an intrigued and nontrivial way.

Our paradigm is as follows. Starting from any fault intolerant PRAM algorithm, we increase the total number of processors, and allocate a subset S of processors to each operation O with a schedule decided off-line. The operation O is executed concurrently by all the processors in S which are still alive (this requires a COMMON CRCW-PRAM variant). The cardinality of S is chosen to guarantee that the operation is completed with a given probability.

Let p be the probability that an arbitrary processor E_j completes the t-th step of its program, given that it has completed all the previous steps (shortly, E_j is alive when entering step t). We assume that p is a constant with respect to t and is the same for all processors. Formally, for any processor index j and time step i, define the event

$$C_i^j = \text{"Processor } E_j \text{ completes the } i\text{-th step of its program"},$$

and, for any $t > 0$ and any given j, let

$$\Pr\left(C_t^j \mid \bigcap_{i=1}^{t-1} C_i^j\right) = p. \tag{9}$$

As an additional condition, we assume that distinct processors behave independently, that is, for any choice of indices (i, j) and (h, k) with $j \neq k$, the events C_i^j and C_h^k are independent. Note that relation (9) captures the common assumption on the exponential distribution of hardware failures in a model with discrete time [10].

Consider any fault intolerant PRAM algorithm A running in time T and performing a total number X of operations. At each step t, the algorithm performs the operations O_t^k, $1 \leq k \leq X_t$, $\sum_{t=1}^{T} X_t = X$. We will allocate a *cluster* S_t^k of processors to each operation O_t^k, so that the operation is executed with at least a fixed constant probability $\bar{p}$. For $\bar{p}$ to be constant, the size of S_t^k must increase with t, because the probability that a processor in S_t^k is still alive decreases with t.

The value of $\bar{p}$ clearly influences the overall probability that the new fault tolerant algorithm $\bar{A}$ is completed successfully. Let $C_{\bar{A}}$ be the event "algorithm $\bar{A}$ is completed successfully". For $1 \leq t \leq T, 1 \leq k \leq X_t$, define the event:

$$I_t^k = \text{"No processor in } S_t^k \text{ completes } O_t^k\text{"}.$$

We have $\Pr(I_t^k) \leq 1 - \bar{p}$, therefore

$$\Pr(C_{\bar{A}}) = 1 - \Pr\left(\bigcup_{t=1}^{T} \bigcup_{k=1}^{X_t} I_t^k\right) \geq 1 - X(1 - \bar{p}) \tag{10}$$

We require that $\Pr(C_{\bar{A}}) \geq r$, for fixed r. Then it suffices that $\bar{p}$ satisfies the relation:

$$1 - X(1 - \bar{p}) \geq r. \tag{11}$$

We are now ready to determine the size s_t^k of the clusters S_t^k. For this purpose, define the event:

$$Y_t^k = \text{"at least one of the processors in } S_t^k \text{ is alive after the first } t \text{ steps"}.$$

By unfolding relation (9), we have that the probability that an arbitrary processor completes the first t steps of its program is p^t, therefore:

$$\Pr(Y_t^k) = 1 - \Pr\left(\bigcap_{h=1}^{s_t^k} \overline{\bigcap_{j=1}^{t} C_t^h}\right) = 1 - \left(1 - p^t\right)^{s_t^k}.$$

We require that, for any t and k, $\Pr(Y_t^k) \geq \bar{p}$. Then it suffices that s_t^k be such that $1 - (1 - p^t)^{s_t^k} \geq \bar{p}$, whence

$$s_t^k \geq \frac{\log_e(1 - \bar{p})}{\log_e(1 - p^t)}. \tag{12}$$

Note that the right hand side of relation (12) is independent of k. Hence all the s_t^k, $1 \le k \le X_i$, can be set to the same value s_t. It follows that the number of processors s required to complete algorithm $\bar{A}$ with probability at least r is

$$s = \max\{X_t s_t, 1 \le t \le T\}. \tag{13}$$

The above results can be applied to the solution of any problem in Paradigm 2. As an example, let us apply the paradigm to solve Problem 1 of section 2 with constant data size N, as a framework for any census problem. The problem can be solved on a P-processor PRAM, $1 \le P \le N$, by a uniform family of fault intolerant parallel algorithms $\{A_P\}$, whose computation is organized in two phases. In the first phase, the initial set of data is subdivided into P disjoint sections, one for each processor, and the sum in each section is computed sequentially in time $\lceil \frac{N}{P} \rceil - 1 \le \frac{N}{P}$. In the second phase, the processors perform a tree-like computation on the P partial results in time $\lceil \log P \rceil - 1 \le \log P$. The overall time requirement of A_P is $\frac{N}{P} + \log P$, while the total number of operations, including the ones of idling processors, is $X = N + P$.

If the processors may fail, each algorithm A_P must be transformed into a corresponding fault tolerant algorithm $\bar{A}_P$. Recall that A_P and $\bar{A}_P$ require the same time, since the operations of $\bar{A}_P$ are the same as in A_P. However, each operation O_t^k is executed in $\bar{A}_P$ in parallel by all the processors still alive in cluster S_t^k. In the framework of Paradigm 2, $\bar{A}_P$ requires a number $s(P)$ of processors given in relation (13). Through relations (11) and (12), we have that $s(P)$ depends on the required probability r of successful completion. As customary in randomized algorithms, we set $r \ge 1 - \frac{1}{N^c}$, for a given constant c, independently of the value of P.

From relation (11) we have $1 - X(1 - \bar{p}) = 1 - (N + P)(1 - \bar{p}) \ge 1 - \frac{1}{N^c}$, whence

$$\bar{p} \ge 1 - \frac{1}{N^c(N + P)}. \tag{14}$$

From relation (12) we then derive the number of processors $s_t^k = s_t$ for operation O_t^k, namely:

$$s_t = \frac{\log_e(N^c(N + P))}{\log_e \frac{1}{1 - p^t}}. \tag{15}$$

Given that $\log_e \frac{1}{1 - p^t} \ge p^t$ for any $t > 0$, and recalling that $P \le N$, we have $s_t \le (c + 2)\log_e N \left(\frac{1}{p}\right)^t$. To apply relation (13) we still have to determine the values of X_t for the two phases of the algorithm. We have $X_t = P$, $1 \le t \le \frac{N}{P}$ (first phase), and $X_{N/P+i} = \frac{P}{2^i}$, $1 \le i \le \log P$. Therefore:

$$s(P) \le \max \left\{ \begin{array}{ll} (c + 2)P \left(\frac{1}{p}\right)^t \log_e N, & 1 \le t \le \frac{N}{P} \\ (c + 2)P \left(\frac{1}{p}\right)^{\frac{N}{P}} \left(\frac{1}{2p}\right)^i \log_e N, & 1 \le i \le \log P \end{array} \right\} \tag{16}$$

From relation (16), we derive with easy calculations:

Proposition 4. *For any* $p > \frac{1}{2}, c > 0$ *and* $P \leq N$, *Problem 1 with constant data size* N *admits a family of fault tolerant algorithms with success probability* $\geq 1 - \frac{1}{N^c}$, *requiring time* $\frac{N}{P} + \log P$ *and a number of processors* $s(P) \leq (c+2)P \left(\frac{1}{p}\right)^{N/P} \log_e N$.

Note that the assumption $p > \frac{1}{2}$ is plausible, since p is the probability that a processor completes a single step. For example, for $P = N$, algorithm $\bar{A}_P$ solves the problem in time $\log N$ with probability $\geq 1 - \frac{1}{N^c}$, with $O(cN \log N)$ processors.

Proposition 4 puts into evidence an unexpected property of our paradigm. As the number of processors P of the fault intolerant algorithm A_P increases, hence the running time T of A_P and $\bar{A}_P$ decreases, the number of processors $s(P)$ of $\bar{A}_P$ may increase or decrease for proper values of p and N. Hence, the total work $s(P)T$ may decrease for increasing P, against all the bounds on parallel speed-up. For example note that, for fixed p, we have $s(\frac{N}{\log_{1/p} N}) = \Omega(cN^2)$, from (12) and (14), and $s(N) = O(cN \log N)$ from Proposition 4, that is $s(N) = o(s(\frac{N}{\log N}))$.

In fact, formula (1) should now express a $\leq$ relation between $s(P)T(P, N)$ and $s(1)T(1, N)$, which can hold in any direction for proper values of p and N (note that the fault tolerant version $\bar{A}_1$ of a sequential algorithm A_1, requires $s(1) > 1$ processors). Against a fair expectation from relation (1), we have that $s(P)T(P, N) \leq s(1)T(1, N)$ for $P \to N \to \infty$ and fixed p, thereby proving the inherent power of the parallel solution.

4 Computing in a secure environment (Paradigm 3)

The theory of computing relies on the assumption that computable problems can be solved sequentially. There are situations, however, where the intrinsic power of parallel computation may be necessary. A classical request is that an action be performed by several distinct agents to certify the result reliably. A similar request may be raised for security reasons. Different schemes of computation thus arising are grouped in Paradigm 3.

For a given computation, consider a *Data Dependency DAG* (DDD) of V vertices, where vertices correspond to a single operations and edges specify data dependencies [1]. The set of vertices is partitioned into *strata* $S_0, \ldots, S_{h-1}$, such that u is in S_i if i is the length of the longest path from a source to u (source vertices are in S_0). The resulting structure is called SDDD. Let $P \geq 1$ processors be available, and assume that each operation can be performed by any processor in unit time. A *scheduling* of SDDD is an assignment of a processor $q(u)$ and a time $t(u)$ to each vertex u such that:

1. $q(u) \neq q(v)$ for $t(u) = t(v)$;
2. $t(u) < t(v)$ for $u \in S_i$, $v \in S_j$, $i < j$.

If $P \geq \max\{|S_i|, 0 \leq i \leq h - 1\}$, there is a straightforward scheduling with $t(u) = i$ for each $u \in S_i$, $0 \leq i \leq h - 1$. The *duration* of the scheduling (i.e., the time required by the computation) is h and is obviously optimal. For $P < \max\{|S_i|, 0 \leq i \leq h-1\}$, each stratum S_i can be divided into $\left\lceil \frac{|S_i|}{P} \right\rceil$ new strata, and the above scheduling applied to the resulting SDDD. The duration is then $\leq \frac{V}{P} + h$, distant from optimal within a factor of 2.

We now introduce our new paradigm. Let $Q = \{q_1, \ldots, q_P\}$ be the set of processors, and $\{v_1, \ldots, v_s\}$ be an arbitrary stratum of SDDD. Any single operation v_i must be executed by a subset of processors, according to the following design rules:

A1: an integer n_i, $0 < n_i \leq P$, is assigned to v_i, with the intention that n_i arbitrary processors must be employed;

A2: a fixed subset $Q_i \subseteq Q$ is specified for v_i;

B1: the processors assigned to v_i may operate at different times;

B2: all the processors assigned to v_i must operate at the same time.

We construct a scheduling of SDDD by scheduling the operations of each stratum $S = \{v_1, \ldots, v_s\}$ independently of the other strata, under the following combinations of the above rules. Let d be the number of parallel steps required for S:

A1,B1 *Easy.* An optimal scheduling is trivially attained by a linear time assignment procedure. We have $d = \left\lceil \sum_{i=1,s} n_i / P \right\rceil$.

A1,B2 *Difficult.* The scheduling is equivalent to bin-packing, where the n_i's are to be packed into bins of size P. Applying known bin-packing heuristics we attain $d < \left\lceil 2 \sum_{i=1,s} n_i / P \right\rceil$, and d is within a constant factor from optimal.

A2,B1 *Easy.* The scheduling can be reformulated as a sequence of max-flow problems on a bipartite graph built on the sets S and Q, with edges $[v_i, q_j]$ for $q_j \in Q_i$, augmented with a source and a sink vertex. However, this max-flow problems are particularly easy, and can be collectively solved in time $\sum_{i=1,s} |Q_i|$, by a linear scan of the Q_i's. We have $d = \max\{k_i, 1 \leq i \leq P\}$, where k_i is the number of occurrences of q_i in $Q_1, \ldots, Q_s$. Note that d is clearly optimum.

A2,B2 *Open.* The scheduling of S reduces to an Open Shop Scheduling with tasks of length 0 or 1 [3]. A (non evaluated) heuristic can be constructed as an extension of the First Fit heuristic for bin-packing, with proper additional constraints on the selection of the subsets of processors to be allocated in each bin.

5   Conclusion and extensions

The main goal of this paper is to stimulate a discussion on parallel algorithm design in non conventional situations, where the increase in the number of processors may result in a drastic improvement of performance. We have restricted our analysis to three computational paradigms. Variations and alternatives to our schemes are possible and desirable. Referring to Paradigm 1, we may assume that a problem has fixed data size, but variations of the data values occur with time. An algorithm must now be capable of changing the effect of its previous operations which involve a datum D, if D is later modified. A theory similar to the one for d-algorithms can be developed.

Paradigm 1 is unsatisfactory if the data arrived after completion of the algorithm cannot be ignored. Rather, the stream of data must be considered without an end, as required for example in operating systems and data base maintenance [7]. The time can be divided in slots of length T. Each slot consists of an updating phase, during which the data accumulated in the previous slot are treated, followed by a free phase where other routines may be run. If t and t_p are the sequential and parallel times to solve a problem, define the free time gain $G = \frac{T-t_p}{T-t}$. Unexpectedly G may assume any value between 1 and ∞ for certain families of problems and for proper values of the parameters.

Several variations of Paradigm 2 are significant. In particular, we may consider an on-line allocation strategy such that, at each time step, the subset of processors assigned to each operation is chosen at random, or is taken deterministically from the set of processors that are still alive [8]. The analysis of these cases, and the implications on the bounds of parallel speed-up, are challenging open problems.

Finally, Paradigm 3 is centered on scheduling problems, which have been approached independently on single SDDD strata. A global optimization strategy on SDDD as a whole is likeley to yield better results.

References

[1] A. Aggarwal and A.K. Chandra. Communication Complexity of PRAMs. *Proc. 15th Int. Colloquium on Automata, Languages and Programming* (1988) 1-18.

[2] S.G. Akl, M. Cosnard and A.G. Ferreira. Data-movement-intensive problems: two folk theorems in parallel computation revisited. *Theoretical Computer Science* **95** (1992) 323-337.

[3] M.R. Garey and D.S. Johnson. *Computers and Intractability*. Freeman, San Francisco, 1978.

[4] P.C. Kanellakis and A.A. Shvartsman. Efficient parallel algorithms can be made robust. In *Proc. 8th Annual ACM Symp. on Principles of Distributed Computing* (1989) 211-222.

[5] R.M. Karp and V. Ramachandran A survey of parallel algorithms for shared memory machines. In *Handbook of Theoretical Computer Science* North Holland, New York NY (1990) 869-941.

[6] Z.M. Kedem, K.V. Palem and P.G. Spirakis. Efficient robust parallel computations. In *Proc. 22nd Annual ACM Symp. on Theory of Computing* (1990) 590-599.

[7] F. Luccio and L. Pagli. *The p-shovelers problem. (Computing with time-varying data).* *SIGACT News* **23**, 2 (1992) 72-75

[8] C. Martel, R. Subramonian, A. Park. Asynchronous PRAMs are (almost) as good as synchronous prams. In *Proc. 31st Symp. on Foundations of Computer Science* (1990) 590-599.

[9] W. Paul. On line simulation of $k+1$ tapes by k tapes requires nonlinear time. *Information and Control* **53** (1982) 1-8.

[10] K.S. Trivedi. *Probability and statistics with reliability, queueing, and computer science applications.* Prentice-Hall, Englewood Cliffs NJ (1982).

[11] U. Vishkin. Can parallel algorithms enhance serial implementation?. *SIGACT News* **22**, 4 (1991) 63.

Scalable Parallel Computers and Scalable Parallel Codes: From Theory to Practice

Marc Snir

IBM T. J. Watson Research Center

P. O. Box 218, Yorktown Heights, NY 10598, USA

snir@watson.ibm.com

1 Introduction

Massively parallel computing technology offers two outstanding promises: The promise for top performance that exceeds the top performance of conventional supercomputers, at a fraction of the cost; and the promise for linear scaling of performance as function of cost, over a very wide range. This last aspect of parallel computing is captured by the idea of *scalable parallel computing*. The computer industry has thrived since the early days of the IBM S/360 by offering the same basic architecture in wide range of models, with different cost/performance tradeoffs. However, never before was there the opportunity for a linear trade-off between cost and performance over a range spanning more than three orders of magnitude, with one basic technology. This opportunity, if fully realized, could revolutionize the computer industry.

Clearly, a massively parallel processor (MPP) assembled from a thousand conventional microprocessors is, by some measure, a thousand times more powerful than a conventional microprocessor. But can this computing power be effectively harnessed? Will such machine deliver to the user a thousand times the performance of a uniprocessor? Can this performance improvement be achieved without significant redesign of the software? And can this be done while keeping the overall cost of the parallel machine no higher than a thousand time the cost of the uniprocessor?

An affirmative answer to the questions of the last paragraph requires the following three ingredients.

Scalable architectures: Multiprocessor architectures with cost and performance linear in the number of nodes, for each significant performance parameter.

Scalable algorithms: Algorithms with performance that improves linearly in the number of nodes used.

Scalable programs: Programs that express scalable algorithms.

We shall focus in this paper on the last two topics.

2 Scalable Algorithms – Computation

2.1 Performance of Parallel Algorithms

We shall focus initially on the computation aspect of parallelism, using the shared-memory PRAM model. Access to shared memory as assumed to take constant time.

The time complexity of an algorithm in this model is a function of two parameters: n, the problem size, and p, the number of processors. We denote by $T(n, p)$ the running time of an algorithm for problem size n and p processors.

Consider the following two sorting algorithms: The first is based on an emulation of a bitonic sorting network by a parallel machine, with one processor allocated to each comparator. Each

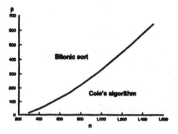

Figure 1: Phase Diagram for Parallel Sorting

comparator is fed by two sorted lists of size $n/2p$ and outputs the top half and bottom half of the merged list [2]. This algorithm has running time

$$T(n,p) = \frac{n \log n}{p} + \frac{n}{2p} \log^2 p.$$

The second algorithm is the elegant but somewhat complex algorithm due to Cole [3]. It has runing time

$$T(n,p) = \frac{5n \log n}{p} + 3 \log n.$$

(In both case we consider only comparisons.) Which is better? If we ignore the second term in Cole's algorithm then we find that Cole's algorithm is better when $8 \log n \leq \log^2 p$, worse otherwise. Thus, each algorithm can dominate the other, for different values of n and p. This behavior can be illustrated, as shown in Figure 1 by a *phase diagram* that indicates the superior algorithm for each combination of values of n and p. A good sorting routine would use a *polyalgorithm*, resorting to either of the two sorting methods in the domain where its performance is superior. This is not altogether a surprising phenomenon, as it occurs for sequential algorithms, too: Strassen's matrix multiply algorithm performs better than the n^3 algorithm for large values of n, worse for small values.

A polyalgorithm for matrix multiplication on a sequential machine will decide which method to use according to problem size. We are accustomed to see programs parameterized by problem size – there is no surprise in seeing in the code a branch based on problem size. A polyalgorithm for parallel sorting will need to choose the appropriate method, according to the current values of n and p. Thus, machine size has to be one of the program parameters, if the code has to port over machines of different sizes. It cannot be hidden, cannot be dealt only by the compiler or the operating system, since an *algorithmic* decision, namely which of two sorting methods to use, depend on the value of p.

To the same extent that code that ports over a range of problem sizes need to be cognizant

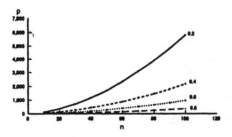

Figure 2: equi-efficiency contours for Gaussian elimination algorithm

of the problem size, code that ports over a range of machine sizes need to be cognizant of the machine size.

Note that, for any values of n and p, the running time of Cole's algorithm is at most worse by a constant factor that the running time of the second sorting algorithm. Thus, in a theoretical sense, this algorithm can be said to be superior overall. But constant factors cannot be ignored, in practice. Furthermore, one can easily derive examples where each algorithm can be arbitrarily faster than the other.

2.2 Scalable Parallel Algorithms

Intuitively, an algorithm is scalable if p processors improve running time by a factor of p, as compared to a sequential algorithm. Let $T(n)$ be the running time of a sequential algorithm for the same problem. The *speedup* of the algorithm is the ratio $T(n)/T(n, p)$ and its *efficiency* is the ratio $T(n)/(p \cdot T(n, p))$. An algorithm *scales* if the speedup achieved with p processors is close to p or, equivalently, the efficiency is close to one. We shall assume that $T(n)$ is the running time of the best known sequential algorithm.

Clearly, a parallel algorithm cannot preserve constant efficiency for all values of n and p. We can fix an efficiency threshold, say 50%, and consider which values of n and p achieve efficiency above this threshold. The algorithm is scalable if that efficiency is achieved for all "interesting" values of p and n. Figure 2 shows equi-efficiency contours for the obvious parallel version of the Gaussian elimination algorithm. We find that an efficiency of 50% is achieved on 1,000 processors or less by Gaussian elimination on matrices of size ≥ 80. Smaller problems are unlikely to be of much interest, and the performance of the machine on smaller problems is unlikely to be critical. Thus, for all practical purposes, the algorithm is scalable (this assumes, of course, that our model is adequate – an assumption we shall revisit latter).

A fixed efficiency can be preserved by increasing problem size, as machine size is increased. A natural choice is to assume that problem size increases linearly with the number of processors. This choice makes pragmatic sense: Often parallel machines are constrained by the size of their memories (because of slow I/O) and are used to solve the largest problem that can fit in the machine memory. The amount of memory used is most often proportional to problem size, and the amount of memory available increases linearly in the number of processors.

An algorithm *scales with fixed size* if

$$T(mp)/(pT(mp,p)) \geq \epsilon ,$$

for some fixed positive m and ϵ.

An algorithm scales with fixed size if

$$T(n, n) = O(T(n)/n);$$

up to n processors can be used efficiently to run the algorithm. This is not achievable, in general, when sequential complexity $T(n)$ is linear – it would require constant time parallel complexity. For the purpose of theoretical study we propose the following amended definition: An algorithm *scales with quasi fixed size* if

$$T(f(p)p)/(pT(f(p)p,p)) \geq \epsilon ,$$

for some fixed positive ϵ and a polylog bounded function $f()$. Thus, we allow a modest increase in problem size, when machine size increases.

An algorithm scales with quasi fixed size if

$$T(n, n/f(n)) = O(T(n)f(n)/n),$$

for some polylogarithmically bounded function $f()$. Up to $n/polylog(n)$ processors can be used efficiently to run the algorithm.

Another natural choice is to assume that the total compute time is to stay constant. The pragmatic motivation for such choice is that there are often external constraints on the time one can devote to a computation, based on what is reasonable turnaround time for various users of a computer. For example, NASA bases its analysis of its compute requirements on the assumption that a simulation done as part of engineering design should take no more than 15 minutes, and a simulation done as part of scientific research should take no more than 200 hours [5].

An algorithm scales with quasi fixed time iff it can be solved efficiently in polylogarithmic time. Note that both definitions (constant size and constant time scaling) coincide for problems with linear sequential complexity.

A well-known conjecture claims that P-complete problems do not belong to the class NC, the class of problems that can be solved in parallel in polylogarithmic time. Some P-complete problems have linear time algorithms (e.g., lexicographic first maximal independent set). If the conjecture is true, then such problems cannot be solved by an algorithm that scales with quasi fixed size.

Even problems in NC may fail to qualify, as a scalable algorithm must be efficient. Single source shortest path, reacheability in graphs, and many other related problems can be solved in linear time sequentially; they can be solved in parallel in polylogarithmic time, but not efficiently so. It has been conjectured that one cannot obtain for these problems an efficient, polylogarithmic time parallel algorithm (the *transitive closure bottleneck*). If this conjecture stands, then these problems cannot be solved by algorithms that scale with quasi constant size.

2.3 Scalable Codes

How can we write codes that express scalable algorithms? We have shown that p, the number of processors, must be an explicit parameter of scalable parallel algorithms. This, because the choice of the right solution method may depend in a nontrivial manner on the relation between n, the problem size, and p. However, it is conceivable that this is a discrete choice between few competing methods, whereas each of these methods can be coded independently of p.

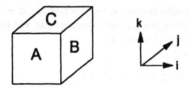

Figure 3: Graphical Representation of Matrix Product Computation

2.3.1 Implicit Parallelism

Consider the case of matrix product. The standard n^3 algorithm is expressed by the following sequential Fortran program.

```
DO J = 1, N
  DO I= 1, N
    C(I,J) = 0
    DO K=1, N
      C(I,J) = C(I,J) + A(I,K)*B(K,J)
    END DO
  END DO
END DO
```

Any decent compiler will identify that the two outer loops are independent, and derive a parallel algorithm with running time $O(n^3/p+n)$. A reasonable compiler will also have knowledge of parallel linear recurrence solving, which will allow to parallelize the inner loop, and derive a parallel algorithm with running time $O(n^3/p+\log n)$. The number of processors p need not be explicit in the program, and will be bound at run-time. We can consider the triple nested Fortran loop as a *specification* of the matrix product computation: The code specifies the operations to be executed and the dependencies among these operations. A parallelizing compiler derives a minimal equivalent specification from that code, thus allowing code moves. The compiler can derive an efficient parallel algorithm from this Fortran code because the code is easy to analyze. The computation is *oblivious*: The computation graph depends on n, but not on the matrix entries. The graph has a simple structure: The iteration space is a 3-dimensional cube of size n^3, with one add-multiply computed at each node; see Figure 3. Entries of A are broadcast in the j dimension; entries of B are broadcast in the i dimension; and sums are accumulated in the k dimension. The partition indicated in Figure 4 (a) corresponds to a distribution of the outer loop; this achieves a running time of $O(n^3/p+n^2)$; partition (b) in the same figure corresponds to a distribution of both outer loops; it achieves running time $O(n^3/p+n)$; an improved running time of $O(n^3/p+\log(n))$ is achieved by partition (c), where the sum accumulation is also parallelized.

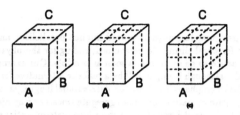

Figure 4: Partition of Matrix Computation

2.3.2 Explicit Parallelism with Virtual Processors

Consider, by contrast, Cole's sorting algorithm. This algorithm is non oblivious: The set of comparisons performed and the dependencies between these comparisons depend on the values of the entries. The partition of comparisons to processors is a nontrivial part of the algorithm. Thus, it is highly unlikely that Cole's algorithm could be derived by a compiler from a sequential sorting algorithm. Explicit parallelism must be used to express this algorithm. The algorithm is efficient for any number of processors up to $n/\log(n)$. Given an algorithm written for q processors, a compiler can easily derive an algorithm for $p < q$ processors that emulates efficiently the first one. Thus, it is acceptable to write the algorithm for a problem dependent number of virtual processors, and rely on the compiler (or the run-time system) to map this algorithm on the actual number of physical processors.

2.3.3 Explicit Parallelism with Physical Processors

Consider the sorting algorithm derived from a bitonic network. The algorithm, for p processors, is derived from the emulation of a bitonic network with $2p$ lines. It is hard to see how this can be expressed in a manner that is independent of p: The emulation of a network with n lines will yield a much less efficient algorithm, with order $n\log^2 n$ comparisons. Thus, it would seem in this case that p must be an explicit parameter of the code.

A counter argument can be made that this predicament is of our own make: The bitonic sort algorithm we used to derive a parallel sort is not efficient, unlike Cole's algorithm. However, this algorithm can outperforms Cole's algorithms by a significant (constant) factor, for some values of n and p. While constant factors are not a major point of interest in theoretical algorithmic analysis, they can be very significant, in practice.

2.4 Conclusion

The evolution in parallel programming languages is toward implicit parallelism, and toward virtual parallelism: Explicitly coding for parallelism is to be avoided; coding for the physical machine size is a low-level programming practice to be overcome as soon as possible. Our examples indicate this may not be possible in general – although it might well be a realistic alternative for many numerical codes with simple structure. Much emphasis is now put on *data-parallel* languages, where parallelism is implied from the use of aggregate operations on data aggregate (mostly array operations on data arrays); parallelism is derived from parallel execution of these aggregate operations or derived from a data partition. Our examples imply that control parallelism, where parallelism is derived from explicit user allocation of operations to (virtual or physical) processors is necessary to express certain algorithms.

3 Scalable Algorithms – Communication Bandwidth

The algorithmic analysis outlined in the last section ignores one important access of parallel computing, namely communication. It is not practical to construct a shared memory memory with hundreds of ports, that would offer bandwidth and access time per port similar to the bandwidth and access time of a single port memory; conflicting memory accesses will further impede performance. Thus, communication has to be promoted to the rank of a "first order" computational resource, to be dealt explicitly by the user.

We refine our PRAM model, so as to allow us to consider the impact of limited global bandwidth on computations. In the LPRAM model, the shared memory is physically distributed across processors. A memory can supply one word per cycle to the local processor, but only one word per b cycles to a remote processor. (the global memory has bandwidth b^{-1} per processor; e.g., b may be the ratio between the width of the local memory bus and the width of channels to remote memories). We shall assume that the bandwidth b^{-1} does not change as the number of processors is increased.

We can assume that a parallel computation consists of separate computation steps, where only local accesses occur, and communication steps where each memory is accessed by a remote processor. We denote by $C(n, p)$ the number of communication steps with input of size n and p processors. The total execution time is $T(n, p) + bC(n, p)$. The ratio $T(n, p)/C(n, p)$ is defined to be the *locality* of the algorithm. The algorithm is compute bound if the locality is $\geq b$, communication bound, otherwise.

Suppose that the computation time of an algorithm scales with fixed size. The total execution time scales, independent of b, only if communication time increases no faster than computation time (i.e., locality does not decrease). The following condition has to be fulfilled:

$$C(mp, p)/C(m) = O(T(mp, p)/T(m)),$$

or, equivalently,

$$C(mp, p) = O((mT(mp))/(pT(m))).$$

Consider the matrix product algorithms schematically shown in Figure 4. Communication essentially occurs at the boundaries between subcubes. There are p subcubes. If the subcubes are chosen to be of equal shape, then the total communication is $\Omega(n^2p)$ for partition (a), $\Omega(n^2\sqrt{p})$ for (b) and $\Omega(n^2\sqrt[3]{p})$ for (c). We shall show that communication can be "load balanced", resulting in a total communication time of $\Omega(n^2)$ for (a) $\Omega(n^2/\sqrt{p})$ for (b), and $\Omega(n^2/p^{2/3})$ for (c). Computation time is $\Omega(n^3/p)$. One can see that algorithm (a) has decreasing locality if problem size n^2 scales linearity in p; the locality of algorithm (b) is preserved, and the the locality of algorithm (c) increases. In fact, the locality in algorithm (c) is preserved when, more stringently, the algorithm is scaled with fixed time (i.e., n^3, rather than n^2, is proportional to p).

Consider a recursive algorithm such that a problem of size mp can be solved efficiently on p processors by solving subproblems of size m, each on one processor; assume that the bulk of the computation and communication occurs in the solution of the subproblems. Then the number of subproblems solved is $O(T(mp)/T(m))$ and the total communication is $O(mT(mp)/T(m))$. If the communication can be load balanced then the algorithm fulfils the last condition. This covers the case of algorithms such as FFT, matrix product using either the n^3 algorithm or Strassen's product, and many others. Also, algorithms with linear sequential running time (no locality) trivially fulfils the last condition.

It seems that, whenever a scalable algorithm can be developed for a problem, one can also make sure that communication scales correctly. Tradeoffs between communication and computation occur provably, for artificially constructed examples [1]. They seem to occur in practice, as often different methods are used when communication is expensive. Thus, b has to be an explicit parameter in algorithm design, if different machines have widely different bandwidth. One can hope that market pressure will establish rules of thumbs for a "balanced parallel architecture" (e.g., one byte bandwidth for each flop), that will lead to roughly similar values of b on most machines.

3.1 Scalable Codes

3.1.1 Implicit Parallelism

Consider the matrix product algorithm implied by partition (b) in Figure 4. Assume, for simplicity that $p = n^2$, so that each processor $P_{I,J}$ is assigned to the computation of one entry $C(I,J)$ (the general case is obtained by replacing entries with submatrices). The computation is described by the following pseudocode, that is executed by each processor $P_{I,J}$. (We use Fortran 90 notation for array sections: A(I,:) denotes row I of array A.)

```
Read  A(I,:);
Read  B(:,J);
C(I,J) = DOT_PRODUCT(A(I,:), B(:,J))
```

A naive implementation of this parallel algorithm will lead to conflicting memory accesses, where each entry is simultaneously accessed by $\sqrt{p}$ processors. These conflicting accesses are prevented by skewing each of the matrices A and B, and shifting each vector circularly among the processors that access it; at any time, each processor holds only one entry of A and one entry of B. This is the well known systolic algorithm for matrix product [6]. Assume that all three matrices are distributed, with entry (I,J) at processor $P_{I,J}$; further assume that the code is compiled using the *owner compute rule*: assignments are executed by the processor where data resides. Then the systolic matrix product algorithm can be expressed as follows, in Fortran 90, using array operations. (The function CSHIFT performs a circular shift on a vector or on the indicated dimension of an array.)

```
REAL, DIMENSION(N,N) :: A, B, C

!HPF$ ALIGN WITH A :: B, C
!HPF$ DISTRIBUTE(BLOCK, BLOCK) :: A

DO K = 2, N
   CALL CSHIFT( A(K,:), K-1)
   CALL CSHIFT( B(:,K), K-1)
END DO

C = 0

DO K = 1, N
  C = C + A*B
  CALL CSHIFT( A, 1, 1)
  CALL CSHIFT( B, 1, 2)
END DO
```

Fortran 90 does not provide a mechanism for enforcing a particular distribution of arrays. High Performance Fortran is an extension to Fortran 90 that provides such mechanism. The two comment lines starting with !HPF$ indicate that all three arrays are aligned and distributed into sub-blocks; this yields the desired layout. The HPF directives effect the mapping of data and, indirectly, the mapping of computation to processors. However, they do not affect the semantics of the Fortran program. In this case, these are simple, declarative directives. The approach can be extended to cover more complex, executable directives, that control data mapping algorithmically [4].

3.1.2   Explicit Parallelism

Consider, again, Cole's sorting algorithm. This algorithm can be implemented to run on the LPRAM model with optimal communication time $C(n,p) = O(n \log n/(p \log(n/p))$ [1]. This, however, requires additional algorithmic work to redistribute data dynamically. This redistribution work depends very specifically on p, the number of processors (data is resdistributed among processors after each $log n(n/p)$ stages of Cole's algorithm); the algorithm has to be coded to the number of physical processors.

Suppose Cole's algorithm is coded for a problem dependent number of processors, say n, which are then emulated by p physical processors. There is $\Omega(n \log n)$ total communication between virtual processors. Communication between virtual processors that map to the same physical processor results in no physical communication. Is it possible to organize the algorithm and the mapping so that the remaining communication will be optimally $O(n \log n/\log(n/p))$? If this goal is achievable then it would motivate a programming style similar to that illustrated by our HPF fragment code, in the previous section: Code is developed for a problem dependent number of processors; directives are then used to map virtual processors onto physical nodes. This directives may be executable, and may incorporate nontrivial algorithmics; however, they do not affect the semantics of the unadorned code, only its performance.

Acknowledgements

This presentation was inspired by discussions with several participants of the 92 Gordon Research Conference on Software,Tools and Libraries for Concurrent Supercomputing.

References

[1] Aggarwal A. , Chandra A. K. and Snir M. , Communication Complexity of PRAMs. *Theoretical Computer Science 71* (1990), 3-28.

[2] Baudet, G. and Stevenson, D. Optimal sorting algorithms for parallel computers. *IEEE Trans. Comput. C-27* (1978), 84-87.

[3] Cole, R.. Parallel merge sort. *SIAM J. Comput. 17* (1988), 770-785.

[4] Fox G. *et. al.* . Fortran D language specification. Tech. Rep. COMP TR90079, Computer Science, Rice Univ. , March 1991.

[5] Peterson, V. L.
et. al. . Supercomputing requirements for selected disciplines important to aerospace. *Proc. IEEE 77* (1989) 1038-1055.

[6] Ullman J. D. Computational aspects of VLSI. Computer Science Press, 1984.

A Framework for Analyzing Locality and Portability Issues in Parallel Computing

(Extended Abstract)

Abhiram Ranade

Computer Science Division
University of California
Berkeley, CA 94720

How to reduce communication overhead is a central concern in parallel computation. Indeed, most applications that run well on existing machines do so because they have locality – processors work on local data most of the time, and require data from remote processors only infrequently. Much work has gone into organizing programs so that they have locality; and notable success has been acheived when problems have regular, predictable data access patterns, such as in linear algebra (e.g. dense matrix multiplication). High performance is usually acheived by low level programming and customizing the algorithm to fit the interconnection topology of the parallel computer. Program portability is typically lost. For general, unstructured applications, it is completely unclear whether we can acheive high performance, even if we are willing to customize algorithms to architectures and give up portability.

Another approach is to ignore locality issues at an algorithmic level, and instead build parallel computers using networks that are so powerful that frequent interprocessor communication can be efficiently supported. This frees the programmer/algorithm designer to use models such as PRAMs which are easier to work with; and the powerful communications network guarantees that the PRAM algorithm can be efficiently *simulated* on the parallel computer. Most of the existing parallel computers do not have communication hardware capable of efficiently simulating PRAM programs, and hence can be thought of as favoring the first approach; while some machines currently being designed, such as the Saarbrucken PRAM[1, 2] and the TERA[5] provide very powerful communication networks which will enable efficient PRAM simulation and hence be able to free the programmer of worrying about the issue of communication locality. This approach provides portability implicilty, since the programmer always worries only about a single model: the PRAM.

The goal of this paper is to explore the first approach at length. If we can determine that it is a viable approach, then we potentially save the cost of a powerful communications network that is required by the second approach. The principal questions we consider are (1) Can we formally define what it means to algorithmically exploit locality? (2) Are there inherently nonlocal problems which cannot be efficiently solved in parallel without fast communication networks? (3) If we can determine that a given problem may possess locality, are there algorithmic techniques that allow us to exploit the locality in implementations on real machines? (4) Can we write portable parallel programs that exploit locality?

* Supported in part by NSF-DARPA grant # CCR-9005448 and Air Force Office of Scientific Research, Grant # F49620-90-C-0029.

0.1 Overview and Summary

In this paper, we outline an approach for answering these questions. This preliminary version of the paper only presents the main ideas in a somewhat informal manner. We begin in section 1 with a description of the different architectural/programming models we consider, and conclude in section 5 by examining the implications of the ideas described. The paper has three main parts summarized below.

0.2 Inherently Nonlocal Problems

In section 2 we define a formal measure for the inherent or *gross locality* of a problem. Our measure is related to the well studied notion of communication complexity, and enables us to show that several simple problems (e.g. sparse graph connectivity, parallel expression evaluation[16]) are inherently nonlocal. This result is very general, and applies to implementations on all parallel computers, and for all values of *parallel slackness*[21], the ratio of the problem size to the number of processors, also referred to as the *virtual processor ratio*. In particular, our result shows that for several interesting problems the best strategy on *any parallel computer* and for *any parallel slackness* is to use a simulation of PRAM algorithms for these problems.

0.3 Problems In Which Locality can be exploited

In section 3 we show that there are many problems in which it is in fact possible to exploit locality. While locality exploitation techniques are well known for algorithms in which the dataflow pattern is regular and known beforehand, the problems we consider here relate to irregular, and often even dynamic data structures. In particular, this means that by using appropriate algorithmic techniques it is possible to acheive efficiencies as high as those obtainable on PRAMS[2] on sparse processor networks.

Several of these problems, however, possess only limited locality, e.g. determining the convex hull of points in a plane, searching data structures in parallel. It is possible to get efficient implementations for these problems only on relatively powerful communication networks, e.g. a Butterfly. On weaker communication networks such as a mesh, we show that it is impossible to acheive linear speedup for these problems without having exponentially large (in the number of processors) parallel slackness.

0.4 How to develop portable parallel algorithms that exploit locality

Much work has been done on simulating one model of parallel computation on another and using such simulations it is possible (automatically, if only in theory) to port algorithms developed for one model to another, e.g. Butterfly network algorithms to shuffle-exchange networks, or PRAM algorithms to meshes. However, these simulations typically do not preserve efficiency. For example, for many problems we can develop a more efficient mesh algorithm by working directly on a mesh, rather than by simulating (efficient) PRAM or Butterfly algorithms.

---

[2] Note that we cannot improve upon PRAM efficiencies, since any reasonable parallel computation model can be simulated on a PRAM with constant (essentially unit) slowdown.

Our notion of gross locality of a problem precisely outlines the circumstances under which simulations of one model on another will give efficient algorithms. In fact, as we will demonstrate, for each problem we can designate a *native model* such that once we get efficient implementations of the problem on its native model, we can use simulations to port it to other models. If we have efficient simulations between models (which we do), we will be guaranteed that the algorithm obtained by simulating the algorithm from the native model cannot be improved. So for instance, we shall show that the native model for the convex hull problem is the Butterfly. If we can find an efficient Butterfly algorithm (which we can), it is sufficient to simulate the Butterfly algorithm on a mesh (or any other model); the simulated algorithm cannot be improved upon by any other (possibly customized) mesh algorithm.

Informally, our conclusion is that it is possible to write portable parallel programs – unfortunately, there is not a universal parallel computing model that we can use. Each problem has its own native model, but since we have mechanisms for porting from that model we do have (automatic) portability. We discuss these ideas in section 4.

1 Models

In this paper we consider two classes of parallel computation models. The first class is that of PRAMs. Since we will only use simulations of PRAM algorithms, and since the cost of simulating PRAMs on networks is the same for different PRAM variants, we will typically consider the most powerful variant: CRCW PRAMs augmented with the Multiprefix capability[20]. Often, however, simpler variants will suffice.

The second class of models is that of sparse processor networks. In fact, these will be our models of realistic machines. All the network algorithms we mention use standard network models, i.e. processors connected together by a bounded-degree network, e.g. Butterflies, Shuffle-exchanges, fat-trees, constant dimension grids. Following standard practice, we will assume that in a single time step, each processor can execute a single (standard) instruction, or exchange a single word of data with a neighbor. We will assume a word to be $\theta(\log p)$ bits wide, with p the number of processors. Since we will assume that the problem size n is no more than polynomially larger, a word is also $\theta(\log n)$ bits wide.

For the purpose of proving lower bounds, we will characterize processor networks using essentially just a single parameter called the *relative bisection bandwidth*. Let $B(p)$ denote the bisection bandwidth, i.e. the minimum number of words transmitted in unit time across any bisection of the network. The relative bisection bandwidth, denoted by $b(p)$ is simply $B(p)/p$. For instance, the relative bisection bandwidth for a standard butterfly is $\theta(1/\log p)$. We also allow non-standard networks, e.g. networks in which not all vertices have processors, or networks in which channels are bit-wide. For instance a Butterfly with bit-wide channels has relative bisection $\theta(1/\log^2 p)$. We will define the relative bisection of the PRAM to be 1.

Intuitively, networks with larger relative bisection bandwidth are more powerful. This intuition is backed by simulation between models[8, 7, 15]. We allow deterministic as well as randomized simulations. Typically, we find that a model i with higher relative bisection bandwidth b_i can simulate a single (arbitrary) step of model

j with lower relative bisection bandwidth b_j with constant slowdown. However, in general, simulating an arbitrary step of model i must require at least b_i/b_j steps on model j. We shall say that the simulation is bandwidth efficient if this lower bound is achieved, i.e. if any single step of model i can be simulated using $\theta(b_i/b_j)$ steps of model i. As a result of substantial work in this area, we know bandwidth-efficient simulations between most network models, as well as between PRAMs and network models. For instance, Koch et al show how a p processor Butterfly with relative bisection $\theta(1/\log p)$ can simulate a single step of a two dimensional mesh having relative bisection $\theta(1/\sqrt{p})$ with constant slowdown. The reverse simulation is easily seen to require $\theta(\sqrt{p}/\log p)$ steps of the mesh for a single step of the Butterfly, and is thus bandwidth efficient.

For any network model i we will use $S_i(p)$ to denote the time to simulate a single step of a PRAM, both with p processors. A PRAM simulation is bandwidth efficient if $S_i(p) = \theta(1/b_i(p))$. Typically we will drop the subscript i if it is clear by the context.

A third class of models has recently been proposed as bridging models between networks and PRAMS. These include the Bulk Synchronous PRAM[21], the logP model[12], and the LPRAM[4]. These models also fit into our framework. For instance the logP model has a parameter g called the gap which is essentially the reciprocal of the relative bisection bandwidth as per our definition. Bandwidth efficient simulations can be defined between the other models and these bridging models; but these simulations typically require that the number of processors in the model being simulated is substantially larger than the model on which the simulation is performed. We defer this discussion to the full version.

2   A Formal Definition of Locality

It is certainly clear how to design algorithms for realistic parallel computers (sparse networks) without exploiting locality: use the PRAM model, and then run the algorithms on the target network by using a simulation of the PRAM model. The simulation overhead is $S(p)$, so that if the best time on the PRAM is T, then the simulation time is $S(p)T$. It is natural then, to ask if the time on the network could be improved to $\theta(T)$, by designing an algorithm that is customized to the network topology and reduce the overhead of communication. We shall say that a network algorithm exploits locality if its running time on a network is $o(S(p)T)$, i.e. smaller than the time to simulate the best PRAM algorithm on the network. So for example, on a p processor butterfly, we know $S(p) = \theta(\log p)$, or on a p processor mesh, $S(p) = \theta(\sqrt{p})$, so that algorithms that run in time $o(T \log p)$ on the Butterfly or $o(T\sqrt{p})$ on a mesh will be considered as exploiting locality. We shall say locality is fully exploited if the network time is $\theta(T)$.

We can prove lower bounds on the extent to which locality can be exploited by defining a quantity called the *gross locality* (locality for short) of a computational problem.

2.1 Gross Locality

Simply stated, the gross locality of a problem is the ratio: parallel work $W = pT$ required to solve the problem using the best PRAM algorithm, divided by the two processor communication complexity of the problem.

Our notion of communication complexity is standard, except we require input and output to be distributed, as described below. Our model consists of two processors connected together by a communication link. We assume that the processors have unlimited computing power and that local computation at each processor is free. However we are charged for each word ($\theta(\log n)$ bits, for problem size n) that is communicated along the link. The inputs and outputs to the problem being solved must be specified in a where and when oblivious manner (i.e. where and when each input bit is read and output generated is specified in advance, independent of the value of the bits). In addition, we shall assume that the inputs and the outputs are distributed, i.e. each processor inputs half the bits and outputs half the bits. Which bits to input/output at each processor is at the discretion of the algorithm designer, but this must be specified in advance. The number of bits transmitted across the link will depend upon the algorithm used, as well as the problem instance. The communication complexity of a problem is the minimum over all possible algorithms of the maximum (over problem instances) number of words transmitted by the algorithm to solve the problem.

Let $C(n)$ denote the communication complexity for the given problem, with problem size n. Let $W(n)$ denote the work required to solve the problem on a PRAM. Then the gross locality of the problem is $L(n) = W(n)/C(n)$.[3]

Theorem 1. *Let the minimum time for solving a problem on a p processor PRAM be T, with n denoting the problem size. Let the gross locality of the problem be $L(n)$, and let $b(p)$ denote the relative bisection bandwidth of a p processor network. Then the time required on the network is $\Omega(T(1 + \frac{1}{L(n)b(p)}))$. Suppose $S(p)$ denotes the cost of simulating a PRAM step on the given network, with the simulation being bandwidth efficient. Then the time required on the network is $\Omega(T(1 + \frac{S(p)}{L(n)}))$.*

Proof: The communication time on the network must be $\Omega(C(n)/B(p))$, but $C(n)/B(p) = T(\frac{C(n)}{pT} \cdot \frac{p}{B(p)}) = T(\frac{1}{L(n)b(p)})$. Adding the computation time which must at least be T gives the first result. The second follows since $b(p) = \theta(1/S(p))$. ∎

An obvious corollary is:

Corollary 2. *Suppose the gross locality $L(n)$ of a problem P is $O(1)$, and suppose that a bandwidth efficient PRAM simulation is available for a given network. Then the simulation of the fastest PRAM algorithm on the network is the fastest algorithm for P on the network.*

---

[3] The ratio of the amounts of computation to communication performed by a program is commonly used to analyze its quality, especially in scientific computing. The intuition behind our measure is similar; the difference being that we are seeking to characterize the intrinsic locality of problems rather than particular algorithms.

In some sense our comparison of the best deterministic network algorithm with a possibly randomized simulation of a deterministic PRAM algorithm is unfair. We believe that it should be possible to extend our definition of locality by considering randomized communication complexity. An additional technical issue concerns W. Ideally, we should define it to be the optimum sequential work. This is useful however, only if we know an optimum sequential algorithm. Our definition on the other hand is practically more useful, since we can work with nonoptimal parallel algorithms. We will discuss these issues at more length in the full version.

2.2 Examples of Inherently Nonlocal Problems

As shown by JaJa[14], the communication complexity of determining whether or not an n vertex graph is connected is $\Omega(n \log n)$ bits, or $\Omega(n)$ words. This is true even for sparse graphs, i.e. those having $m = O(n)$ edges. The best deterministic algorithm for sparse graphs is due to Cole and Vishkin[11] and requires time $T = O(\log n)$ and uses $n\alpha(m, n)/\log n$ processors, where $\alpha(m, n)$ is the inverse Ackerman function. Thus $W(n) = n\alpha(m, n)$. The problem thus has locality $\alpha(m, n)$. Thus the best possible network time (achieved thorough exploitation of locality) must be at least $\Omega(TS(p)/\alpha(m, n))$, which is hardly better than $O(TS(p))$, the time acheived using PRAM simulation.

We conjecture that the randomized communication complexity of connectivity is also $O(n)$ words, in which case the locality of the sparse graph connectivity problem is $O(1)$ using the efficient parallel algorithm by Gazit[13]. In this case it is clear that a direct network implementation will be no more efficient than a straightforward simulation of the PRAM algorithm, i.e. the problem is inherently nonlocal.

Using a Multiprefix based PRAM[20], sorting n integers of size $\theta(\log p)$ requires $\theta(n)$ work. Since the communication complexity is easily seen to be $\theta(n)$ words, the problem has gross locality $\theta(1)$, and hence is inherently nonlocal.

It has been shown, that while the problem of evaluating arithmetic expressions having n terms and arbitrary parenthesization can be solved in $\theta(\log n)$ time on an $n/\log n$ processor PRAM[3], it has communication complexity $\theta(n)$ words[16]. Since the work on a PRAM is the optimal $\theta(n)$, its locality is $\theta(1)$, i.e. it is inherently nonlocal.

3   Problems Having Locality

Most regular problems such as comparison-based Sorting, Matrix multiplication, FFT have locality. We can conclude this indirectly from the fact that there are numerous good network implementations for these problems in the literature, and also by considering their communication complexity. Our main concern in this paper, however, is irregular or dynamic problems. In what follows, we point out several examples of these that have locality.

The problem of computing convex hulls is intimately related to sorting. Using this relation, it is possible to show that the optimum work for a PRAM algorithm is $\theta(n \log n)$, and further, that the communication complexity is $\theta(n)$. Thus the locality is $\theta(\log n)$. Note further that there are algorithms for solving the convex hull problem on a PRAM having linear speedup over the best sequential algorithm[6]. Using theorem 1 we can also conclude that while there may exist implementations with linear speedup on the Butterfly, the speedup on a two dimensional mesh can be at most $O(\sqrt{p}/\log n)$, i.e. $o(p)$ unless n is superpolynomial in p.

We have recently shown that a p processor Butterfly network can compute the convex hull of $n = p \log^2 p$ points in the plane in $O(\log^3 p)$ time[18]. This algorithm fully exploits locality – the time on the Butterfly is the same as the time on a PRAM with the same number of processors.

Optimally efficient network algorithms have been found recently for several problems, demonstrating not only that their gross locality is larger than one, but that it can also be exploited. Examples include backtrack search for solving combinatorial problems, and maintenance of ordered set data structure[17, 19]. Recently, Cheriyan, Hagerup, and Mehlhorn[10] have shown that using polynomial slack, it is possible to fully exploit locality for the maxflow problem.

Parallel slackness (polylogarithmic or polynomial) has been found to be crucial for developing algorithms that exploit locality. As has been observed, parallel slackness is also useful to reduce synchronization costs[21]. In addition, we have recently found that it can give astonishingly simple sorting algorithms[9].

In the past, enormous amount of research has been directed toward solving problems in polylogarithmic time, possibly using a number of processors polynomially larger than the size of the problem. While this is of great theoretical interest, in practice, we have very few processors as compared to the problem size. Because of economic issues (silicon real estate as well as market forces) coarse grained processors with relatively large memories are popular and will continue to remain popular for the foreseeable future. Further, because of ever increasing computational needs, we expect that as sizes of parallel computers increase, they will be used to solve even larger problems, allowing large parallel slackness.

4 Locality and Portability

We shall say that a problem P of size n is native to a model i if the relative bisection b_i of model i is inversely proportional to L, where L is the gross locality of a problem P, i.e. $b_i L = \theta(1)$. We shall say that an algorithm A for P is portable if A runs on the native model of P and fully exploits locality. We show that if an efficient simulation is available for the native model of A on another model j, then the simulation of A on j gives the best possible algorithm for P on j. Notice that we do not claim that $A(j)$ gives linear speedup; only that $A(j)$ cannot be improved.

Theorem 3. *Suppose A is a portable algorithm for a problem P running on the native model i of P. Suppose b_i and b_j denote the relative bisection of i and some model j. Suppose that (a) $b_i < b_j$, and that we have a constant time simulation of model i on model j, or (b) $b_i \geq b_j$, and we have a bandwidth efficient simulation of model i on some model j. In either case the simulation $A(j)$ of A on model j is the fastest possible algorithm for P on j.*

Proof: Let T denote the minimum time to solve problem P on a p processor PRAM. Since A fully exploits locality on model i, we know that it runs in time

$O(T)$. If $b_i < b_j$, we have a constant time simulation of i on j, i.e. $A(j)$ runs in optimal $O(T)$ time. Alternatively, suppose that $b_i \geq b_j$. Since the simulation of i on j is bandwidth efficient, we know that a single step of i is simulated in time b_i/b_j on model j, so that the time for $A(j)$ is $O(T(b_i/b_j))$. But by theorem 1 the time for any algorithm running on model j must be $\Omega(T\left(1 + \frac{1}{Lb_j}\right)) = \Omega(T(b_i/b_j))$, since $L = \theta(1/b_i)$. ∎

Notice that this is a very strong notion of portability — not only can you automatically generate an algorithm for model j, but you get the best possible algorithm — so that there is no incentive whatsoever to redevelop a customized algorithm for the target architecture. Also note that the native model for problems with locality $O(1)$ is the PRAM. In this case the above theorem reduces to corollary 2.

As an example we consider the problem of finding the convex hull of n points in the plane. As mentioned, the locality of this problem is $O(\log n)$. So the Butterfly network with p processors having relative bisection $O(1/\log p) = O(1/\log n)$ is native for this problem. Although we do not know of efficient algorithms with $p = n$, from [18] we know that there exists an algorithm (with $n = p\log^2 p$) which we will call A that solves this problem in $O(\log^3 p)$ time while exploiting locality fully. As per our definition, A is a portable algorithm. Now if we wish to construct an algorithm for convex hulls on a 2 dimensional mesh, all we need is a bandwidth efficient simulation of the butterfly on the mesh. Such a simulation is well known, and can be used to derive a convex hull algorithm $A(\text{mesh})$ for the mesh from the Butterfly algorithm A. Further, we are guaranteed that no algorithm for finding convex hulls of n points on a p processor mesh can be faster than $A(\text{mesh})$ to within constant factors.

In fact, our notion of portability extends to simulations involving different number of processors in the two models. We will consider this issue at greater length in the full version.

5 Conclusions and Summary

This work potentially affect two areas: interconnection network design, and parallel programming methodology.

A key issue in designing parallel computers is the balance between computing power and communication capacity. As we have observed, there exist several problems that are inherently nonlocal, and therefore require high communication capability for efficient implementation. We also listed several problems for which fast network implementations can be designed. Some of these problems, however, possess only limited locality, and thus require relatively powerful communication networks (e.g. Butterflies). To summarize, we cannot give a clear answer to the question of how powerful communication networks we must build; but as more results become known about locality of different problems and as we develop locality exploiting algorithms for more problems, we will have a more complete answer.

Our ideas provide a methodology for developing portable parallel programs. The first step given a problem is to determine its gross locality. This determines a native architecture for the problem. The next step is to design an algorithm on the native model that fully exploits locality. This algorithm can now be simulated on different architectures, and is guaranteed to have good efficiency.

Acknowledgements: I am grateful to Abhijit Sahay for comments on a previous version.

References

1. F. Abolhassan, R. Drefenstedt, J. Keller, W. Paul, and D. Scheerer. On the physical design of PRAMS. In J. Buchmann, H. Ganziger, and W. Paul, editors, *Informatik - Festschrift zum 60. Geburstag von Gunter Hotz.* Teubner Verlag, 1992.
2. F. Abolhassan, J. Keller, and W. Paul. On the cost-effectiveness of PRAMS. In *IEEE Symposium on Parallel and Distributed Processing*, pages 2–9, December 1991.
3. K. Abrahamson, N. Dadoun, D. Kirkpatrick, and T. Pryztycka. A simple parallel tree contraction algorithm. Technical Report 87-30, University of British Columbia, 1987.
4. Alok Aggarwal, Ashok Chandra, and Marc Snir. Communication Complexity of PRAMS. *Theoretical Computer Science*, pages 3–28, March 1990.
5. Robert Alverson, David Callahan, Daniel Cummings, et al. The TERA Computer System. In *Proceedings of Supercomputing 90*, pages 1–6, 1990.
6. M. Atallah and M. Goodrich. Efficient parallel solutions to some geometric problems. *Journal of Parallel and Distributed Computing*, 3:492–507, 1986.
7. S. N. Bhatt, F. R. K. Chung, J. W. Hong, F. T. Leighton, and A. L. Rosenberg. Optimal Simulations by Butterfly Networks. In *Proceedings of STOC 88*, pages 192–204, 1988.
8. S. N. Bhatt, F. R. K. Chung, F. T. Leighton, and A. L. Rosenberg. Optimal simulations of tree machines. In *Proceedings of the IEEE Annual Symposium on The Foundations of Computer Science*, pages 274–282, 1986.
9. David Blackston and Abhiram Ranade. Snakesort: A family of optimal randomized sorting algorithms, 1993. manuscript.
10. Joseph Cheriyan, Torben Hagerup, and Kurt Mehlhorn. Can maximum flow be computed in $o(nm)$ time? Technical Report A 90/07, Universitat des Saarlandes, May 1990.
11. R. Cole and U. Vishkin. Approximate and exact parallel scheduling with application to list, tree and graph problems. In *Proceedings of the IEEE Annual Symposium on The Foundations of Computer Science*, pages 478–491, 1986.
12. D. Culler, R. Karp, D. Patterson, A. Sahay, K. Schauser, E. Santos, R. Subramonian, and T. Eicken. LogP: Towards a realistic model of Parallel Computation. In *Principles and Practice of Parallel Programming*, 1992. To appear.
13. H. Gazit. An optimal randomized parallel algorithm for finding connected components in a graph. In *Proceedings of the IEEE Annual Symposium on The Foundations of Computer Science*, pages 492–501, 1986.
14. Joseph Ja'Ja'. The VLSI Complexity of Selected Graph Problems. *Journal of the ACM*, 31:377–391, April 1984.
15. R. Koch, T. Leighton, B. Maggs, S. Rao, and A. Rosenberg. Work-preserving emulations of fixed-connection networks. In *Proceedings of the ACM Annual Symposium on Theory of Computing*, pages 227–240, May 1989.
16. Ernst Mayr, 1992. Personal Communication.
17. Abhiram G. Ranade. Optimal speedup for backtrack search on a butterfly network. In *Proceedings of the ACM Symposium on Parallel Algorithms and Architectures*, pages 40–48, July 1991.

18. Abhiram G. Ranade. Communication efficient algorithms for some geometric problems. In preparation., 1992.
19. Abhiram G. Ranade. Maintaining dynamic ordered sets on processor networks. In *Proceedings of the ACM Symposium on Parallel Algorithms and Architectures*, pages 127–137, June-July 1992.
20. Abhiram G. Ranade, Sandeep N. Bhatt, and S. Lennart Johnsson. The Fluent Abstract Machine. In *Proceedings of the Fifth MIT Conference on Advanced Research in VLSI*, pages 71–94, March 1988. Also available as Yale Univ. Comp. Sc. TR-573.
21. L. G. Valiant. A Bridging Model for Parallel Computation. *Communications of the ACM*, 33(8):103–111, August 1990.

Optimal Implementation of General Divide-and-Conquer on the Hypercube and Related Networks

Ernst W. Mayr   Ralph Werchner

Fachbereich Informatik
J.W. Goethe-University
Frankfurt am Main
Germany

Abstract. We show how to implement divide-and-conquer algorithms without undue overhead on a wide class of networks. We give an optimal generic divide-and-conquer implementation on hypercubes for the class of divide-and-conquer algorithms for which the total size of the subproblems on any level of recursion does not exceed the original problem size. For this implementation, appropriately sized subcubes have to be allocated to the subproblems generated by the divide-step. We take care that these allocation steps do not cause unbalanced distribution of work, and that, asymptotically, they do not increase the running time. Variants of our generic algorithm also work for the butterfly network and, by a general simulation, for the class of hypercubic networks, including the shuffle-exchange and the cube-connected-cycles network. Our results can also be applied to optimally solve various types of routing problems.

Topics: *Theory of Parallel and Distributed Computation, Algorithms and Data Structures*

1 Introduction

The divide-and-conquer approach is one of the most successful programming paradigms. Especially in the field of parallel processing one of the most natural methods to solve problems is to divide a problem into subproblems, solve these in parallel and then, combine the solutions to a solution of the given problem instance.

The complete execution of a divide-and-conquer algorithm can be visualized as a tree, the root representing the given instance of the problem and the other nodes representing subproblems. In this tree we can associate with each node (subproblem) the set of processors dealing with the corresponding subproblem. From this point of view, the problem of efficiently allocating sets of processors to the subproblems (nodes of the tree) becomes evident. Our goal in this paper is to solve this problem in a way causing minimal overhead in addition to the running time needed by the divide- and conquer-steps themselves. Unlike for PRAM's [FW78] which provide complete processor interconnection and hence simple processor allocation mechanisms (but see also [vG89]), this problem is much more difficult on network architectures. Two major hurdles are (i) allocating appropriately sized subnetworks to subproblems and (ii) routing the subproblems to their subnetworks.

These two objections are conflicting with each other. If we want to find appropriately sized subnetworks leaving only very few processors idle, the subproblems might have to be routed over long distances. On the other hand, keeping routes short may imply that not enough suitably sized subnetworks are available. We show that a compromise between these two extremes of the trade-off yields asymptotically optimal results for a wide class of divide-and-conquer algorithms.

Results concerning closely related allocation problems on the hypercube can be found in [CL90], [CS87], and [KDL89]. These papers consider the problem of allocating appropriately sized subcubes to incoming tasks in an on-line fashion on a hypercube that is already partially allocated. Our approach differs since we allocate subcubes to all subproblems on the same level of recursion simultaneously.

In [ZRL91] an implementation of divide-and-conquer is considered where each divide or conquer step is executed by a single processor. Thus, if a divide step always creates two subproblems, the resulting dependency structure between processors is a binomial tree, whose embeddings into de Bruijn and other networks are discussed.

2 Fundamental Concepts and Notation

2.1 Networks

Consider networks consisting of p processors interconnected by bidirectional communication channels capable of transmitting $\Theta(\log p)$ bits per step. In particular we consider the family of boolean hypercubes and the family of butterfly networks. Our main results also hold for the so called *hypercubic networks*, such as the shuffle-exchange network, the de-Bruijn network, and the cube-connected-cycles network, by a general simulation given in [S90].

A *d-dimensional hypercube* contains 2^d processors. Their id's are the strings in $\{0,1\}^d$. Two processors are connected iff their id's differ in exactly one bit. If we associate with each processor the integer represented by its id, the set of processors can be ordered according to this numbering. Let an interval $[a, b)$ of processors in a hypercube denote the set of processors with numbers $a, a+1, \ldots, b-1$. This interval is an i-dimensional subcube iff $2^i \big| a$ and $a + 2^i = b$. In this paper we consider only subcubes that are intervals in this sense, though there are many more subcubes.

A *d-dimensional butterfly* contains $(d + 1) 2^d$ processors named by tupels from $[0, d] \times \{0, 1\}^d$. Connections are between processors (i, a) and $(i + 1, b)$ iff $a = b$ or a and b differ only in position $i+1$. The set of processors $[0, i] \times [a, b)$ is an i-dimensional subbutterfly iff $2^i \big| a$ and $a + 2^i = b$. By cutting all edges between the nodes of level i and level $i + 1$ the d-dimensional butterfly is disconnected into 2^{d-i} i-dimensional butterflies and 2^{i+1} $(d - i - 1)$-dimensional butterflies. These subbutterflies will be used in our construction. We assume that the nodes in the butterfly network are ordered lexicographically, with the second component more significant than the first. An extensive collection of results concerning hypercubes and hypercubic networks can be found in [L92].

In the following sections we will focus on hypercube algorithms. In section 6 we then show how to modify our results for the butterfly network.

2.2 Restrictions on the Divide and the Conquer-Implementations

In this paper we consider divide-and-conquer algorithms with the following properties:

- In the divide-step each problem is split into subproblems with sizes adding up to no more than the size of the given problem; size is measured in processor words;
- The solution to each subproblem is no longer than the subproblem itself;
- Each subproblem is treated in a subcube at least its size. The input of the divide-step is assumed to be stored contiguously in a subcube (interval) starting at the first processor, and the output is a sequence of subproblems each stored in an interval of processors. The conquer-step works in an analogous manner. Note however that the subproblems are generally not subcubes.

Let the running time of the divide-step and the conquer-step for inputs of size n be bounded by $T(n)$, let the sizes of the generated subproblems be bounded by $s(n)$, and let c be the size of problems solved without any more recursive steps. Then an obvious lower bound for the running time of any divide-and-conquer algorithm is

$$\bar{T}(n) = T(n) + T(s(n)) + T(s(s(n))) + \ldots + T(c)$$

In the sequel we show how to reach this bound asymptotically for hypercubes and hypercubic networks.

From the properties we agreed on for the divide-step and the conquer-step the following algorithmic problems become apparent:

- The generated subproblems in general don't match the sizes of subcubes (resp. subbutterflies);
- subproblems in general are stored in intervals which are not subcubes; rather, the intervals have to be routed to subcubes.

We define the *subcube allocation problem with expansion x* as follows:

Suppose we are given a sequence of intervals of total length $\leq n$ where each interval length is a power of 2. Then the intervals have to be aligned with subcubes in the interval $[0, xn)$. The algorithm has to be executed on a hypercube with a size of the next power of 2 greater than or equal $x n$.

3 The Subcube Allocation Problem

In this section we consider several subcube allocation algorithms for the hypercube. In the algorithms we use the following primitive operations for which logarithmic time algorithms are known:

- parallel-prefix (for a sequence $a_1, a_2, \ldots, a_p$ and an associative operator $\circ$, have, for all i, the i-th processor compute the value of $\bigcirc_{1 \leq j \leq i} a_j$) [S80];
- pipelined parallel-prefix ($\log p$ independent parallel-prefix operations) [PM89];

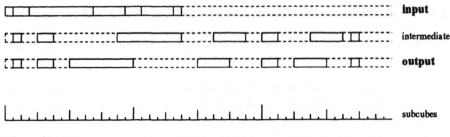

Fig. 1. Subcube allocation by a monotone routing

- concentration routing, inverse concentration routing, monotone routing (each processor is the source and the destination of at most one data item, the order of the data items is preserved by the routing, and, in concentration routings, the data items are concentrated to the leftmost processors, one item per processor) [NS81].

Lemma 1. *There is an $O(\log\log n \log n)$ time algorithm for the subcube allocation problem with expansion 1.*

Proof. It is sufficient to sort the given intervals according to their size in descending order, and to concentrate the resulting sequence to the left. As the length of each interval is a power of 2, a simple induction shows that the sorted intervals are aligned with subcubes.

Using parallel-prefix computations and monotone routings each data item computes the length of its associated interval. There are at most $\log n$ distinct lengths. The intervals are divided into groups according to their lengths. Using parallel-prefix operations and concentration routings the upper half of groups is concentrated to the left and the lower half to the right. This process is recursively repeated within the two halves until the intervals are sorted according to their lengths. The depth of the recursion is bounded by $\log\log n$. □

If the running time of the given divide-step and conquer-step is only logarithmic in n the above method leads to a suboptimal algorithm due to the $\log\log n$ factor. Our next lemma shows how to achieve an optimal running time at the cost of a somewhat larger expansion.

Lemma 2. *There is an $O(\log n)$ time algorithm for the subcube allocation problem with expansion 2.*

Proof. Assume that the sequence of intervals (each with length a power of 2) with a total length of n is stored in the leftmost processors of a hypercube of size at least $2n$. We first route the intervals to the right so that immediately to the left of each interval there is empty space equal to the size of the interval. Then each interval is shifted to the left until it is aligned with an appropriately sized subcube. In this shift operation no two intervals interfere with each other (see Figure 1).

It is obvious that the final destinations of the intervals can be computed in advance and only one inverse concentration route has to be carried out. □

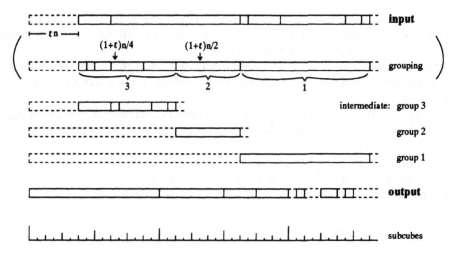

Fig. 2. Subcube allocation in groups

The following result shows that the two previous lemmata can be viewed as the extreme points of a trade-off between the expansion and the time required for the routing. For notational convenience let $\log x$ be 1 for $x \leq 2$.

Theorem 3. *The subcube allocation problem with expansion $1 + \varepsilon$ can be solved in $O(\log \log 1/\varepsilon \, \log n)$ steps, for $\frac{1}{n} \leq \varepsilon \leq 1$.*

Proof. The main observation for this algorithm is that in an embedding of large intervals by the previous method the gaps between the intervals can be used to embed smaller intervals. Furthermore this process can be repeated.

Let g_i be the total size of all intervals of length 2^i for $0 \leq i \leq \lfloor \log n \rfloor$, and let

$$G_i = \varepsilon n + \sum_{0 \leq k \leq i} g_k$$

$$r = \lceil \log(1/\varepsilon + 1) \rceil$$

$$h_j = \min \left\{ i \, \middle| \, G_i \geq (1 + \varepsilon)n/2^j \right\} \qquad (0 \leq j < r)$$

We divide the intervals into r groups (see figure 2). The j-th group contains all intervals of size a with $2^{h_j} < a \leq 2^{h_{j-1}}$ (setting $h_r = -\infty$). The groups can be identified, separated and sorted in $O(\log r \log n)$ steps by the method given in the proof of Lemma 1.

Assume that we have a hypercube of size at least $\sum_{1 \leq j \leq r} G_{h_j}$ processors (we can simulate such a cube by the given cube with constant slowdown since $\sum_{1 \leq j \leq r} G_{h_j} < 3(1 + \varepsilon)n$). We insert empty space between the groups so that for the j-th group an interval of length G_{h_j} is available. Using the method given in the proof of Lemma 2 (treating the largest intervals separately) an embedding for each group in $[0, G_{h_j})$ is computed.

Now we use the observation mentioned at the beginning of this proof. Suppose we have two embeddings of the following form:

The first embedding maps a set of intervals, each of size at least 2^i, to an interval $[0, a)$ leaving empty space b; the second embedding maps intervals of size less than 2^i in the interval $[0, b)$ leaving empty space c.

Then we can merge, in a straightforward way and using two monotone routings, the two embeddings into one embedding of all intervals in the interval $[0, a)$ leaving empty space c.

Applying this step repeatedly, the r embeddings computed above are merged into one embedding of all intervals in the interval $[0, (1 + \varepsilon)n)$. This process requires $O(\log r \log n)$ steps. □

It turns out that it is also possible to embed intervals into subcubes with expansion 1 using only logarithmic time. For this algorithm we use our generic divide-and-conquer method presented in the following section as a bootstrap.

4 A Generic Divide-and-Conquer Algorithm

4.1 A Suboptimal Solution

As already noted in the introduction a divide-and-conquer algorithm can be viewed as a tree with the root corresponding to the given problem, the other nodes corresponding to the subproblems, and the leaves corresponding to subproblems solved directly. Our first implementation of the divide-and-conquer paradigm proceeds in phases corresponding to the levels of the tree. Each phase consists of the following steps:

A1. All subproblems at the present level of the tree are padded in size to the next power of 2 and are stored contiguously from the left of the hypercube. Using the algorithm of Lemma 2 each subproblem is routed to its own subcube;

A2. for each subproblem the divide-step is executed within its associated subcube.

When all subproblems are of some constant size, they are solved directly. In the ascending ("conquer") part of the algorithm we recombine these solutions to the subproblems. To guarantee correct combination of the computed results we have to remember the data movements made in the subcube allocation routines of the descending part, and reverse them. Suitable techniques to remember moves with just a small amount of additional memory are proposed in (the full version of) [MW92]. We only need a constant number of bits per processor for each phase to store the moves.

Note that for the algorithm to work correctly the size of the hypercube must be at least $4n$ for inputs of size n.

Each of the subcube allocation steps in the above algorithm takes $O(\log n)$ steps. Thus, the total running time is

$$T(n) + O(\log n) + T(s(n)) + O(\log n) + T(s(s(n))) + \ldots + O(\log n) + T(c)$$

where again $T(n)$ is a bound on the running time of the divide-step and the conquer-step, $s(n)$ is the maximum size of a subproblem, and c is the size of problems solved directly.

Since the time required for the subcube allocation steps does not decrease on deeper levels of recursion this running time may be significantly larger than the lower bound $\bar{T}(n)$. In our next algorithm we manage to solve this problem by restricting the subproblem allocation routings to smaller subcubes.

To solve this problem one could try to allocate subcubes to subproblems generated out of a problem a only within the subcube allocated to a. But in this way the maximum load of subcubes on each level of recursion would grow exponentially with the depth in the worst case. A real solution of this problem is to allocate subcubes within ranges that are small enough to use fast allocation algorithms, and large enough to bound the growth of unbalance in the distribution of the data items on deeper levels of recursion. The details of this method are given in the following subsection.

4.2 An Optimal Solution

We describe the descending part of our optimal algorithm. For an i-dimensional cube C, which is initially the whole cube, the algorithm consists of the following steps:

1. Execute steps A1 and A2 on C until all subproblems are smaller than $2^{\lfloor i/4 \rfloor}$.
2. Divide the subproblems in C into $2^{\lceil i/2 \rceil}$ roughly equally sized groups as follows: Concentrate all intervals comprising the subproblems to the first processors in C, say $[a, a + n')$. For all j with $0 \le j < 2^{\lceil i/2 \rceil}$, assign to group j all intervals beginning in

$$\left[a + \left\lfloor j\frac{n'}{2^{\lceil i/2 \rceil}} \right\rfloor , a + \left\lfloor (j+1)\frac{n'}{2^{\lceil i/2 \rceil}} \right\rfloor \right)$$

Route the intervals of group j into the j-th $\lfloor i/2 \rfloor$-dimensional subcube of C, i.e. the subcube starting at processor $a + j\, 2^{\lfloor i/2 \rfloor}$. Call this algorithm recursively for each of these subcubes provided that their dimension $\lfloor i/2 \rfloor$ is not below some appropriately chosen constant d_0. Otherwise all subproblems are of constant size and are solved directly.

To guarantee that the subcube allocation steps in the phases can be executed correctly, we had to assume in the previous subsection that the cube was at least 4 times as large as the input size, or, as we shall say subsequently, the initial load of the cube was at most $1/4$.

Lemma 4. *With an initial load ≤ 0.183 and $d_0 = 8$ the above algorithm is never invoked on a subcube with a load $> 1/4$.*

Proof. Consider an i-dimensional subcube C invoking in step 2 the algorithm recursively for an i'-dimensional subcube C'. Let $l(C)$ and $l(C')$ denote the load of C and C', then we have

$$l(C') < \left(\frac{l(C)\, 2^i}{2^{i-i'}} + 2^{\lfloor i/4 \rfloor} \right) \frac{1}{2^{i'}}$$

$$= l(C) + 2^{\lfloor i/4 \rfloor - i'}$$

$$= l(C) + 2^{\lfloor i/4 \rfloor - \lfloor i/2 \rfloor}$$

$$\le l(C) + 2^{-i'/2}$$

Thus the load of an i-dimensional subcube, for which the above algorithm is recursively invoked starting from a d-dimensional hypercube, is bounded by

$$0.183 + 2^{-\lfloor d/2 \rfloor /2} + 2^{-\lfloor \lfloor d/2 \rfloor /2 \rfloor /2} + \ldots + 2^{-i/2}$$

$$\leq 0.183 + \sum_{j \geq 0} \left(2^{-i/2} \right)^{\left(2^j \right)}$$

An easy computation shows that this sum is less than $1/4$ for $i \geq 8$. □

To analyze the running time of this divide-and-conquer algorithm, we only have to consider the descending part, because the ascending part is symmetrical.

Let us at first estimate the running time of step 2, the grouping and routing of subproblems. These operations need $O(i)$ steps in an i-dimensional subcube. But as the dimension of the subcubes is halved on each level of recursive calls, the sum of these running times is $O(\log n)$.

Secondly the time needed for the subcube allocation algorithm (step A1) executed in an i-dimensional subcube is also $O(i)$. We want to compare this time with the time needed for the immediately following divide-step (step A2) in the largest allocated subcube, which must be at least of size $2^{\lfloor i/4 \rfloor}$ by our termination criterion for the loop of step 1. Provided that the running time of the divide-step or conquer-step is $T(n) = \Omega(\log n)$, we spend $\Omega(i)$ steps for this divide-step or the corresponding conquer-step. Therefore, the subcube allocation step cause only a constant factor overhead in the running time.

We want to note here that the authors could hardly think of a divide-step and conquer-step for any nontrivial problem running in $o(\log n)$ time on the hypercube.

Theorem 5. *Given a divide-step and a conquer-step satisfying the assumptions listed in section 2, with running times $T(n) = \Omega(\log n)$ on the hypercube, there is an algorithm solving problems of size n on a $\lceil \log n \rceil$-dimensional hypercube in time $O(\bar{T}(n))$, with*

$$\bar{T}(n) = T(n) + T(s(n)) + T(s(s(n))) + \ldots + T(c)$$

for some constant c and a bound $s(n)$ on the size of subproblems.

Proof. We have given an algorithm achieving the time bound on a hypercube with an initial load of at most 0.183. This larger hypercube can be simulated by a $\lceil \log n \rceil$-dimensional hypercube with a slowdown factor of at most 8. □

5 Applications

In [MW92] a divide-and-conquer algorithm is given that performs a special class of partial permutations called *parentheses-structured routings* in logarithmic time on hypercubes. In a well-formed string of parentheses, these partial permutations map each opening parenthesis to its matching closing parenthesis. The method used in [MW92] employs specific properties of this problem in order to obtain an efficient algorithm. The generic approach presented in this paper gives an alternative algorithm with the same running time.

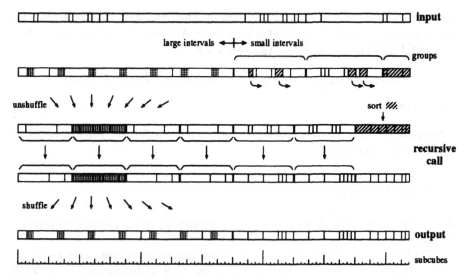

Fig. 3. Recursive subcube allocation algorithm

As another application of Theorem 5, we present a subcube allocation algorithm with expansion 1 for hypercubes which runs in logarithmic time.

Let d be the dimension of the cube. We execute the following steps (see Figure 3):

1. Separate the *small* intervals of size $< 2^{\lceil d/3 \rceil}$ from the *large* intervals concentrating the large intervals to the left and the small to their right.

2. Let n' denote the total size of the large intervals, and set $n'' = n'/2^{\lceil d/3 \rceil}$. Redistribute the large intervals by performing an *unshuffle permutation*, i.e. route the data item stored in processor $i + j\, 2^{\lceil d/3 \rceil}$ (for $0 \le i < 2^{\lceil d/3 \rceil}$ and $0 \le j < n''$) to processor $j + i\, n''$, using a bit-permute-permutation [NS82a] and a concentration routing.

   Now consider each of the intervals $[i\, n'', (i+1)\, n'']$ as a new subproblem *for our subcube allocation algorithm*, whose corresponding (and identical) subsolutions can be combined by reversing the above routing.

3. Cut the sequence of small intervals into groups of contiguous intervals, each of length between $2^{\lfloor \frac{2}{3} d \rfloor}$ and $2^{\lfloor \frac{2}{3} d \rfloor} + 2^{\lceil d/3 \rceil}$ (only the last group may be smaller). This can easily be done by cutting near multiples of $2^{\lfloor \frac{2}{3} d \rfloor} + 2^{\lceil d/3 \rceil - 1}$.

4. Use a pipelined segmented parallel prefix operation to find the distribution of interval sizes within the groups. Then, in each group of size s mark a set of intervals with a total size of $s - 2^{\lfloor \frac{2}{3} d \rfloor}$.

5. Concentrate the marked intervals to the right. Sort them together with the last group in order of descending sizes. Since there are $O(2^{\frac{2}{3} d})$ data items to be sorted, this step can be performed in logarithmic time using *sparse enumeration sort* [NS82b].

   Again note that each group of size $2^{\lfloor \frac{2}{3} d \rfloor}$ comprises a subproblem; after solving these subproblems, all small intervals are embedded into subcubes.

The divide-step and the conquer-step just outlined can both be implemented in logarithmic time on a d-dimensional hypercube. All generated subproblems are of size $\leq 2^{\lfloor \frac{2}{3}d \rfloor}$. Thus we can apply Theorem 5 with

$$T(n) = O(\log n), \quad s(n) \leq n^{2/3}, \quad \text{and hence} \quad \bar{T}(n) = O(\log n),$$

and obtain:

Theorem 6. *There exists an $O(\log n)$ time algorithm for the subcube allocation problem with expansion 1.*

6 The Butterfly

For the butterfly network we require two modifications of the method presented in section 4.

The first modification is due to the fact that butterflies cannot easily be divided into subbutterflies. As noted in section 2, a butterfly of dimension $2i + 1$ can be divided into 2^{i+2} i-dimensional butterflies whereas a butterfly of dimension $2i$ has to be divided into 2^i i-dimensional and 2^{i+1} $(i-1)$-dimensional butterflies. Thus step 2 (grouping of subproblems) has to be adjusted appropriately so as to distribute the load roughly equally to the subbutterflies.

The second problem is that the subnetwork allocation for the butterfly is slightly more complicated than for the hypercube. There is a solution to the subnetwork allocation problem for the butterfly with a constant expansion. But the problem to route each subproblem into its allocated subnetwork seems to be much easier if we additionally demand the subproblems to be at least of size $(\lfloor i/4 \rfloor + 1) 2^{\lfloor i/4 \rfloor}$ in an i-dimensional butterfly.

For the following lemma assume that the intervals to be embedded have lengths matching the sizes of butterflies.

Lemma 7. *The subnetwork allocation problem with expansion 8 for butterflies can be solved in $O(\log n)$ steps if each of the intervals given in a d-dimensional butterfly is at least of size $(\lfloor d/4 \rfloor + 1) 2^{\lfloor d/4 \rfloor}$.*

Proof. Let a sequence of intervals be given, and let the length of the j-th interval be $(d_j + 1) 2^{d_j}$. Since the expansion is at least 8, we have

$$\sum_j (d_j + 1) 2^{d_j} \leq \frac{1}{8}(d + 1) 2^d$$

$$\implies \qquad \sum_j 2^{d_j} \leq \frac{1}{2} 2^d$$

Using the simple technique of Lemma 1, we can embed a sequence of intervals with lengths 2^{d_j} into subcubes of a d-dimensional hypercube without changing the order of the intervals. If, instead, in the hypercube the j-th interval is embedded in $[a_j, a_j + 2^{d_j})$, then we solve our problem for the butterfly by routing the j-th interval to the set of processors $[0, d_j] \times [a_j, a_j + 2^{d_j})$. This routing is monotone in our lexicographic order of the d-dimensional butterfly. □

For the i-dimensional butterfly we substitute the upper bound for the subproblem sizes that we could guarantee after step 1 by $(\lfloor i/4 \rfloor + 1) \, 2^{\lfloor i/4 \rfloor}$. We can also achieve this bound by collecting after each execution of steps A1 and A2 those subproblems that are already smaller than $(\lfloor i/4 \rfloor + 1) \, 2^{\lfloor i/4 \rfloor}$ to one end of the butterfly and subdividing further only those subproblems that are still too large.

In this way we can guarantee the condition of Lemma 7.

A proof very similar to that of Theorem 5 (and therefore omitted) yields:

Theorem 8. *We are given a divide-step and a conquer-step for a problem P satisfying the assumptions given in section 2 with running times $T(n) = \Omega(\log n)$ on a butterfly of size $b(n)$, where $b(n)$ is the smallest size $\geq n$ of a butterfly. Then P can be solved for instances of size n on a butterfly of size $b(n)$ in time $O(\bar{T}(n))$.*

There are a many networks with a structure very similar to the butterfly. These *hypercubic networks* include the cube-connected-cycles network, the Benes network, the shuffle-exchange network, and the de Bruijn network. The analogue of Theorem 8 is valid for each of these networks. This follows from a result shown by Schwabe in [S90] stating that a network of one of these types can be simulated by a similar size network of any other type with a constant factor slowdown. To obtain Theorem 8 for some family F, we have to simulate the divide-step and the conquer-step by a butterfly, apply Theorem 8, and simulate the complete butterfly divide-and-conquer algorithm on the given network of type F.

A direct proof of Theorem 5 for each of the hypercubic networks seems to be difficult, because the subnetwork allocation problem can become quite complicated. Indeed, for the cube-connected-cycles this problem is even unsolvable, because no connected regular network can contain a regular subnetwork of the same degree.

7   Conclusion and Open Problems

In this paper we have implemented divide-and-conquer on the hypercube and the hypercubic networks with an asymptotically optimal running time. If the goal is minimizing the constant factor in the overhead caused by our method, there is a number of design decisions that can be made, depending on the parameters $T(n)$ and $s(n)$. We have presented a number of different subcube allocation algorithms, one could use different subcube sizes for the recursive calls and different parameters for allocating subcubes. The choices given in this paper work relatively well in all cases. Indeed it is not even necessary to know the bounds $T(n)$ and $s(n)$.

A more general (and, of course, more complicated) approach to the problems considered in this paper would be to allow the total size of subproblems generated on any one level to exceed the original problem size and/or to allow the number of processors performing a divide-step or conquer-step to depend non linearly on the problem size.

Another interesting open question is whether there is a direct optimal algorithm for the subcube allocation problem with expansion 1.

References

[CL90]   M.Y. Chan and S.-J. Lee. Subcube recognition, allocation/deallocation and relocation in hypercubes. *Proceedings of the 2nd IEEE Symposium on Parallel and Distributed Processing*, 87–93, 1990.

[CS87]   M.-S. Chen and K.G. Shin. Processor allocation in an N-cube multiprocessor using Gray codes. *IEEE Transactions on Computers*, C-36:1396–1407, 1987.

[FW78]   S. Fortune and J. Wyllie. Parallelism in random access machines. *Proceedings of the 10th ACM Symposium on Theory of Computing*, 114–118, 1978.

[vG89]   A. van Gelder. PRAM processor allocation: A hidden bottleneck in sublogarithmic algorithms *IEEE Transactions on Computers*, C-38:289–292, 1989.

[KDL89]   J. Kim and C.R. Das and W. Lin. A processor allocation scheme for hypercube computers. *Proceedings of the 1989 International Conference on Parallel Processing. Vol. 2 Software*, 231–238, 1989.

[L92]   F.T. Leighton. *Introduction to Parallel Algorithms and Architectures*. Morgan Kaufmann Publishers, 1992.

[MW92]   E.W. Mayr and R. Werchner. Optimal routing of parentheses on the hypercube. *Proceedings of the 4th Annual ACM Symposium on Parallel Algorithms and Architectures*, 109–117, 1992.

[NS81]   D. Nassimi and S. Sahni. Data broadcasting in SIMD computers. *IEEE Transactions on Computers*, C-30:101–107, 1981.

[NS82a]   D. Nassimi and S. Sahni. A self-routing Benes network and parallel permutation algorithms. *IEEE Transactions on Computers*, C-31:148–154, 1982.

[NS82b]   D. Nassimi and S. Sahni. Parallel permutation and sorting algorithms and a new generalized connection network. *JACM*, 29:642–667, 1982.

[PM89]   C.G. Plaxton and E.W. Mayr. Pipelined parallel prefix computations and sorting on a pipelined hypercube. Technical Report STAN-CS-89-1269, Stanford University, 1989. To appear in J. Parallel Distrib. Comput..

[S90]   E.J. Schwabe. On the computational equivalence of hypercube-derived networks. *Proceedings of the 2nd Annual ACM Symposium on Parallel Algorithms and Architectures*, 388–397, 1990.

[S80]   J.T. Schwartz. Ultracomputers. *ACM Transactions on Programming Languages and Systems*, 2:484–521, 1980.

[ZRL91]   X. Zhong, S. Rajopadhye and V.M. Lo. Parallel implementations of divide-and-conquer algorithms on binary de Bruijn networks. Technical Report CIS-TR-91-21 University of Oregon, 1991.

Parallel Implementations of Graph Embeddings
(extended abstract)

Fred S. Annexstein

Department of Computer Science
University of Cincinnati
Cincinnati, OH 45221-0008

Abstract. This paper addresses the problem of how to efficiently implement a certain class of network emulations. We provide a framework for studying and implementing graph embeddings at a fine level of abstraction, suitable for the specification of pseudocode. Our results show that many networks with regular structure, including meshes, complete-binary trees, butterflies, X-trees, and mesh-of-trees can be efficiently embedded within a hypercube using SIMD-style parallel algorithms for translating node labels.

1 Introduction

Designers of nonshared memory parallel programs recognize that the communication patterns of their program solutions often match well to particular interconnection topologies. There are a number of programming environments (e.g., Parallaxis [2] and Poker [10] projects) that allow programs to explicitly specify such topological information. Compilers for programs written in such languages can often take advantage of this information to produce efficient code for tightly-coupled parallel computers.

One unavoidable step in the compilation process is the generation of software that "reconfigures" the physical architecture, given the specified logical interconnection topology. A popular approach taken to model solutions to this problem is via graph embeddings. Indeed, recent years have seen a wealth of papers on embedding one "guest" network into another "host" network [1, 3, 5, 6]. The reader is referred to [8, 9] for many more references.

The hypercube, in particular, has received much attention as a host network. Its popularity and versatility as a network underlying parallel computers is due in large part to its recursive structure that is well suited to divide-and-conquer applications. No less important is the fact that many computational structures are subgraphs, or nearly subgraphs of the hypercube. Such containment results include meshes [3, 5], binary trees [1, 7], butterflies [6], X-trees, and mesh-of-trees (see [8, 9]). These results are often specified in the literature by embedding algorithms that run in time linear in the size of the networks. This may not be useful in practice, especially when implementing sub-linear time algorithms. However, in this paper we develop a framework and a set of results that demonstrate that embeddings of the previously mentioned graphs can be implemented using parallel algorithms (without communication), where each node of the host computes the label of the node of the guest that it will emulate, along with the physical location of the logical neighboring processes. The algorithms we describe all run in parallel-time logarithmic in the size of the network. This time bound is exponentially faster than an implementation of the associated sequential algorithms.

We identify the problem of embedding one network in another as one of re-labeling the nodes of graphs. The problem can be stated as follows: given a pair of labeled graphs (representing a host and a guest network), find an algorithm that takes as input a node-label of the guest graph and outputs a node-label of the host graph subject to certain objectives. We also need to obtain the inverse mapping: an "unlabeling" algorithm that when presented with a node-label of the host as input produces as output the node-label of the inverse image under the original labeling algorithm. Herein we consider the case where the host network is the boolean hypercube and the guest networks are a variety of popular computational structures. We provide labeling and unlabeling algorithms that meet the objective that labels of adjacent nodes of the guest graphs are translated into bit-strings of small hamming distance apart—*hamming distance* is the number of bit positions that a pair of bit-strings differ. The existence of such algorithms demonstrate that the hypercube networks can be quickly reconfigured in software to logically resemble these guest topologies.

In the following section we provide our formal framework. In the Sections 3,4,5, and 6 we examine parallel-embeddings of a number of common computational structures that, hopefully, demonstrates the eminent practicality of this framework.

2 Formal Framework

A. Parallel Graph Embeddings   Let $\mathcal{G}$ and $\mathcal{H}$ be undirected graphs. An *embedding* of $\mathcal{G}$ into $\mathcal{H}$ is a (one-to-one) mapping $\alpha : V_{\mathcal{G}} \rightarrow V_{\mathcal{H}}$ of the nodes of $\mathcal{G}$ to the nodes of $\mathcal{H}$. If $\mathcal{G}$ and $\mathcal{H}$ are node-labeled graphs we say that there is a *parallel-embedding of $\mathcal{G}$ into $\mathcal{H}$ (realizing α)* if there is a pair of algorithms that effect the mapping α, specified as follows:

- a *labeling algorithm* $\mathcal{A}$ which inputs a node-label g of $V_{\mathcal{G}}$ and outputs the node-label of $\alpha(g)$ of $V_{\mathcal{H}}$
- an *unlabeling algorithm* $\mathcal{A}'$ which inputs a node-label h of $V_{\mathcal{H}}$ and outputs the node-label of $\alpha^{-1}(h)$ of $V_{\mathcal{G}}$.

To measure the quality of a parallel graph embedding, there are two cost measures that we are primarily concerned with. The *dilation* of an embedding is the maximum distance in $\mathcal{H}$ that any pair of adjacent nodes in $\mathcal{G}$ are mapped to by α. The *run-time* of the parallel embedding is the number of (parallel) bit-operations necessary to implement the algorithms $\mathcal{A}$ and $\mathcal{A}'$. The parallel-embeddings we present are all *efficient* in that the dilation is $O(1)$ and both algorithms run in time *linear* in the length of the input. In general, labeling algorithms work by generating each bit of a label in constant time. For notational convenience, bit-strings will be indexed right to left (e.g., an n-bit string w will be written $w_n \cdots w_2 w_1$),

B. Transformation Graphs   We assume that programmers specify the logical interconnect of their programs using one or more *transformation graphs*. This is typical of what is done in languages like Parallaxis [2]. Such specifications allow the use of symbolic names for communication directions. First, the specification encodes (labels) the set of nodes V_G (typically using subranges of integers). Second, a fixed set of transformations $\{\phi_i\}$ describes the adjacency relations using simple operations (e.g. arithmetic) on the node-labels, with the interpretation that there is a directed arc labeled ϕ_i from g to $\phi_i(g)$ for each $g \in V_G$.

C. Compilation Scenario Suppose a program is written with the logical process-interconnection specified explicitly using a transformation graph. During the compilation process, the compiler first invokes an appropriate unlabeling algorithm — in parallel each physical (host) processor h computes the label of the logical-process $\alpha^{-1}(h)$ it emulates. In effect each host processor-node-label (HID) is translated into a guest process-node-label (GID). Second, the compiler directs each host-processor to compute the labels of the logical neighbors by applying the set of transformations $\{\phi_i\}$ to the computed GID. Next, by invoking the labeling algorithm, each of these neighbor-labels is translated into a corresponding physical address and stored in a local register set.

D. Hypercube Networks and Gray Codes The hypercube is the host network we focus on for this study. The *order-n hypercube* $Q(n)$ has 2^n nodes labeled by distinct n-bit strings. Pairs of nodes are adjacent if their labels are at hamming distance 1.

Fact 1: For all pairs of integers h, k, the hypercube $Q(h + k)$ is isomorphic to the product graph $Q(h) \times Q(k)$.[1]

Fact 2: There is (circular) list of all 2^n distinct n-bit strings such that each adjacent pair in the list is at hamming distance 1.

Such a list is called a *Gray code*, and they are succinctly specified by what are called Gray code transition sequences (GCTS). A GCTS of order-n is defined as a list of $2^n - 1$ integers from the set $\{1, 2, \ldots, n\}$ that identifies the sequence of bit-positions to flip in constructing a Gray code. The reader is referred to [11] for more on Gray-like sequences.

The following recursive definition yields the *standard* GCTS of order n (sometimes called binary-reflexive). The reader may verify that it indeed produces a valid GCTS.

$$G_1 := 1 \qquad G_n := G_{n-1}, n, G_{n-1} \quad (n > 1)$$

We place an ordering on the elements of this Gray code by beginning the sequence with 0^n.

3 Parallel-Embedding Rings and Meshes

The standard transformation graph for the Ring is given as follows:

Ring $[0 \ldots 2^n - 1]$

---

[1] The product graph $G \times H$ has as vertex set the cartesian product $V_G \times V_H$. There is an edge between (g, h) and (g', h') when $g = g'$ and $(h, h') \in E_H$, or $h = h'$ and $(g, g') \in E_G$.

$$\phi_{\text{c-wise}} : \text{Ring}[k] \longrightarrow \text{Ring}[k+1 \bmod 2^n]$$
$$\phi_{\text{cc-wise}}: \text{Ring}[k] \longrightarrow \text{Ring}[k-1 \bmod 2^n]$$

The fact that such a graph is a subgraph of a hypercube follows from Fact 2 above. However, to specify a parallel-embedding of the Ring we need an algorithm to determine for any given $0 \leq k < 2^n$ the kth bit-string in the Gray code. The ith bit of the rank-k bit-string can be determined by the computing the exclusive-or of the ith and the $i+1^{\text{st}}$ bits of the binary representation of k.

procedure **Rank-to-Gray**(k, n)

Input: integer k — — *ring-node given by its rank*
integer n — — *denoting the order of the Gray code*
Output: bit-string w — — *string of rank k in the order-n Gray code*

1. For $i := 1$ to n do — — *calculate each bit*
   $w_i := k_i + k_{i+1} \pmod 2$
2. Return w

It is easy to invert the previous procedure to produce the unlabeling algorithm, since, for each ℓ, the sum of the most significant ℓ bits of w is a telescoping series that evaluates to the ℓth bit of k.

procedure **Gray-to-Rank**(w)

Input: bit-string w — — *string representing a node of the hypercube*
Output: integer k — — *the rank of that node in the Gray-code*

1. Initialize $k := 0$; Sum $:= 0$
2. For $\ell := \text{length}(w)$ downto 1 do — — *calculate each bit*
   Sum $:=$ Sum $+ w_\ell \pmod 2$
   $k := 2k + \text{Sum}$
3. Return k

Theorem 1. *There is a dilation 1 parallel-embedding of the 2^n-node Ring (or linear-array) into the hypercube $Q(n)$.*

Meshes are graphs that are direct products of linear arrays. Every 2-dimensional mesh can be embedded into an optimal size hypercube with dilation 2 [3]. Recently, Chan and Chin have shown that this embedding can be adapted to yield and an efficient parallel-embedding [4].

Next we turn to the problem of deriving efficient parallel-embeddings of the complete binary tree into the hypercube.

4 Parallel-Embedding Complete Binary Trees

The *complete binary tree* of height n, denoted CBT(n), is an ordered, rooted tree of $2^{n+1}-1$ nodes in which all non-leaf nodes have two children. The ith-level $(0 \leq i \leq n)$

of CBT(n) consists of 2^i nodes each at a distance of i from the root. The standard transformation graph for CBT(n) is given as follows:

Tree $[1 \ldots 2^{n+1} - 1]$
ϕ_{left} : **Tree**$[i] \longrightarrow$ **Tree**$[2 * i]$
ϕ_{right} : **Tree**$[i] \longrightarrow$ **Tree**$[2 * i + 1]$
ϕ_{up} : **Tree**$[i] \longrightarrow$ **Tree**$[i$ div $2]$

This standard labeling of CBT(n) can effectively be used for implementing tree-based algorithms on an order-($n + 1$) hypercube when such algorithms are specified in a level-by-level fashion, i.e., only the tree nodes on one level are active during any step of the algorithm.[2] To wit, assign the CBT node with standard-label w (in binary) to the hypercube-node labeled $w0^{n+1-\lfloor \log(w) \rfloor}$ with the msb deleted.[3] It then follows that the tree node with standard label w and its left child $w0$ are assigned to nodes at hamming distance 0 (i.e., they are assigned to the same node), and the node w and its right child $w1$ are assigned to nodes at hamming distance 1. For the unlabeling algorithm, a node of the hypercube simply needs to be informed which level is active in the next computation step. If the next active level is level i, then the processor "unlabels" by removing, if possible, the $n - i$ rightmost 0s from its HID and appends a 1 on the left. If it is not possible to do the removal, then the inverse image is empty and the processor will remain idle for the next computation step.

For more general tree-based algorithms there is a labeling scheme that within the framework of parallel-embeddings is quite effective, although tedious for a programmer to employ directly using transformations.

Definition. In the *inorder* labeling of the CBT(n) each node is labeled with its (binary numbered) rank in the inorder traversal of the tree (beginning at 0).

Induction can be used to establish the following proposition.

Proposition 2. *In the inorder labeling of the CBT(n), the labels of each non-leaf node and its left child are at hamming distance 1. The labels of each non-leaf node and its right child are at hamming distance 2.*

Hence, the inorder labeling yields an embedding with good dilation. Also, there are simple labeling and unlabeling algorithms for translating between the standard and inorder labels. The CBT node with standard-label w (in binary) is translated to the node-labeled $w01^{n-\lfloor \log(w) \rfloor}$ with the msb deleted. To translate from inorder labels to the standard labels, simply identify and remove the unique suffix of the form 01^k for some $0 \le k \le n$, followed by appending a 1 bit on the left. Hence, we have the following result.

Theorem 3. *There is a dilation 2 parallel-embedding of CBT(n) into the hypercube $Q(n + 1)$.*

---

[2] Parallel prefix computations, for example, fall into this category of tree algorithms.
[3] All logarithms are base 2.

5 Parallel-Embedding Doubly Rooted Binary Trees

There is a labeling scheme and an effective translation algorithm for the CBT such that only one pair of labels of adjacent nodes are at hamming distance 2 (all other adjacent pairs are at hamming distance 1). Such a result is the best possible since the $CBT(n)$ is not a subgraph of $Q(n + 1)$. To produce such a labeling we will encode a related structure, the double-rooted-binary-tree (DRBT). The $DRBT(n)$ of height-n is obtained from $CBT(n)$ by subdividing one of the edges adjacent to the root, or equivalently replacing the root with a path of length 2. We refer to the nodes of the new path as the left root ℓ and the right root r. The standard transformation graph and labeling for the DRBT is nearly identical to that for the CBT except we label ℓ with 0 and r with 1 (see Fig. 1).

Proposition 4. *The $DRBT(n)$ is a spanning tree of the hypercube $Q(n + 1)$ ([7]).*

Our goal is to find a labeling scheme that demonstrates Prop. 4 via a parallel-embedding. We will show that there is such a labeling which we call a *cube-labeling*. We also show that there are efficient algorithms to translate between the cube-labeling and the standard labeling of the DRBT. To this end, we use the inorder labeling of the DRBT as an intermediate step.

Definition. The *inorder listing* of the $DRBT(n + 1)$ is defined as follows:

$$\{L_n, \ \ell_n, \ R_n, \ r_n\}$$

where L_n is the left $CBT(n)$-subtree listed inorder, ℓ_n is the left root, R_n is the right $CBT(n)$-subtree listed inorder, and r_n is the right root.

To effect a cube-labeling of the DRBT one uses an inductive construction. In this construction two operators on strings are employed. We use an operator called $\mathcal{Z}$ that appends on the left a 0-bit to all bit-strings, and an operator called $\mathcal{F}$ that appends on the left a 1-bit after first interchanging the leading (leftmost) two bits. For the base of the induction (height-1 version), we label $L_0 := 11, \ell_0 := 10, R_0 := 01, r_0 := 00$. For the inductive hypothesis label $r_n := 0^{n+2}$, $\ell_n := 10^{n+1}$, and the $\text{root}(R_n) := 010^n$. Using the string operations $\mathcal{F}, \mathcal{Z}$, and the fact that interchanging bits in node-labels yields a graph automorphism of the hypercube, the induction can be extended, and a proof of Prop. 4 follows.

Observation 1. The inorder listing of cube-labeled nodes of the $DRBT(n + 2)$ can be given inductively as follows

$$
\begin{array}{ll}
L_{n+1} := \mathcal{F}(L_n), \ \mathcal{F}(\ell_n), \ \mathcal{Z}(R_n) & \ell_{n+1} := \mathcal{F}(r_n) \\
R_{n+1} := \mathcal{Z}(L_n), \ \mathcal{Z}(\ell_n), \ \mathcal{F}(R_n) & r_{n+1} := \mathcal{Z}(r_n)
\end{array}
$$

Figure 1 shows the various labelings of DRBT(2), and Figure 2 shows the application of the string operations $\mathcal{F}, \mathcal{Z}$ to the cube-labeling,

We now demonstrate that one can effectively translate between inorder-labels and the cube-labels of DRBT nodes by applying consequences of Observation 1. The form expressed above suggests a natural recursive algorithm. The translation of an n-bit inorder-label can be reduced to the translation of the $n - 1$ low-order bits followed by an application of the appropriate operator ($\mathcal{Z}$ or $\mathcal{F}$). Hence, recursively consider consecutive leading pairs of bits of the inorder-label to determine which quarter it is ranked. If the rank number is in the first or fourth quarters, then the $\mathcal{F}$ operator is applied, otherwise the $\mathcal{Z}$ operator is applied. There are two stopping conditions in the recursive procedure. The recursion stops if either the length of the input integer is two (base case) or if all the low-order bits are all 1, which implies that we are at one of the root nodes, and thus the translation follows from the induction above.

procedure **Inorder-to-Cube** (w)

Input: binary integer w $--$ *tree node given by inorder labeling*
Output: bit string w' $--$ *same tree node given by cube labeling*

1. Initialize $k := \text{length}(w)$
2. If $k = 2$ $--$ *the base case*
    then case w of
          $00 = L_0 : w' := 11;$ $01 = \ell_0 : w' := 10;$
          $10 = R_0 : w' := 01;$ $11 = r_0 : w' := 00$
3. Else if $(w \bmod 2^{k-1} = 2^{k-1} - 1)$ do $--$ *if the $k-1$ lsbs are all 1*
    if $w \text{ div } 2^{k-1} = 0$ $--$ *then w labels a root*
        then $w' := 10^{k-1}$ $--$ *w labels ℓ_k*
        else $w' := 0^k$ $--$ *w labels r_k*
4. Else if $(w \text{ div } 2^{k-2}) \in \{1, 2\}$ $--$ *determine which quarter w resides*
    then $w' := \mathcal{Z}(\text{Inorder-to-Cube}(w \bmod 2^{k-1}))$
                   $--$ *recursive calls on the $k-1$ low order bits*
    else $w' := \mathcal{F}(\text{Inorder-to-Cube}(w \bmod 2^{k-1}))$
5. Return w'

The procedure to translate from a cube-label to an inorder-label operates in two stages. In the first stage we discover the sequence of operators $\{\mathcal{F}, \mathcal{Z}\}$ that lead to the input node label. In this search we only need consider one bit at a time, i.e., a leading 0-bit implies the application of the $\mathcal{Z}$ operator, and a 1-bit implies the application of the $\mathcal{F}$ operator (followed by a swap of the next two leading bits). In the second stage we use this sequence in a suffix computation to generate each bit of the inorder-label. That is, for each i we compute which "tree-state" from the set $\{L, \ell, R, r\}$ is produced by the length-i suffix of the $\{\mathcal{F}, \mathcal{Z}\}$-sequence. This information along with Observation 1 determines the next leading bit of the inorder label. The following uses the function $\text{cons}(,)$ to concatenate a pair of strings,

procedure **Cube-to-Inorder** (w)

Input: bit string w $--$ *tree node given by cube labeling*
Output: binary integer w' $--$ *tree node given by inorder labeling*

1. Initialize $k := \text{length}(w)$
2. For $i := k$ downto 3 do $--$ *compute expression $O_k \cdots O_4 O_3(w_2 \ w_1) = w$*
    if $w_i = 0$ $--$ *where each $O_i \in \{\mathcal{Z}, \mathcal{F}\}$*

then $O_i := \mathcal{Z}$
   else $O_i := \mathcal{F}$; swap(w_{i-1}, w_{i-2})
{ *Next do a suffix computation on this expression generating each bit of the output.* }
3. Case $w_2 \, w_1$ of   – – *Base condition*
   11 : **State** $:= L$; $w' := 00$;   10 : **State** $:= \ell$; $w' := 01$
   01 : **State** $:= R$; $w' := 10$ 00 : **State** $:= r$; $w' := 11$
4. For $i := 3$ to k do   – – *Applying Observation 1*
      If $O_i = \mathcal{Z}$ – – *we can determine the* i^{th}*-bit of* w'
         then case **State** of   – – *and the next "tree-state"*
            L, ℓ : cons$(1, w')$; **State** $:= R$
            R : cons$(0, w')$; **State** $:= L$
            r : cons$(1, w')$; **State** $:= r$
      If $O_i = \mathcal{F}$
         then case **State** of
            L, ℓ : cons $(0, w')$; **State**$:= L$
            R : cons$(1, w')$; **State**$:= R$
            r : cons$(0, w')$; **State**$:= \ell$
5. Return w'

Theorem 5. *There is a dilation 1 parallel-embedding of the DRBT(n) into the hypercube $Q(n + 1)$.*

Corollary 6. *There is a (single edge) dilation 2 parallel-embedding of the CBT(n) into the hypercube $Q(n + 1)$.*

6   Embedding Other Networks

6.1   Butterfly-like Networks

Three common networks fall into the category of Butterfly-like networks: FFT, butterfly, and cube-connected-cycles. All are considered bounded-degree relatives of the hypercube. In fact each is a subgraph or nearly a subgraph of the product graph of a cycle and a hypercube. Previous results show that such networks can be embedded in the optimal-size hypercube with optimal dilation [6]. Our results from the previous sections can be applied to these embeddings and developed into parallel-embeddings with the same parameters. We sketch how this is done, but leave the details for the full paper.

A. Cube-connected-cycles
In the standard transformation graph for the *order-n cube-connected-cycles* the $n2^n$ nodes of the graph are labeled by the set $\{0, 1, \ldots, n-1\} \times \{0, 1\}^n$, and three transformation functions $\{\phi_{\text{cycle}}, \phi_{\text{cross}}\}$ (and inverses) are defined as follows: ϕ_{cycle} maps node-label (i, w) to $(i + 1 \bmod n, w)$, and ϕ_{cross} maps (i, w) to (i, w^i), where w^i represents the bit-string w with the bit in the ith position flipped. A node labeled (i, w) is said to lie on level i, and in column w.

¿From this labeling it is clear that (for even values of n) the order-n cube-connected-cycles is a subgraph of the hypercube $Q(\lceil \log n \rceil + n)$. This follows from Fact 1 and the fact that any length-$2k$ cycle can be found in the hypercube by applying k-length prefixes of a GCTS. A simple modification of the **Rank-to-Gray** algorithm and its inverse yield an effective parallel-embedding.

B. FFT and Butterfly

In the standard transformation graph for the *order-n FFT graph* the $(n + 1)2^n$ nodes of the graph are labeled by the set $\{0, 1, \ldots, n\} \times \{0, 1\}^n$, and a set of four transformation functions $\{\phi_{plus}, \phi_{cross}\}$ (and inverses) are defined as follows: ϕ_{plus} maps (i, w) to $(i + 1, w)$, and ϕ_{cross} maps (i, w) to $(i + 1, w^i)$.

In [6] it is shown that the FFT network is a subgraph of the smallest hypercube with as many nodes. The construction of the embedding is based on the use of the standard GCTS. Consequently, the embedding algorithm found in [6] can be developed into a parallel-embedding.

The butterfly graph can be viewed as the FFT network with the input and output vertices (i.e., the top and bottom levels) identified. The techniques used for the FFT naturally extends to the butterfly graph. Hence, there is a dilation 2 parallel-embedding of each of the butterfly-like networks in the smallest hypercube with as many nodes.

6.2 X-trees

An X-tree of height-n, denoted by $X(n)$, is a $CBT(n)$ with additional edges between pairs of nodes on the same level. The standard transformation graph for $X(n)$, includes two transformation functions in addition to those defined for the $CBT(n)$. The additional transformation and its inverse, connect pairs of nodes whose integer-labels differ by 1. It is convenient for a concise specification to allow the edges to wrap across levels, however, the use of wrap-edges in programs must be avoided for the sake of efficiency.

By combining the results of Sections 3 and 4 we can achieve a dilation 2 parallel-embedding of $X(n)$ into the hypercube $Q(n + 1)$. First translate the standard labels into inorder labels. One can show by induction that the inorder-labeling has the property that adjacent nodes of $X(n)$ on the same level differ by powers of 2, specifically 2^{n-i+1} for nodes on level i. Next translate each inorder label k into the rank-k string in the Gray-code sequence using **Rank-to-Gray**. By induction, one can show that the standard Gray-code sequence has the property that two code words that differ in rank by any power of 2, can be at most a hamming distance 2 apart. Hence, there is a dilation 2 parallel-embedding of $X(n)$ into the hypercube $Q(n + 1)$.

6.3 Mesh-of-trees

In the standard transformation graph for a *mesh-of-trees* network of height-n, denoted by $MT(n)$, each node is labeled by a pair of integers (x, y) each satisfying $1 \leq x, y < 2^{n+1}$, and at least one larger than $2^n - 1$. A set of four transformations are defined as follows: there is a connection from (x, y) to (w, z) precisely when $y = z$ and $w = 2x + b$; or when $x = w$ and $z = 2y + b$ (for $b \in \{0, 1\}$).

One may observe from this labeling that $MT(n)$ is a subgraph of the direct product of two $CBT(n)$s. By applying the translation algorithms between standard and cube-labelings of the CBT to each component we find that we can there is a dilation 2 parallel-embedding of the Mesh-of-Tree $MT(n)$ in the hypercube $Q(2n+2)$.

Acknowledgments. I would like to George Purdy and Tarun Kumar for helpful discussions.

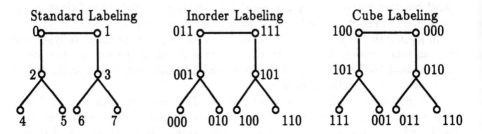

Fig. 1. *Various labelings of DRBT(2)*

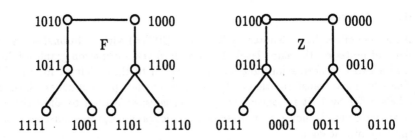

Fig. 2. *Application of $\mathcal{F}$ and $\mathcal{Z}$ to cube-labeled DRBT(2)*

References

1. S.N. Bhatt, F.R.K. Chung, F.T. Leighton, A.L. Rosenberg (1991): Efficient embeddings of trees in hypercubes. *SIAM J. Comput.*, to appear.
2. T. Bräunl (1989): Structured SIMD programming in Parallaxis. *Structured Programming 10/3*, 121-132.
3. M.Y. Chan (1988): Dilation-2 embedding of grids into hypercubes. *Intl. Conf. on Parallel Processing*, 295-298.
4. M.Y. Chan and F.Y.L. Chin (1990): Parallelized simulation of grids by hypercubes. Tech. Rpt. TR-90-11, Univ. Hong Kong.
5. D.S. Greenberg (1987): Minimum expansion embeddings of meshes in hypercubes. Tech. Rpt. DCS/RR-535, Yale Univ.
6. D.S. Greenberg, L.S. Heath and A.L. Rosenberg (1990): Optimal embeddings of butterfly-like graphs in the hypercube. *Math. Syst. Th. 23*, 61-77.
7. I. Havel and P. Liebl (1973): Embedding the polytomic tree into the n-cube. *Časopis pro Pěstování Matematiky 98*, 307-314.
8. F.T. Leighton (1992): *Introduction to Parallel Algorithms and Architectures.* Morgan Kaufmann, San Mateo.
9. B. Monien and I.H. Sudborough (1990): Embedding one interconnection network on another. In *Computational Graph Theory* (G. Tinhofer et al., eds,) Springer Verlag, 257-282.
10. L. Snyder (1990): The XYZ abstraction levels of Poker-like languages. In *Languages and Compilers for Parallel Computing* (D. Gelernter et al., eds.) MIT Press, 470-489.
11. H.S. Wilf (1989): *Combinatorial algorithms: an update*, CBMS-55, SIAM.

On Sorting by Prefix Reversals and the Diameter of Pancake Networks.

by

Mohammad H. Heydari and I. Hal Sudborough
Department of Computer Science
The University of Texas at Dallas
Richardson, TX 75083-0688
USA

Abstract

We show that the conjectured hardest stack of burnt pancakes, $-I(n)$, can be sorted in $\frac{3(n+1)}{2}$ steps, for all $n \equiv 3 \pmod 4$ with $n \geq 23$. If $-I(n)$ is indeed hardest, then both the "burnt" and "unburnt" pancake networks of dimension n have diameter at most $\frac{3(n+1)}{2}$. We also describe a $\frac{9}{8}n + 2$ step sorting sequence for Gates and Papadimitriou's unburnt stack of pancakes, χ_n, thus disproving their conjecture that $\frac{19}{16}n$ steps are required.

1   Introduction

The "pancake problem" was stated in [2] as follows:

> The chef in our place is sloppy, and when he prepares a stack of pancakes they come out all different sizes. Therefore, when I deliver them to a customer, on the way to the table I rearrange them (so that the smallest winds up on top, and so on, down to the largest at the bottom) by grabbing several from the top and flipping them over, repeating this (varying the number I flip) as many times as necessary. If there are n pancakes, what is the maximum number of flips (as a function of n) that I will ever have to use to rearrange them?

Let $f(n)$ denote the maximum number of steps needed to sort a stack of n pancakes. Garey, Johnson, and Lin [3] describe $f(n)$, for $n \leq 7$; David Robbins [6] describes $f(n)$, for $8 \leq n \leq 9$. Recently, Cohen and Blum [1] and, independently the current two authors describe $f(n)$, for $10 \leq n \leq 12$. (See *Appendix 1.*) Gates and Papadimitriou [4] show that $\frac{17}{16}n \leq f(n) \leq \frac{5n+5}{3}$, conjecture that their permutation χ_n, used to show the $\frac{17}{16}n$ lower bound, requires $\frac{19}{16}n$ flips, and introduce a *burnt pancake* version of the problem. This problem stipulates a stack of pancakes not only of different sizes but with one side burnt. Again for aesthetic reasons, one wants to sort the stack by size, but also now with all burnt sides downward. Let $g(n)$ denote the maximum number of flips needed to sort into the desired order any stack of n burnt pancakes. Cohen and Blum [1] describe $g(n)$, for $n \leq 10$. (See *Appendix 1.*) Gates and Papadimitriou [4] show that any stack of n burnt pancakes can be sorted in at most $2n + 3$ steps, and the stack consisting of n decreasing size pancakes (*i.e.* largest on top), all with their burnt side down, denoted by $-I_n^U$, requires $\frac{3}{2}n - 1$ steps. Cohen and Blum [1] recently conjecture that $-I(n)$, *i.e.* obtained from $-I_n^U$ by a flip of the entire stack, is hardest. They describe beautiful properties of $-I(n)$ and considerable computer search evidence to support the conjecture. Let $T(n)$ denote the number of steps needed to sort $-I(n)$. Cohen and Blum describe $T(n)$, for $n \leq 18$, and show that $T(n) \leq \frac{23}{14}n + c$ and, hence, under the conjecture, $f(n), g(n) \leq \frac{23}{14}n + c$, for all n. (See *Appendix 1* for values of $T(n)$, for $n \leq 17$.)

Aside from being an interesting combinatorial problem, the number of flips required to sort a stack of n burnt or unburnt pancakes is the diameter of the n-dimensional *burnt pancake network* and *pancake network*, respectively. These Cayley graph networks, based on permutation groups or the product of a permutation group with the group $Z_2 \times Z_2 \times \cdots Z_2$ (n times), where Z_2 is $GF(2)$, are obtained by appropriate choices of generators. Such networks have been proposed recently [5], as they have better diameter and vertex degree than the popular hypercube [7]. For example, the burnt pancake network of dimension n, $BP(n)$, has $2^n n!$ processors, is regular of degree n, and has diameter at most $2n$ [1]. In fact, under the Cohen and Blum conjecture [1], $BP(n)$'s diameter is $T(n)$ and we show that $T(n) \leq \frac{3(n+1)}{2}$, for all $n \geq 27$ such that $n \equiv 3 \pmod 4$. (Cohen and Blum also note that $T(n) \geq \frac{3}{2}n$, so our bound is tight.)

As noted by Cohen and Blum [1], one reason to focus on sorting burnt pancakes rather than unburnt pancakes is greater simplicity of analysis. Consider the process of sorting a stack of unburnt pancakes. If two pancakes of consecutive size are brought together and never later separated, then they can be considered as a single burnt pancake. That is, they form a single pancake with an orientation, namely the side corresponding to the larger of the two is burnt, as it needs to have that side down at the end. Thus one can view the stack shrinking as such adjacencies are formed until the entire stack is transformed into a final single burnt pancake.

We represent a stack of n burnt pancakes by a permutation of the integers $\{1, \ldots, n\}$ with a $+$ or $-$ to denote whether the pancake has its burnt side down or up, respectively (usually we omit the $+$ for ease of notation.) Such signed permutations are represented by column vectors. The symbol ":" represents one or more pancakes. For example,

$$I_n = \begin{bmatrix} 1 \\ 2 \\ \vdots \\ n \end{bmatrix} \quad and \quad -I_n = \begin{bmatrix} -1 \\ -2 \\ \vdots \\ -n \end{bmatrix}$$

represent the sorted configuration of n pancakes, I_n, and the (conjectured) hardest burnt pancake sequence $-I_n$, respectively. The symbol $\vdash$ between two such vectors represents that a single flip transforms the first into the second. For example,

$$\begin{bmatrix} 3 \\ -1 \\ 2 \\ -4 \\ 5 \end{bmatrix} \quad \vdash \quad \begin{bmatrix} 4 \\ -2 \\ 1 \\ -3 \\ 5 \end{bmatrix}$$

since flipping the top four pancakes transforms the first into the second. Similarly, let $\vdash^m$ be placed between two vectors to represent that there is a sequence of m flips that transforms the first into the second. Given an arbitrary stack of pancakes A, the stack obtained by flipping all of A is denoted by A^U.

A substack formed by (1) a maximum length downward sequence of consecutively increasing sized pancakes with burnt side down, or (2) a maximum length upward sequence of consecutively increasing sized pancakes with burnt side up is called a *block*. Similarly, a substack formed by (1) a maximum length downward sequence of consecutively decreasing sized pancakes with burnt side down or (2) a maximum length upward sequence of consecutively decreasing sized pancakes with burnt side up is called a *clan*. For example, in the stack

$$\begin{bmatrix} 3 \\ 2 \\ 1 \\ 4 \\ 5 \\ -6 \end{bmatrix} \quad \text{the substack} \quad \begin{bmatrix} 3 \\ 2 \\ 1 \end{bmatrix} \quad \text{is a clan of size 3 and the substack} \quad \begin{bmatrix} 4 \\ 5 \end{bmatrix} \quad \text{is a block.}$$

An *adjacency* in a stack exists between consecutive elements of a block and nowhere else. (One caveat: We shall say that an adjacency exists also when the largest pancake is at the bottom.) A flip sequence has no *wastes* if every flip in the sequence creates a new adjacency without destroying any old adjacencies. Clearly a flip sequence is optimum if it has no wastes, as the sorted stack $I(n)$ has n adjacencies, and each flip creates at most one new adjacency. That is, if m adjacencies are needed to reach $I(n)$, at least m steps are required. For example, the flip sequence $10, 4, 6, 14, 6, 4, 10$ is the unique optimum sorting sequence (without wastes) for the stack

$$[-8, -7, -4, -3, -14, -13, -2, -1, 11, 12, 9, 10, -6, -5, 15].$$

2 $-I(n)$ can be sorted in $\frac{3(n+1)}{2}$ steps.

Theorem 1 *For all $n \geq 23$ such that $n \equiv 3 (mod\ 4), T(n) \leq \frac{3(n+1)}{2}$.*

Proof: We show first a weaker result, namely that for all $n \equiv 3 (mod\ 12), T(n) \leq \frac{3(n+1)}{2}$. The sequences $3, 2, 3, 2, 3, 2$ and w^3, where $w = 15, 10, 4, 6, 14, 6, 4, 10$ are flip sequences to sort $-I(3)$ and $-I(15)$, respectively. Cohen and Blum [1] observed this earlier. In fact, they showed, by computer search, that $T(3) = 6$ and $T(15) = 24$. It follows that $T(n) = \frac{3(n+1)}{2}$, for both $n = 3$ and $n = 15$.

We now show that $T(n) = \frac{3(n+1)}{2}$, for all values of $n > 15$ such that $n \equiv 3 (mod\ 12)$. Consider the flip sequence $\xi(n) = n, \{n - 5 - 6i\}_{0 \leq i \leq \frac{n-9}{6}}, \{6 + 12i\}_{0 \leq i \leq \frac{n-15}{12}}, n - 1, 6,$ $4, \{n - 5 - 12i, 6, 4\}_{0 \leq i \leq \frac{n-27}{12}}, 10$. Note that $\xi(n)$ has length $\frac{n+1}{2}$. Let $p(n)$ be the stack obtained from $-I(n)$ by the flip sequence $\xi(n)$ and let $q(n)$ denote $p(n)^U$. We claim that $q(n)$ is:

$$q(n) = \begin{bmatrix} -1 \\ (\sigma_1) \\ (\sigma_2) \\ \vdots \\ (\sigma_s) \\ 9_s \\ 8_s \end{bmatrix}, \quad \text{where } s = \frac{n-3}{12} \text{ and, for } 1 \leq j \leq s, \ \sigma_j = \begin{bmatrix} 11_j \\ 10_j \\ -6_j \\ -7_j \\ -4_j \\ -5_j \\ 15_j \\ 14_j \\ 3_j \\ 2_j \\ 13_j \\ 12_j \end{bmatrix},$$

$$\text{where} \quad i_j = \begin{cases} i + 6(j - 1), & \text{if } 2 \leq i \leq 7, \\ i + 6(\frac{n-3}{12} - j + 1), & \text{if } 8 \leq i \leq 15. \end{cases}$$

The proof is completed by showing that $q(n)$ can be sorted in n steps. First, consider the flip sequence $\tau(n) = \{10 + 12i, 4, 6\}_{0 \le i \le \frac{n-15}{12}}, n - 1$ of length $\frac{n+1}{4}$. $\tau(n)$ transforms the stack $q(n)$ into the stack

$$r(n) = \begin{bmatrix} -7_s \\ \gamma_s \\ -\sigma_{s-1} \\ \gamma_{s-2} \\ \vdots \\ -\sigma_1 \\ -\gamma_1 \\ \vdots \\ \sigma_{s-2} \\ -\gamma_{s-1} \\ \sigma_s \\ (9_s) \\ (8_s) \end{bmatrix}, \text{ where } \gamma_i = \begin{bmatrix} -4_i \\ -3_i \\ -14_i \\ -15_i \\ 5_i \\ 6_i \\ -10_i \\ -11_i \end{bmatrix}, \text{ and } \sigma_i = \begin{bmatrix} 1_i \\ 2_i \\ 13_i \\ 12_i \end{bmatrix}. \text{ Let } t(n) = \begin{bmatrix} -9_s \\ -\sigma_s \\ \gamma_{s-1} \\ -\sigma_{s-2} \\ \vdots \\ \gamma_1 \\ \sigma_1 \\ \vdots \\ -\gamma_{s-2} \\ \sigma_{s-1} \\ -\gamma_s \\ (7_s) \\ (8_s) \end{bmatrix}.$$

(Note that $t(n)$ is the stack obtained from $r(n)$ by a flip of all but the bottom element, i.e. a flip of size $n - 1$.)

Consider the flip sequence $\chi(n) = \{n - 9 - 6i, n - 11 - 12i, n - 5 - 6i\}_{0 \le i \le \frac{n-15}{12}}$, of length $\frac{n-3}{4}$. $\chi(n)$ transforms $t(n)$ into $u(n)$, where $u(n)$ is of the form:

$$u(n) = \begin{bmatrix} -15_1 \\ \alpha_1 \\ \vdots \\ \alpha_s \\ \beta_s \\ \vdots \\ \beta_1 \\ \lambda_1 \\ \vdots \\ \lambda_s \\ (7_s) \\ (8_s) \end{bmatrix}, \text{ where } \lambda_i = \begin{bmatrix} 1_i \\ 2_i \\ 13_i \\ 14_i \\ 3_i \\ 4_i \end{bmatrix}, \alpha_i = \begin{bmatrix} 5_i \\ 6_i \\ -10_i \\ -9_i \end{bmatrix}, \text{ and } \beta_i = \begin{bmatrix} -12_i \\ -11_i \end{bmatrix}. \text{ Let } v(n) = \begin{bmatrix} -8_s \\ -7_s \\ -\lambda_s \\ \vdots \\ -\lambda_1 \\ -\beta_1 \\ \vdots \\ -\beta_s \\ -\alpha_s \\ \vdots \\ -\alpha_1 \\ 15_1 \end{bmatrix}.$$

(Note that $v(n) = u(n)^U$.)

Finally, the sequence $10 + 8(s - 1), \{4 + 8(s - i - 1), 6 + 8(s - i - 1), 14 + 8(s - 1) + 4i, 6 + 12i, 4 + 12i, 10 + 8(s - 1) + 4i\}_{0 \le i \le s-1}$, of length $\frac{n-1}{2}$, transforms $v(n)$ into sorted order, i.e. into $I(n)$.

The complete flip sequence is: $n, \{n - 5 - 6i\}_{0 \le i \le \frac{n-9}{6}}, \{6 + 12i\}_{0 \le i \le \frac{n-15}{12}}, n - 1, 6, 4,$
$\{n - 5 - 12i, 6, 4\}_{0 \le i \le \frac{n-27}{12}}, 10, n, \{10 + 12i, 4, 6\}_{0 \le i \le \frac{n-15}{12}}, n - 1, \{n - 9 - 6i, n - 11 - 12i,$
$n - 5 - 6i\}_{0 \le i \le \frac{n-15}{12}}, n, 10 + 8(s - 1), \{4 + 8(s - i - 1), 6 + 8(s - i - 1), 14 + 8(s - 1) + 4i,$
$6 + 12i, 4 + 12i, 10 + 8(s - 1) + 4i\}_{0 \le i \le s-1}$, where $s = \frac{n-3}{12}$.

It has length $1 + (\frac{n-9}{6} + 1) + (\frac{n-15}{12} + 1) + 3 + (3(\frac{n-27}{12}) + 3) + 2 + (3(\frac{n-15}{12}) + 3) + 1$
$+ (3(\frac{n-15}{12}) + 3) + 2 + 6(\frac{n-3}{12}) + 6 = \frac{3(n+1)}{2}$. So, $T(n) \le \frac{3(n+1)}{2}$, for all $n \equiv 3 \pmod{12}$.

Let us now describe how such flip sequences were found. In fact, each sequence above satisfies certain structural properties. For example, consider the portion of the above flip sequences transforming $q(n)$ into $u(n)$. The stack $q(n)$ has -1 at the top and otherwise is a collection of clans of size 2. The stack $u(n)$ has $-n$ at the top and otherwise is a collection of blocks of size 2. Moreover, $q(n) \vdash^{\frac{n+1}{2}} u(n)$ and, for all $1 \le i \le \frac{n+1}{2}$, at the ith step the stack has $-(2i - 1)$ on top. A stack such as $q(n)$ is called *2-good*. That is, it is a stack with -1 on top and $\frac{n}{2}$ clans of size 2 below, for some n, that can be converted with the minimum number of flips, *i.e.* $\frac{n+1}{2}$, into a stack with $-n$ on top and $\frac{n}{2}$ blocks of size 2 below. Note that if a stack is *2-good* then there is a unique way to reach the stated goal with $\frac{n+1}{2}$ flips. That is, the first flip must bring -3 to the top, the second -5 to the top, ... and so on. A *2-good* sequence $q(n)$ itself is its *input* and the uniquely defined goal stack with $-n$ on top and $\frac{n+1}{2}$ blocks of size 2 is called its *output*.

Moreover, in the sequences described above the stack $v(n) = u(n)^U$ can be sorted optimally, *i.e. without any wastes*, and the stack $p(n) = q(n)^U$ can be sorted into $-I_n^U$, *i.e.* backwards order, optimally. A 2-good stack is called *2-perfect*, if a flipping of its input and output, namely $q(n)^U$ and $u(n)^U$ above, results in stacks that can be sorted optimally into $-I(n)^U$ and $I(n)$, respectively. Each $q(n)$ described above is 2-perfect.

There is a "cut and paste" operation that allows one to take two 2-perfect stacks, $q(m)$ and $q'(n)$, both m and n odd, and produce another 2-perfect stack, say $q^*(m+n -3)$ of $m+n-3$ pancakes. (The operation is not described here due to page constraints.) However, all our flip sequences are obtained by manipulating 2-perfect stacks by such a cut and paste operation.

Moreover, computer search has found other examples of 2-perfect stacks of sizes 23, 27, 31, and 35. Using the cut and paste operation and some of these alternative 2-perfect stacks, we have found flip sequences for $-I(n)$ of length $\frac{3(n+1)}{2}$, for all sufficiently large values of $n \equiv 7(mod\ 12)$, $n \equiv 11(mod\ 12)$, and $n \equiv 3(mod\ 28)$. These are given below:

The flip sequence, for all $n \geq 35$ and $n \equiv 11(mod\ 12)$, is:

$$n, n-5, n-13, n-17, n-15, n-11, n-15, \{10+12(s-i-2), 4+12(s-i-2)\}_{0\leq i\leq s-2},$$
$$\{6+12i\}_{0\leq i\leq s-2}, 12s+2, 12s+10, \{6,4,10+12(s-i-1)\}_{0\leq i\leq s-1}, n, 18, 4, 8, 14, 12,$$
$$\{30+12i, 4, 6\}_{0\leq i\leq s-2}, n-1, \{n-9-6i, n-11-12i, n-5-6i\}_{0\leq i\leq s-2}, \frac{n+1}{2}, \frac{n+1}{2}+2,$$
$$\frac{n+1}{2}-4, 4, \frac{n+1}{2}+6, n, 8s+2, 8s-4, 8s-2, 8s+6, 6, 4, 8s+2, 8s-12, 8s-10,$$
$$\{12s-2-4(s-i-3), 12s-18-12(s-i-3), 12s-20-12(s-i-3), 12s-6-4(s-i-3),$$
$$4+8(s-i-3), 6+8(s-i-3)\}_{0\leq i\leq s-3}, n-1, n-9, n-15, n-11, n-15, n-17, n-13, n-5,$$
$$(\text{where } s = \frac{n-11}{12}),$$

the flip sequence, for all $n \geq 55$ and $n \equiv 7(mod\ 12)$, is:

$$n, \{n-9-10i\}_{0\leq i\leq 3}, \{n-45-6i\}_{0\leq i\leq \frac{n-49}{6}}, \{6+12i\}_{0\leq i\leq s-3}, n-17, n-1, 10, 8, 12, 10, 14,$$
$$12, n-5, 10, 8, 12, 10, 14, 12, n-25, \{6, 4, 10+12(s-i-4)\}_{0\leq i\leq s-4}, n, 10, 14, 18, 8, 10, 30,$$
$$34, 38, 8, 10, \{50+12i, 4, 6\}_{0\leq i\leq s-4}, n-1, n-9, n-11, n-5, \{n-15-6i, 44+12(s-i-5),$$
$$n-11-6i\}_{0\leq i\leq s-5}, 6s+12, 28, 6s+20, 6s+16, 6s+12, 6s-2, 8, 6s+6, 6s+2, 6s-2,$$
$$n, 8s+10, 8s+4, 8s+6, 8s+14, 6, 4, \{8s+10+4i, 8s-4-8i, 8s-2-8i, 8s+18+4i,$$
$$18+12i, 16+12i\}_{0\leq i\leq s-5}, 12s-6, 28, 30, 26, 28, 24, 26, 12s+2, 12s-30, 12s-32, 12s-6,$$
$$12, 14, 10, 12, 8, 10, n-1, 12(s-1)+2, 12(s-1), 12(s-1)+10, (\text{where } s = \frac{n-7}{12}),$$

and the flip sequence, for all $n \geq 31$ and $n \equiv 3(mod\ 28)$, is:

$$n, \{18+28(s-i-1), 12+28(s-i-1), 24+28(s-i-1), 20+28(s-i-1), 26+28(s-i-1),$$
$$22+28(s-i-1)\}_{0\leq i\leq s-1}, \{6+28i, 12+28i, 14+28i, 18+28i, 24+28i\}_{0\leq i\leq s-1}, n-1,$$
$$\{14, 12, 18+28(s-i-1)\}_{0\leq i\leq s-1}, n, \{26+28i, 12, 22, 16, 12, 10, 6\}_{0\leq i\leq s-1}, n-1,$$
$$\{n-25-6i, n-21-6i, n-19-6i, n-15-6i, n-9-6i, 12+28(s-i-1),$$
$$n-5-6i\}_{0\leq i\leq s-1}, n, 2+16s, \{12+16(s-i-1), 14+16(s-i-1),$$
$$n-1-12(s-i-1), n-7-12(s-i-1), n-13-12(s-i-1), n-17-12(s-i-1),$$
$$n-19-12(s-i-1), 6+28i, n-9-12(s-i-1), n-5-12(s-i-1),$$
$$n-11-12(s-i-1), n-7-12(s-i-1), 12+28i, n-13-12(s-i-1)\}_{0\leq i\leq s-1},$$
$$(\text{where } s = \frac{n-3}{28}).$$

3   A Conjecture Disproved.

Gates and Papadimitriou [4] describe a permutation χ_n of length n, for all $n > 0$ and $n \equiv 0 (mod\ 8)$, and prove that any flip sequence to sort χ_n must have length at least $\frac{17}{16}n$. They conjecture that, in fact, $\frac{19}{16}n$ is necessary. We disprove the conjecture by showing that $\frac{9}{8}n + 2$ flips are sufficient.

The permutation χ_n is defined as $\tau_1\, \tau_2^R\, \dots\, \tau_{m-1}\, \tau_m^R$, for even $m \geq 1$, where $n = 8m$ and τ_i is defined as follows: Let τ_1 be the sequence $1, 7, 5, 3, 6, 4, 2, 8$. For each positive integer $k > 1$, let τ_k be the sequence $1_k, 7_k, 5_k, 3_k, 6_k, 4_k, 2_k, 8_k$, where $i_k = i + 8(k-1)$, for each $i \in \{1, \dots, 8\}$ and let τ_i^R denote the reversal of τ_i.

We show, contrary to the conjecture, that $f(\chi_n) \leq \frac{9}{8}n + 2$, for all even $n > 0$. First we show that $\chi_n' = \tau_1\, \tau_2^R\, \dots\, \tau_{m-2}^R\, \tau_{m-1}$ can be done in $9(m-1)$ steps. The stated result follows, as one can sort $\chi_n = \chi_n'\, \tau_m^R$ by

$$\chi_n = \chi'_n\, \tau_m^R \vdash \tau_m\, \chi'^R_n \vdash^8 \tilde{\tau}_m \chi'^R_n \vdash (\tilde{\tau}_m)^R \chi'^R_n \vdash \chi'_n \tilde{\tau}_m \vdash^{9(m-1)} \tilde{\chi}'_n\, \tilde{\tau}_m = [1\ \dots\ n]$$

where $\tilde{\chi}'_n$ and $\tilde{\tau}_m$ represent the sorted versions of χ'_n and τ_m, respectively. (τ_m can be sorted in 8 steps, as observed in [4]).

Now, for a given odd number $m > 0$ and integer $i, 1 \leq i \leq \frac{m-1}{2}$, let Π_i denote the flip sequence:

$$8i, 8i+7, 6, 3, 5, 4, 3, 2, 8i+9, 8i+14, 3, 2, 4, 3,$$

and ρ_i the flip sequence:

$$6(m-1)+4(i-1)+9, 6(m-1)+4(i-1)+2, 6(m-1)+4(i-1)+11, 6(m-1)+4(i-1)+6.$$

Then χ_m is sorted by the sequence:

$$(\star) \qquad 6, 2, 3, \Pi_1, \dots, \Pi_{\frac{m-1}{2}}, 6(m-1)+5, 6(m-1)+7, 6(m-1)+2, \rho_1, \dots, \rho_{\frac{m-1}{2}}, 6, 2, 6$$

This can be seen as follows. After the flips $6, 2, 3,$ χ_m is transformed into: $(3, 4), (6, 5), 7, (1, 2), 8, \tau_2^R, \tau_3, \dots \tau_{m-1}^R, \tau_m$. By induction on i, it can be shown that, after the flips in the sequence $6, 2, 3, \Pi_1, \dots, \Pi_i$, χ_m is transformed into:

$$(3_{2i+1}..7_{2i+1}), (2_{2i}..8_{2i}), \dots, (3_3..7_3), (2_2..8_2), (3, 4), (6, 5), 7, (1, 2), (8, 1_2), (1_3, 2_3),$$
$$(8_3, 1_4), \dots, (8_{2i-1}, 1_{2i}), (1_{2i+1}, 2_{2i+1}), 8_{2i+1}, \tau_{2i+2}^R, \tau_{2i+3}, \dots, \tau_{m-1}^R, \tau_m^R.$$

Then, after the flip sequence $6, 2, 3, \Pi_1, \dots, \Pi_{\frac{m-1}{2}}$, χ_m is transformed into:

$$(3_m..7_m), (2_{m-1}..8_{m-1}), (3_{m-2}..7_{m-2}), (2_{m-3}..8_{m-3}), \dots, (3_3..7_3), (2_2..8_2), (3, 4),$$
$$(6, 5), 7, (1, 2), (8, 1_2), (1_3, 2_3), (8_3, 1_4), \dots, (8_{m-4}, 1_{m-3}), (1_{m-2}, 2_{m-2}), (8_{m-2}, 1_{m-1}),$$
$$(1_m, 2_m), 8_m.$$

And so, after the sequence:

$$6, 2, 3, \Pi_1, \dots, \Pi_{\frac{m-1}{2}}, 6(m-1)+5, 6(m-1)+7, 6(m-1)+2,$$

χ_m is transformed into:

$$(8_2..2_2), (7_3..3_3), \dots, (8_{m-1}..2_{m-1}), (7_m..3_m), (1, 2, 3, 4), (6, 5), (7, 8, 1_2),$$
$$(1_3, 2_3), \dots, (8_{m-2}, 1_{m-1}), (1_m, 2_m), 8_m.$$

By induction on i, again, it can be shown that after the sequence

$$6, 2, 3, \Pi_1, \ldots, \Pi_{\frac{m-1}{2}}, 6(m-1) + 5, 6(m-1) + 7, 6(m-1) + 2, \rho_1, \ldots, \rho_i$$

χ_m is transformed into:

$$(8_{2i+2}..2_{2i+2}), (7_{2i+3}..3_{2i+3}), \ldots, (8_{m-1}..2_{m-1}), \quad (7_m..3_m), (1, 2, 3, 4), (6, 5),$$
$$(7, 8, 1_2, 2_2, \ldots, 8_2, 1_3, 2_3, \ldots, 8_3, \ldots, 1_{2i}, 2_{2i}, \ldots, 8_{2i}, 1_{2i+1}, 2_{2i+1}, \ldots, 8_{2i+1}),$$
$$1_{2i+3}, 2_{2i+3}, \ldots, 8_{2i+3}, \ldots 1_m, 2_m, \ldots, 8_m.$$

Consequently, after the flip sequence

$$6, 2, 3, \Pi_1, \ldots, \Pi_{\frac{m-1}{2}}, 6(m-1) + 5, 6(m-1) + 7, 6(m-1) + 2, \rho_1, \ldots, \rho_{\frac{m-1}{2}}$$

χ_m is transformed into:

$$(1, 2, 3, 4), (6, 5), (7, 8, 1_2, 2_2, \ldots, 8_2, \ldots, 1_m, 2_m, \ldots, 8_m).$$

And so, after the full sequence $(\star)$, the sequence χ_m is sorted.

The length of the sequence $(\star)$ is easily seen to be

$$3 + 14(\tfrac{m-1}{2}) + 3 + 4(\tfrac{m-1}{2}) + 3 = 18(\tfrac{m-1}{2}) + 9 = 9m.$$

As $n = \frac{1}{8}m$, it follows that $(\star)$ has length $\frac{9}{8}n$.

4 A New Conjecture.

An intriguing question remains. Namely, what are hardest stacks of unburnt pancakes? In other words, what are antipodal nodes in the n-dimensional unburnt pancake network?

In the last section it was shown that the hardest stack previously cited in the literature for the unburnt pancake problem, namely χ_n [4], can be sorted in $\frac{9}{8}n + 2 \cong 1.125n$ steps. (We believe, by the way, that $\frac{9}{8}n$ steps are required for χ_n. Computer search, in fact has verified that χ_{16} requires 18 steps and χ_{24} requires 27 steps.) Are there stacks that require more flips, asymptotically, than χ_n?

We offer a conjecture. If true, the answer is yes and, moreover, $f(n) \geq \frac{13}{11}n \cong 1.182n$, for all $n \equiv 0 (mod\ 11)$.

Conjecture: For all $n \geq 1$, $f(n) \geq max\{f(n_1) + f(n_2) \mid n_1 + n_2 = n\}$.

The conjecture is supported by the values currently known for $f(n)$. See *Appendix 1*. For example, $f(12) = 14$ and, among the ways to partition 12, namely $6 + 6$, one obtains $f(12) \geq f(6) + f(6) = 14$. If the conjecture is true, then $f(17) = 20$, as $17 = 11 + 6$, $f(11) = 13$, and $f(6) = 7$. However, we have not yet found a stack of 17 unburnt pancakes that requires 20 flips.

Is there a general method to take hard stacks of length n_1 and n_2 such that $n_1 + n_2 = n$ and obtain a hard stack of length n? For example, there are exactly six stacks of size 11 that require 13 flips, namely

$$
\begin{bmatrix} 1 \\ 5 \\ 3 \\ 10 \\ 2 \\ 6 \\ 9 \\ 11 \\ 7 \\ 4 \\ 8 \end{bmatrix}
\quad
\begin{bmatrix} 1 \\ 11 \\ 3 \\ 6 \\ 9 \\ 4 \\ 7 \\ 10 \\ 5 \\ 8 \\ 2 \end{bmatrix}
\quad
\begin{bmatrix} 1 \\ 11 \\ 3 \\ 8 \\ 5 \\ 10 \\ 7 \\ 4 \\ 9 \\ 6 \\ 2 \end{bmatrix}
\quad
\begin{bmatrix} 7 \\ 2 \\ 9 \\ 6 \\ 11 \\ 4 \\ 1 \\ 10 \\ 3 \\ 8 \\ 5 \end{bmatrix}
\quad
\begin{bmatrix} 1 \\ 3 \\ 11 \\ 5 \\ 8 \\ 6 \\ 2 \\ 9 \\ 7 \\ 10 \\ 4 \end{bmatrix}
\quad
\begin{bmatrix} 1 \\ 7 \\ 2 \\ 11 \\ 4 \\ 6 \\ 9 \\ 5 \\ 8 \\ 10 \\ 3 \end{bmatrix}
$$

$$
\text{(a)} \qquad \text{(b)} \qquad \text{(c)} \qquad \text{(d)} \qquad \text{(e)} \qquad \text{(f)}
$$

and exactly two stacks of size 6 that require 7 flips, namely

$$[4, 6, 2, 5, 1, 3] \quad and \quad [5, 3, 6, 1, 4, 2].$$

Is there a stack of size 17 that requires 20 flips? Is it formed in some way from these?

5   A Routing Heuristic for the Unburnt Pancake Network

We designed a routing heuristic based on (1) prioritizing the operations in the non-deterministic algorithm of Gates and Papadimitriou [4] (used there to show the $\frac{5n+5}{3}$ upper bound) and (2) adding some additional operations, shown in *Appendix 1*. The result was tested on hundreds of thousands of randomly produced stacks of approximately 100 pancakes with no adjacencies and was always able to find a path of length at most 120. Of course, at this stage it is not clear that such short paths always exist, but our heuristic seems to perform well in practice.

6   Concluding Remarks

The six hardest stacks of eleven "unburnt pancakes" shown above are also listed in [1]. Miller, Pritikin, and the second current author have also recently proved [8] that $f(n)$ is asymptotically smaller than $g(n)$.

References

[1] David S. Cohen, Manuel Blum, *Improved Bounds for Sorting Pancakes Under a Conjecture*, Manuscript, Computer Science Division, University of California, Berkeley, California, May 1992.

[2] Harry Dweighter, American Mathematics Monthly, 82 (1) (1975) 1010.

[3] Michael R. Garey, David S. Johnson, and Shen Lin, American Math. Monthly, 84 (4) (1977) 296.

[4] William H. Gates, Christos H. Papadimitriou, *Bounds For Sorting By Prefix Reversal*, Discrete Mathematics 27, pp. 47-57, 1979.

[5] Sheldon Akers, Balakrishnan Krishnamurthy, *A Group-Theoretic Model For Symmetric Interconnection Networks*, IEEE Transactions on Computers, Vol. 38, No. 4, pp. 555-566, April 1989.

[6] David P. Robbins, personal communication, cited in [4].

[7] F. Thomas Leighton, *Introduction to Parallel Algorithms and Architectures: Arrays, Trees, Hypercubes*, Morgan Kaufmann Publishing Inc., 1992.

[8] Z. Miller, D. Pritikin, I.H. Sudborough, personal communication.

Appendix 1

n	2	3	4	5	6	7	8	9	10	11	12	13	14	15	16	17
$f(n)$	1	3	4	5	7	8	9	10	11	13	14	≥ 15	≥ 16	≥ 17	≥ 18	≥ 19
$g(n)$	4	6	8	10	12	14	15	17	18	?	?	?	?	?	?	?
$T(n)$	4	6	8	10	12	14	15	17	18	19	21	22	23	24	26	28

Table 1: Values For $f(n), g(n),$ and $T(n)$

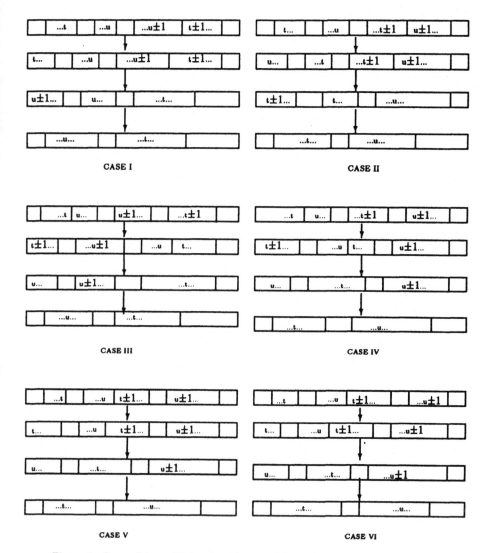

Figure 1: Operations, additional to those in [4], used by our heuristic router.

Springer-Verlag
and the Environment

We at Springer-Verlag firmly believe that an international science publisher has a special obligation to the environment, and our corporate policies consistently reflect this conviction.

We also expect our business partners – paper mills, printers, packaging manufacturers, etc. – to commit themselves to using environmentally friendly materials and production processes.

The paper in this book is made from low- or no-chlorine pulp and is acid free, in conformance with international standards for paper permanency.

Printing: Weihert-Druck GmbH, Darmstadt
Binding: Buchbinderei Schäffer, Grünstadt

Lecture Notes in Computer Science

For information about Vols. 1–610
please contact your bookseller or Springer-Verlag

Vol. 650: T. Ibaraki, Y. Inagaki, K. Iwama, T. Nishizeki, M. Yamashita (Eds.), Algorithms and Computation. Proceedings, 1992. XI, 510 pages. 1992.

Vol. 651: R. Koymans, Specifying Message Passing and Time-Critical Systems with Temporal Logic. IX, 164 pages. 1992.

Vol. 652: R. Shyamasundar (Ed.), Foundations of Software Technology and Theoretical Computer Science. Proceedings, 1992. XIII, 405 pages. 1992.

Vol. 653: A. Bensoussan, J.-P. Verjus (Eds.), Future Tendencies in Computer Science, Control and Applied Mathematics. Proceedings, 1992. XV, 371 pages. 1992.

Vol. 654: A. Nakamura, M. Nivat, A. Saoudi, P. S. P. Wang, K. Inoue (Eds.), Prallel Image Analysis. Proceedings, 1992. VIII, 312 pages. 1992.

Vol. 655: M. Bidoit, C. Choppy (Eds.), Recent Trends in Data Type Specification. X, 344 pages. 1993.

Vol. 656: M. Rusinowitch, J. L. Rémy (Eds.), Conditional Term Rewriting Systems. Proceedings, 1992. XI, 501 pages. 1993.

Vol. 657: E. W. Mayr (Ed.), Graph-Theoretic Concepts in Computer Science. Proceedings, 1992. VIII, 350 pages. 1993.

Vol. 658: R. A. Rueppel (Ed.), Advances in Cryptology – EUROCRYPT '92. Proceedings, 1992. X, 493 pages. 1993.

Vol. 659: G. Brewka, K. P. Jantke, P. H. Schmitt (Eds.), Nonmonotonic and Inductive Logic. Proceedings, 1991. VIII, 332 pages. 1993. (Subseries LNAI).

Vol. 660: E. Lamma, P. Mello (Eds.), Extensions of Logic Programming. Proceedings, 1992. VIII, 417 pages. 1993. (Subseries LNAI).

Vol. 661: S. J. Hanson, W. Remmele, R. L. Rivest (Eds.), Machine Learning: From Theory to Applications. VIII, 271 pages. 1993.

Vol. 662: M. Nitzberg, D. Mumford, T. Shiota, Filtering, Segmentation and Depth. VIII, 143 pages. 1993.

Vol. 663: G. v. Bochmann, D. K. Probst (Eds.), Computer Aided Verification. Proceedings, 1992. IX, 422 pages. 1993.

Vol. 664: M. Bezem, J. F. Groote (Eds.), Typed Lambda Calculi and Applications. Proceedings, 1993. VIII, 433 pages. 1993.

Vol. 665: P. Enjalbert, A. Finkel, K. W. Wagner (Eds.), STACS 93. Proceedings, 1993. XIV, 724 pages. 1993.

Vol. 666: J. W. de Bakker, W.-P. de Roever, G. Rozenberg (Eds.), Semantics: Foundations and Applications. Proceedings, 1992. VIII, 659 pages. 1993.

Vol. 667: P. B. Brazdil (Ed.), Machine Learning: ECML – 93. Proceedings, 1993. XII, 471 pages. 1993. (Subseries LNAI).

Vol. 668: M.-C. Gaudel, J.-P. Jouannaud (Eds.), TAPSOFT '93: Theory and Practice of Software Development. Proceedings, 1993. XII, 762 pages. 1993.

Vol. 669: R. S. Bird, C. C. Morgan, J. C. P. Woodcock (Eds.), Mathematics of Program Construction. Proceedings, 1992. VIII, 378 pages. 1993.

Vol. 670: J. C. P. Woodcock, P. G. Larsen (Eds.), FME '93: Industrial-Strength Formal Methods. Proceedings, 1993. XI, 689 pages. 1993.

Vol. 671: H. J. Ohlbach (Ed.), GWAI-92: Advances in Artificial Intelligence. Proceedings, 1992. XI, 397 pages. 1993. (Subseries LNAI).

Vol. 672: A. Barak, S. Guday, R. G. Wheeler, The MOSIX Distributed Operating System. X, 221 pages. 1993.

Vol. 673: G. Cohen, T. Mora, O. Moreno (Eds.), Applied Algebra, Algebraic Algorithms and Error-Correcting Codes. Proceedings, 1993. X, 355 pages 1993.

Vol. 674: G. Rozenberg (Ed.), Advances in Petri Nets 1993. VII, 457 pages. 1993.

Vol. 675: A. Mulkers, Live Data Structures in Logic Programs. VIII, 220 pages. 1993.

Vol. 676: Th. H. Reiss, Recognizing Planar Objects Using Invariant Image Features. X, 180 pages. 1993.

Vol. 677: H. Abdulrab, J.-P. Pécuchet (Eds.), Word Equations and Related Topics. Proceedings, 1991. VII, 214 pages. 1993.

Vol. 678: F. Meyer auf der Heide, B. Monien, A. L. Rosenberg (Eds.), Parallel Architectures and Their Efficient Use. Proceedings, 1992. XII, 227 pages. 1993.

Vol. 683: G.J. Milne, L. Pierre (Eds.), Correct Hardware Design and Verification Methods. Proceedings, 1993. VIII, 270 Pages. 1993.

Vol. 684: A. Apostolico, M. Crochemore, Z. Galil, U. Manber (Eds.), Combinatorial Pattern Matching. Proceedings, 1993. VIII, 265 pages. 1993.

Vol. 685: C. Rolland, F. Bodart, C. Cauvet (Eds.), Advanced Information Systems Engineering. Proceedings, 1993. XI, 650 pages. 1993.

Vol. 686: J. Mira, J. Cabestany, A. Prieto (Eds.), New Trends in Neural Computation. Procdings, 1993. XII, 746 pages. 1993.

Vol. 687: H. H. Barrett, A. F. Gmitro (Eds.), Information Processing in Medical Imaging. Proceedings, 1993. XVI, 567 pages. 1993.

Vol. 688: M. Gauthier (Ed.), Ada - Europe '93. Proceedings, 1993. VIII, 353 pages. 1993.

Vol. 689: J. Komorowski, Z. W. Ras (Eds.), Methodologies for Intelligent Systems. Proceedings, 1993. XI, 653 pages. 1993. (Subseries LNAI).

Vol. 690: C. Kirchner (Ed.), Rewriting Techniques and Applications. Proceedings, 1993. XI, 488 pages. 1993.

Vol. 691: M. A. Marsan (Ed.), Application and Theory of Petri Nets 1993. Proceedings, 1993. IX, 591 pages. 1993.